D1259195

Designing Effective Organizations

Designing Effective Organizations

'As companies search for all sources of competitive advantage, many are discovering that the ability to organize and execute complex strategies is an important one. Campbell and Goold have again provided us with a good process through which leaders can give organizing its deserved focus.'
Professor Jay Galbraith, author of *Designing the Global Corporation.*

'Campbell and Goold bring much needed clarity and precision to the language of organizational design and show how this can help managers avoid the misunderstandings and differing interpretations that frequently undermine new organization structures.'
Paul Coombes, Director, Organization Practice Area, McKinsey & Company.

'Organization change is close to the top of many companies' agendas. Goold and Campbell's book equips you with ideas and frameworks to take on the journey. The real-world examples help make it both pragmatic and readable.'
Steve Russell, Chief Executive, The Boots Company plc.

'An impressive work. The taxonomy of organizational units and organigram symbols will be especially useful to managers working on structures.'
Philip Sadler, Patron, The Centre for Tomorrow's Company. Author of *The Seamless Organization.*

'Incredibly relevant in helping to pull together a complicated structure based around the dimensions of channels, products, customers and geography – immensely clear and valuable.'
David Roberts, Chief Executive, Personal Financial Services, Barclays plc.

'A welcome breakthrough in designing more effective corporate organization structures. The nine design tests of Goold and Campbell are a valuable addition to an otherwise sparse toolkit.'
Jim Haymaker, Vice President, Strategy & Business Development, Cargill Inc.

'Goold and Campbell have written an insightful, informed, and practical book that can help senior executives pragmatically grapple with both the content and process issues in designing their organizations for competitive advantage. The book has both state of the art ideas as well as detailed examples of their methods in practice.'
Michael Tushman, Professor, Harvard Business School. Author of *Competing by Design* **and** *Winning Through Innovation.*

Designing Effective Organizations

How to Create Structured Networks

Michael Goold
Andrew Campbell

Ashridge Strategic Management Centre, London

JOSSEY-BASS
A Wiley Company
www.josseybass.com

Published by

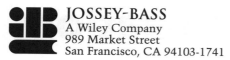

JOSSEY-BASS
A Wiley Company
989 Market Street
San Francisco, CA 94103-1741

www.josseybass.com

Copyright © 2002 by John Wiley & Sons, Ltd.

Jossey-Bass is a registered trademark of John Wiley & Sons, Inc.

Jossey-Bass books and products are available through most bookstores. To contact Jossey-Bass directly, call (888) 378-2537, fax to (800) 605-2665, or visit our website at www.josseybass.com.

Substantial discounts on bulk quantities of Jossey-Bass books are available to corporations, professional associations, and other organizations. For details and discount information, contact the special sales department at Jossey-Bass.

We at Jossey-Bass strive to use the most environmentally sensitive paper stocks available to us. Our publications are printed on acid-free recycled stock whenever possible, and our paper always meets or exceeds minimum GPO and EPA requirements.

ISBN 0-7879-6064-0
Printed and bound in Great Britain by
Biddles Ltd, Guildford and King's Lynn

FIRST EDITION
HB *Printing* 10 9 8 7 6 5 4 3 2 1

Contents

Acknowledgments

Many people have contributed to the ideas presented in this book. We would particularly like to thank the managers who sit on Ashridge Strategic Management Centre's Research Committee in the UK. These managers represent the companies that sponsor the Centre's research, and have provided essential guidance and support throughout the research leading up to the book's publication. We would also like to thank the companies which participated as research sites. Without their co-operation and openness, we would have made little progress. Individuals whose comments, criticisms, and suggestions have been especially valuable include David Bowerin (Citigroup), Neil Donnan (Mars), Jim Haymaker (Cargill), John Ripley (Unilever), David Roberts (Barclays), and Hein Schreuder (DSM).

We would also like to thank the many academic colleagues who have critiqued our work and made valuable inputs to it. We have benefited particularly from dialogues with David Collis, Jay Galbraith, Sumantra Ghoshal, Rob Grant, and Costas Markides. Our co-researchers at Ashridge, Marcus Alexander, Derkjan van der Leest, David Sadtler, and David Young, have also contributed ideas and comments throughout the project.

In the final stages of the work, we benefited from a close collaboration with the Organization Design practice area of McKinsey & Company, working together with a McKinsey project team on the development of an organization design toolkit. The McKinsey consultants pressed us to make our ideas clearer and more practically usable, and were invaluable in shaping our eventual conclusions. Paul Coombes, the McKinsey director in charge of the Organization Design practice area, and Risto Pentinnen, who led the project team and worked most closely with us, deserve special praise for their encouragement, insights, and influence on our thinking.

We have also benefited from a constructive working relationship with the editorial team at Wiley. We would like to thank our editors, Diane Taylor of Wiley (UK) and Susan Williams of Jossey-Bass, for their support and helpful suggestions in the preparation of the manuscript for publication. Thanks should also go to Simon Caulkin for his work in editing the manuscript.

Lastly, we would like to praise our support staff at Ashridge Strategic Management Centre in the UK, who coped with endless redrafts of the manuscript and finally succeeded in producing a legible and intelligible typescript on time. Listra Augustine Joseph, Heidi Caven, Marrion Crooks, Liz Purchase, and Maggie Sampson all made important contributions.

Preface

We embarked on research into the role of the corporate center in strategic decision-making in 1984, nearly 18 years ago. At the time, we were entering largely uncharted waters, since there was little empirical work to show how corporate centers in multi-business firms operate. Our early work produced a rough mapping of the territory, documented in our book, *Strategies and Styles*, which delineates a number of different management styles that we found are commonly adopted by corporate centers.

Subsequently, we have explored the role of the center much more fully. In 1994, we summarized much of our thinking in *Corporate-Level Strategy*, a book which laid out our findings on how the corporate parent can add value to its businesses and how added-value corporate strategies can be developed. In this book, we argued that the objective of corporate strategy should be to create "parenting advantage", that is to say, to add more value to the company's businesses than any other owner could.

During the 1990s, we continued to refine our understanding of corporate parents and the sources of parenting advantage. We have been critical of diversified companies in which the corporate parent adds no discernible value, and have insisted that multi-business corporations only make sense if the corporate parent has a clear strategy for adding value. These views are now widely accepted, and have contributed to the wave of restructurings, de-mergers and break-ups of recent years.

At a conference to mark the tenth anniversary of the

Ashridge Strategic Management Centre in late 1997, we were, however, challenged about the relevance of our ideas to more focused companies. Is the concept of parenting advantage still relevant in companies where the separation of responsibilities between the parent and the businesses is less clear-cut? We therefore embarked on a major project to understand focused companies with more complex relationships between the center and the units.

During the research, we became increasingly interested in the issue of why companies adopt the organizations they do. We found that this important territory was almost as uncharted as the role of the center was in the 1980s. It is widely recognized that organization design can have a profound impact on strategy implementation and competitive success, yet most chief executives have embarrassingly few good answers when pressed to justify their organization designs, and most managers tend to put organization design into the "too difficult" box. This lured us into a change of focus for the project, which has become an exploration of the whole subject of organization design.

This book therefore presents our views on organization design. It also includes the conclusions we have reached on the role of the parent in complex structures, but sets them within the broader context of organizational thinking that we have developed.

1

Structured Networks

Probably the most seductive image of the organization of the future is the self-managed network. It conjures up visions of many highly motivated units, each with a focused expertise, interacting in a creative, bureaucracy-free and cohesive manner. Hierarchy and internal politics are at a minimum. The organization operates like a market, but is more effective than a market due to a set of relationships, ties, commitments, and shared intent that make it a purposeful entity.

This image is seductive because it contrasts so vividly with many of today's complex corporate organizations. These organizations impede decision-making with their ambiguity, kill creativity with their rules and procedures, and sap energy through the heavy hand of hierarchy. Managers know that there has to be a better way; but they do not know how to design it. In companies with extensive and complicated interdependencies between product units, market units, geographical units, functional units, and project units, the simplicity of the self-managed network seems out of reach.

What is more, managers find the whole process of organization design difficult and frustrating. They are overwhelmed by the number of variables they have to consider. They are confused by the advice available from consultants and academics, much of which they find impractical, irrelevant to their concerns, or contradictory. They are constrained to use vague concepts such as "matrix" structures or "dotted-line" relationships because they lack a precise language for specifying the organizations they want to create. And, when it comes to choosing a design, they are unable to resist the influence of personalities and politics because they have no rigorous framework for selecting between alternatives.

This book sets out to provide practical help for managers confronting these difficulties. We have studied the corporate structures of a number of large, complex companies such as ABB, AstraZeneca, British Petroleum (BP), Citigroup, Dow, General Electric (GE), IBM, Mars, Monsanto, Motorola, Philips, Shell, and Unilever, and several smaller, but no less complex, organizations in sectors such as professional services, speciality chemicals, and e-commerce. We have also undertaken consultancy projects for many clients with organization design issues, and we have reviewed the work of leading organization design experts and consultants. From the research, we have developed a new approach to organization design. Our approach not only provides the tools for rigorous decision-making, it also helps managers to create the network-like organizations that they desire. These organizations balance self-management with structure.

Our approach to corporate organization design includes three components:

1. First, we propose nine tests of good design. The tests, which can be applied to any proposed design, highlight weaknesses in design options. They can be used to identify refinements that will overcome the weaknesses, or to rule out seriously flawed options.

2. Second, we provide a language in the form of a taxonomy of different kinds of unit roles and relationships. The taxonomy helps managers to describe and discuss different design options with more clarity. It also helps them develop radical alternatives.

3. Third, we suggest a process that managers can follow when they are facing a design challenge. The process, which builds on the tests and the taxonomy, provides managers with a rigorous but practical approach to organization design. It

also helps them to achieve the outcome they want – an organization with the maximum of self-management, but with sufficient structure and hierarchy to work well. We call this outcome a "structured network".

A structured network has the features of a network – units that are largely self- managing, both in deciding how to achieve their objectives and in their relationships with other units – but sufficient structure, designed-in processes and hierarchy to insure that responsibilities and relationships are clear, that managers can collaborate successfully, and that corporate strategies can be implemented in a purposeful way. At the heart of our thinking is the idea of creating units that are self-managing on all matters except those where influence from the hierarchy or designed-in processes are needed to optimize the working of the network. Our goal is to help managers design organizations that are market-like in much of their behavior, but which are guided by sufficient structure to create more value than markets. Our work over the last 15 years on corporate centers has made us unusually sensitive to the potential that hierarchical structures have both to create and destroy value. A structured network is a design where the value creation potential is amplified and the value destruction potential is minimized.

In this introductory chapter, we will summarize our main messages and identify in which chapters of the book they are developed more fully. This should allow readers to focus their attention on those chapters that are of most interest to them.

Nine Design Tests

Which factors should guide the choice of organization design? (See box: Elements of Organization Design.) There are many informal managerial rules about things such as spans of control and reporting relationships. In addition, academics and consultants have produced a huge amount of work on organization design. But our research told us that managers still lack a practical and systematic framework to guide their organization choices. An important purpose of this book has been to develop a usable framework for guiding organization design choices.

Less an intellectual triumph than a practical checklist for

Elements of Organization Design

Many factors shape the working of an organization. The formal structure, including the allocations of responsibilities to management units and the reporting relationships for these units, provides the basic skeleton. These are the "lines and boxes" of the typical organization chart. The processes and mechanisms through which the units relate to each other, both for hierarchical reporting purposes and for collaboration between sister units, represent the connective tissues. It is through these processes that the components of the organization work together. Then there are the people, the behaviors, the values, and the culture that bring the basic skeleton and its connective tissues to life. A complete organization design must deal with all these factors.

In this book, our emphasis will be on the skeleton and the connective tissues. It is the lines, the boxes, and, crucially, the desired relationships between units that the organization designer must first specify. Softer issues to do with people and corporate culture must be taken into account in the design, but are harder for the organization designer to shape and change. Thus, we will be primarily concerned with:

- responsibility allocation to units
- reporting and lateral relationships
- accountabilities for units
- key reporting and co-ordination processes.

Our advice on the design process will, however, suggest that the organization designer needs to convey intended behavior patterns in the key relationships in the design, and to think carefully about people, incentives, and cultural issues when selecting and finalizing a preferred design.

addressing the most important issues, our framework is grounded on some basic concepts. The first and most important, the fit concept, embraces four drivers of fit – product-market strategies, corporate strategies, people, and constraints. In addition, we have condensed previous ideas on optimal organization design into five good design principles: the specialization principle, the co-ordination principle, the knowledge and competence principle, the control and commitment principle, and the innovation and adaptation principle (Figure 1.1).

The principles are broad in nature and not always easy to convert into prescriptive guidance. They are more valuable in orienting managers than in resolving particular organizational dilemmas. However, as we worked with the principles, we found ways to convert them into some practical tests. Perhaps the most important contribution of this book lies in the insights and understandings that the tests produce. The tests match the fit drivers and the good design principles (see Figure 1.2).

The Fit Tests

One almost universally agreed proposition is that organizations need to be fit for purpose. Strategy, therefore, should be a key

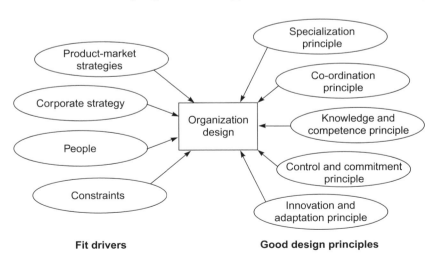

FIGURE 1.1 A Framework for Organization Design

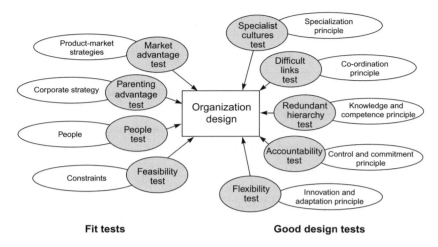

Fit tests   **Good design tests**

FIGURE 1.2 Nine Tests for Organization Design

driver of organization design, and we have found it useful to distinguish between product-market strategies and corporate-level strategy. But strategy is not the only driver of organizational design; at least as important are people. Many authorities counsel against designing an organization around people, preferring to build around the strategy and change the people if necessary. However, people cannot always be changed, and new ones with the required attitudes may be hard to find. So designs should take account of the people available to lead and work in them. Finally, organization design is subject to various constraints, ranging from laws laid down by governments to organizational capabilities or resources that are deeply imbedded. These four drivers of fit are described in detail in Chapter 2.

The fit drivers lead to four fit tests:

- *The market advantage test:* "Does the design allocate sufficient management attention to the operating priorities and intended sources of advantage in each product-market area?"
- *The parenting advantage test:* "Does the design allocate sufficient attention to the intended sources of added value and strategic initiatives of the corporate parent?"

- *The people test:* "Does the design adequately reflect the motivations, strengths, and weaknesses of the available people?"
- *The feasibility test:* "Does the design take account of the constraints that may make the proposal unworkable?"

The fit tests bring out the most important inputs that should guide organization design choices. Provided the design has been selected with these inputs in mind, there should be no problem in passing the fit tests. However, organization design choices are not always so rational. All too often, organizations evolve in ways that are not sufficiently related to the strategy of the company, or else pay scant attention to the limitations of managers who will fill key positions. In one company, we were told that the structure had always been primarily driven by the balance of power between the four barons who ran the main divisions, resulting in business unit groupings that had little to do with the opportunities in the markets being served. Under these circumstances, the organization will be a barrier to successful strategy implementation and will damage competitiveness. The fit tests insure that organizations which are evidently not fit for purpose will be exposed, and that more suitable alternatives will be adopted.

The Good Design Tests

While the four drivers of the fit principle are recognized by most managers, we believe that the good design principles and tests represent more of an advance. They synthesize the vast quantity of academic research and managerial experience about what makes an organization work well into a few basic tests that should guide any organization designer. We devote Chapter 3 to explaining the good design principles in detail.

The specialization principle and co-ordination principle both concern the boundaries between units. The specialization principle states that boundaries should exist to encourage the development of specialist skills, whereas the co-ordination principle emphasizes that activities which need to be co-ordinated should be located within a single unit.

Although these basic principles are clear, there are unfortunately often trade-offs between specialization and co-ordination. A broadly-based product structure may give economies in purchasing and manufacturing, but be detrimental to the development of specialist products for particular markets. A disaggregated geographical structure with many local units may support the special skills needed for different regions, but prevent effective co-ordination in product development or IT infrastructure. Organizational problems arise when there are trade-offs between different ways of grouping responsibilities. In order to help with these trade-offs, we have developed two tests, which give more precision to the principles and make them more practically useful.

- *The specialist cultures test:* "Do any 'specialist cultures', units with cultures that need to be different from sister units and the layers above, have sufficient protection from the influence of the dominant culture?"
- *The difficult links test:* "Does the organization design call for any 'difficult links', co-ordination benefits that will be hard to achieve on a networking basis, and does it include 'solutions' that will ease the difficulty?"

The specialist cultures test questions whether the required specialist skills will thrive only if the managers concerned are insulated from the influence of other parts of the organization. For example, sometimes the best way to develop and market a new product is to set it up as a separate business unit, with little or no contact with the rest of the company. Alternatively, instead of setting up a separate unit, it may be possible for the corporate parent to insure that the specialist culture receives sufficient protection by flexing corporate policies and procedures or by giving it certain powers. The test focuses attention on the dangers of suppressing or damaging activities that fall outside the mainstream corporate culture, dangers which are easy to overlook.

The difficult links test recognizes that many co-ordination benefits can be achieved through spontaneous networking between units, but that others will be more difficult. For example, best practice sharing can often be left to networking between units, whereas the establishment of common technical standards is unlikely without a corporate policy which makes them mandatory. Organization designers should focus only on the few co-ordination benefits that will be difficult: where networking will not deliver the benefits. For these difficult links, it is necessary to develop appropriate co-ordination mechanisms or interventions to overcome the difficulty, or to readjust the design so that the co-ordination lies within the responsibility of a single unit. This test makes managers assess which co-ordination benefits will be difficult to achieve if left to the network, and to think through whether and how any difficulties can be overcome.

Together, the specialist cultures test and the difficult links test give managers a powerful means of assessing the trade-offs between the benefits that can be gained from co-ordination and from specialization. In the 1980s, IBM decided to set up its PC division as a separate unit, free from the influence of the IBM corporate culture and policies. This promoted a specialist PC culture that was highly successful in bringing the new product to market rapidly. Using a similar logic, many commentators argued that, when faced with performance problems in the early 1990s, IBM should break up the whole company into separate, independent units. Lou Gerstner, CEO of IBM, however, believed that the future for IBM lay in providing integrated customer solutions. He therefore kept the company together; but he recognized that co-ordination between separate product divisions was not proving a satisfactory means of offering integrated solutions, due to conflicting divisional priorities and incompatible technologies. He therefore gave authority to IBM's Sales and Distribution division and to a new unit, the Global Services division, to concentrate, respectively, on customer solutions and services, using both IBM and competitor products. These divisions have the power to offer a unified approach to customers, and have dealt well with previously difficult links between IBM divisions. At the same time, Gerstner has encouraged new business activities, such as Business Innovation Services, IBM's e-business initiative, not to be bound by IBM's traditional policies and ways of doing things. IBM's structure now takes account of both the difficult links and the specialist cultures tests.

The difficult links and specialist cultures tests help managers to address the organization design issues faced by companies such as IBM, where there are evident advantages both from specialization and co-ordination. The tests identify the real trade-offs between co-ordination and specialization, and help managers to find ways of gaining the benefits of co-ordination without undermining the development of specialist skills.

The knowledge and competence principle is mainly concerned with delegation. It states that responsibilities should be allocated to the person or team best placed to assemble the relevant knowledge and competence at reasonable cost. The practical test that follows from the principle is:

- *The redundant hierarchy test:* "Are all levels in the hierarchy and all responsibilities retained by higher levels based on a knowledge and competence advantage?"

This test is based on the premise that the default option should be to decentralize to operating units, only retaining responsibilities at higher levels if there is a knowledge and competence rationale. As we have argued in previous work,[1] hierarchy can only be justified if it adds some value to the functioning of the organization. Questions about whether and how the hierarchy adds value have helped numerous companies to sharpen their thinking about the design of their headquarters, group, and division levels. The redundant hierarchy test is a way of formalizing these questions.

The control and commitment principle concerns two challenges that arise in any decentralized organization: how to maintain appropriate control and how to insure high levels of motivation. Units should feel strong pressures to self-correct if they are failing to deliver, and parent-level managers to whom the units report should be able to identify problems easily and promptly. This leads to a further test:

- *The accountability test:* "Does the design facilitate the creation of a control process for each unit that is appropriate to the unit's responsibilities, economical to implement, and motivating for the managers in the unit?"

The accountability test makes managers focus on the pressures that exist for a unit to self-correct. These depend on the relationships the unit has with its internal and external customers, the performance measures for the unit, and the unit's reporting relationship. Market-facing business units with arm's-length customer relationships and bottom-line performance measures are relatively easy to control and motivate. Corporate functions with no external customers, tied internal relationships, and subjective performance measures present more accountability problems. In a complex structure, it is all too easy to create a design that looks good on paper, but leaves unit managers demotivated and unclear about their performance objectives, and parent managers unable to control those who report to them. The accountability test helps managers to design units and establish performance measures that produce effective, low-cost controls that are highly motivating.

The innovation and adaptation principle states that structures should be designed to innovate and adapt as uncertainties become clarified and environments change. An organization design that is perfect for today is of little use if it cannot adapt to cope with the conditions of tomorrow. The principle yields our last test:

- *The flexibility test:* "Will the design help the development of new strategies and be flexible enough to adapt to future changes?"

The test recognizes that some structures allow for evolution and adaptation, whereas others build in rigidity and power bases that resist change. It insures that the designer considers the changes that may be needed, and whether the design will be flexible enough to make them.

Using The Tests

The tests can be used to assess the relative merits of different possible designs. In Chapter 4, we discuss the trade-offs between the sort of simple, SBU-based structures adopted by BP, GE, and Hewlett-Packard and the more complex, interdependent structures of companies such as Citigroup, Monsanto, and ABB. Simple, SBU-based structures have several advantages, but their crucial disadvantage is that they do not fit well with multi-dimensional strategies. Companies whose strategies call for a focus on more than one dimension in order to achieve competitive advantage are likely to need more complex, interdependent structures. We also identify the management challenges typically faced in both simple and complex structures. These challenges influenced the way in which we have formulated our good design tests. The tests therefore help to bring out the advantages and disadvantages of different sorts of structures.

The purpose of the tests is to raise issues. Some can be addressed by refining the structure, by designing process solutions, or by appointing different managers. A key benefit of using the tests comes from the ideas for design improvements that they suggest. For example, a common problem is the creation of a layer of management, for example a geographic region or a product group, without specifying what responsibilities should be retained by this layer and why. The redundant hierarchy test helps to highlight this design weakness, alerting managers to the need either to eliminate the layer or to define the responsibilities, skills, management processes, and leadership style that are needed to make the layer a positive influence on performance.

Some issues raised by the tests point to unavoidable trade-offs: "Do we lose more from under-attending to product or from under-attending to geography?" Often there is no clear answer to these trade-offs, but making sure that the question is asked helps managers to find a reasonable balance between competing interests. By pointing out the trade-offs and weak points in a chosen design, the tests help managers consider in greater depth problems that may occur and future changes that may be needed. The tests also help managers to weigh the pros and cons of different designs and provide a rigorous analytical structure for making design choices.

A Language for Describing Organization Designs

One of the findings from our research was that managers lack a language for describing organization designs. For example, the words used for describing different kinds of units are often ambiguous. The term "business unit" is used universally, but means different things in different companies. Sometimes it refers to a highly autonomous, largely self-contained profit center. In other situations, it is used for units that are much less autonomous, drawing on resources that are shared with other units and accepting the authority of upper levels of management on many key decisions. There is similar ambiguity in terms such as "product group", "division", and "national operating company". This lack of clear language leads to confusion and cross-purposes when managers talk about their organization designs. The problem is particularly acute when managers talk about "matrix" structures, which can mean very different things in different companies.

What is more, a key challenge in organization design is to find a means of defining units in a way that clearly conveys the intentions behind the design. Managers need clarity about what they are supposed to be achieving, in order to provide a context for decentralized, self-managed decisions about specific issues. But manuals that spell out responsibilities in great detail lead to bureaucracy, rigidity, and lack of initiative. Organization designers have faced a difficult choice between too little clarity and too much detail. Our solution is a taxonomy of unit roles that provides a means of describing design intentions, but without excessive detail. By providing a more precise language to express organization design intentions, the taxonomy helps managers to design network organizations where managers are clear about what they should be doing, but not hemmed in with detailed instructions, job descriptions, and rules.

The taxonomy sticks as closely as possible to common usage, but proposes some new terms and gives more precise definitions of others. It embraces eight different unit types:

- *Business units*: market-focused, profit-responsible units with relatively high decision-making autonomy;
- *Business functions*: operating functions, such as manufacturing or sales, that report to a business unit general manager;
- *Overlay units*: market-focused units serving segments defined along dimensions that cut across the business units;
- *Sub-businesses*: market-focused units that serve segments defined at a more disaggregated level than the business units;
- *Core resource units*: units that develop and nurture scarce resources, such as R&D, that are key to competitive advantage for several business units;
- *Shared service units*: units which provide services that are needed by several other units in the company;
- *Project units*: units which carry out tasks or projects that cut across other units, normally for a finite time period; and
- *Parent units*: upper-level units that carry out obligatory corporate tasks, and influence and add value to other units.

Each of these unit types has a different role, with implications for its broad responsibilities, reporting relationships, lateral relationships, and main accountabilities. The differences in unit roles are summarized in Table 1.1, and described in detail in Chapter 5.

The taxonomy of unit roles gives a useful shorthand for communicating about the nature of a unit's intended responsibilities. In Citibank's corporate banking group, for example, there is a complex, interdependent structure, involving customer units, product units, geographical units, and shared infrastructure

TABLE 1.1 A Taxonomy of Unit Roles

Type of unit	Type of responsibility	Relationships Reporting	Lateral	Main accountabilities
Parent ⊘	Obligatory and added-value parenting	Board/parent	Mutual self-interest	Corporate bottom line
Core resource unit	Resource-focused	Hands-on parent/unit	Resource owner/user	Resource development and utilization
Shared service unit	Service-focused	Parent/unit	Service provider/ client	Service cost-effectiveness
Project unit	Project-focused	Parent/unit	Pressure group/ principal	Project delivery
Overlay unit	Market-focused (cut-across)	Parent/unit	Pressure group/ principal	Effectiveness in serving target segments
Business unit	Market-focused	Parent/unit	Mutual self-interest	Bottom line (strong)
Sub-business	Market-focused (disaggregated)	General manager/unit	Quasi-team	Bottom line
Business function	Functional	General manager/ function	Team	Functional effectiveness and contribution

units. It is possible to make the intended working of this structure clearer, by recognizing that, in terms of our taxonomy, the customer units and the product units are supposed to act as "business units", whereas the geographical units are "overlay units" and the infrastructure units are "shared service units". Equally, in many companies, corporate staff departments such as Human Resources and IT are supposed to play a variety of roles. Some staff may be providing a shared service to other units, while others are acting as a core resource, and yet others are assisting the parent. The implications for how these staffs should discharge their responsibilities and relate to other units are very different according to the role they are meant to be playing. Organization designers who were previously failing to make clear their intentions, or struggling to avoid becoming over-involved in too much detail, have found the taxonomy highly valuable.

We have also devised a new type of organization chart, which uses different symbols to give a visual impression of the differences between units and gets away from the traditional hierarchical lines and boxes format (see Figure 1.3).

We believe that the taxonomy provides a simple but powerful means of specifying the vast majority of design concepts that organization designers want to create. An understanding of a unit's role gives essential guidance to unit managers on how to approach specific decisions in accordance with design intentions. For some issues, which will be identified by the tests, it may be necessary to supplement the roles with more detailed responsibility definitions, process maps, and policies. But the roles provide sufficient information for managers to take most decisions on a decentralized basis and to handle most co-ordination through self-managed networking.

We have found the taxonomy very helpful in understanding existing designs, creating new design options, and communicating with managers about the intentions behind different options. It also helps with implementation. Once a management team has been told, for example, that its role is as a shared service unit, the team has much of the information it needs to start work, including how to interact with customer units, what targets to focus on, and what reporting processes to expect with its boss. The taxonomy therefore plays a vital part in the design process we propose.

The Design Process

Most managers find organization design decisions difficult. They recognize that there are no right answers, and that much depends on complicated trade-offs between different possible groupings, processes, and relationships. They also know that people and behaviors matter as much as strategy and logic. They are aware, too, that organization change can be a highly political process, dominated by personalities and power plays. Managers

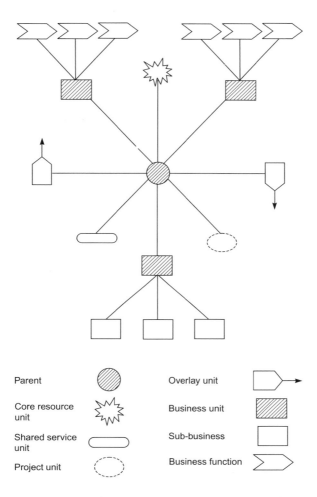

FIGURE 1.3 A New Display Bringing Out Different Roles

can sense when the organization is not working well, but they have little confidence in the outcome of most organization redesign processes.

In addition, most academics and consultants have had little to offer in terms of practical, user-friendly advice. Indeed, a professor at a leading US business school told us that the school had now stopped teaching organization design "because we didn't think we had anything useful to say". The consultants have relied largely on common sense and role models drawn from the successful organization of the moment. They have profited from successive changes in organizational fashions, but have not based their advice on clear and well-grounded principles. Moreover, process re-engineering, the most popular consulting product of the 1990s, is much better at addressing detailed design issues than at getting the overall enterprise architecture right.

As a result, few companies approach organization issues in a systematic manner. When we asked companies why they had chosen their current organization, they were usually able to explain *how* it had come about, but could seldom provide a strong logic for *why*. Whereas good chief executives can almost always provide a clear rationale for their companies' strategies, they are much less articulate when it comes to justifying their structures. They have lacked a rigorous framework and process of analysis for developing and choosing between organization options. One of the main objectives of this book is to fill that void.

Our proposed design process is shown in Figure 1.4. It has three essential steps that must be addressed:

- one or more proposed designs or design concepts need to be developed;
- the preferred option or options need to be tested and refined;
- the chosen design then needs to be finalized to aid communication and implementation.

Creating and Selecting Design Concepts

A design concept is not a full organization design. It consists of the boxes (the units), the lines (who the units report to) and, most important, the unit roles (their broad responsibilities and accountabilities, as well as guidance on their lateral and vertical relationships). It does not contain all the processes and co-ordination mechanisms that will be needed in the final design. These are added in the next two steps in the process.

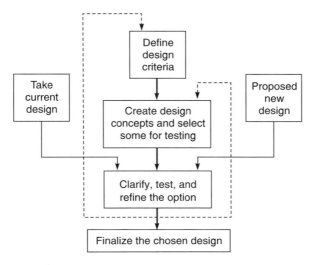

FIGURE 1.4 Making Design Decisions

We believe that it is important to develop a range of different design concept options. Frequently, managers do not consider enough alternatives before making their choice, in part because they do not have the language with which to articulate subtle differences between options. Fortunately, the taxonomy is a powerful tool for generating and articulating different options. New options can be generated by changing the roles of different units. For example, an overlay unit can be converted into a business unit or a shared service unit can become a core resource unit.

To advance to the next step, managers need to choose one or two promising design concepts from the range of options that have been developed. This need not be time consuming. Since any poor judgments will be flushed out when the tests are applied, options can be created and selected in an atmosphere of exploration and experimentation. Managers do not need to agonize about their choices. The next step – testing – will show any weaknesses in the preferred option. For this reason, managers often take the current design or some proposed alternative as their starting point.

Clarifying, Testing, and Refining the Option

Before an option can be tested, it needs to be sufficiently clearly specified. Here the roles taxonomy is essential. Each unit needs a role label. Too often, a proposal is vague about whether, for example, a proposed new customer-facing unit is a business unit, an overlay, or a project unit.

Once the option is clear, it should be put through the tests (see Figure 1.2). The tests are at the heart of our suggested process. We recommend that managers apply the fit tests first, since these tests often identify factors that cause an option to be rejected. Identifying these factors early prevents unnecessary analysis.

The good design tests should follow the fit tests because their value is more to do with helping managers refine and embellish the design concept. The good design tests can result in knock-out factors; but, more normally, processes, mechanisms, or other adjustments can be developed so that issues raised by the tests are resolved. For example, the difficult links test may show that an important co-ordination benefit, such as consistent pricing across national markets, is unlikely to be achieved through networking between nationally focused business units. To insure consistent pricing, a co-ordination mechanism needs to be designed. This might involve a process for bringing the business units together to agree pricing structures, and allowing a corporate-level marketing executive to arbitrate where disagreements arise. The nature of the difficulty should determine the details of the co-ordination solution proposed.

Each issue raised by a good design test normally leads to adjustments that refine and embellish the design concept. Once all the refinements have been added, the design should have just enough structure and process to achieve the appropriate balance between self-management and bureaucracy. The tests, therefore, are not only about judging whether the option will work. They are about helping the designer make the additions, adjustments, and refinements that will turn a design concept into a workable organization.

The danger here is to over- or under-design: creating an

inflexible organization or promoting conflict and confusion. Sufficient, but not too much, structure needs to be provided: sufficient to pass the tests, but not so much that managers feel cramped and constrained. In our experience, organization designers normally start by designing too little. They assume that "we will work it out as we go along", and then, with hindsight, wish that they had spent more time laying out some of the details. Frequently they then flip to the other extreme and design too much. No more structure should be provided than is necessary to pass the tests. Managers should avoid designing those processes and links that can be resolved without top-down input, which are much better left to the participants to work out for themselves.

"Clarify, test, and refine the option" is the pivotal step in our design process (Figure 1.4). It is at this point that a design is challenged and stress-tested. It is also at this point that creativity is often needed to find suitable refinements to the design concept. It is at this point that cross-unit co-ordination processes, top-down policies, behavior norms, and guidance about people decisions are defined. Frequently a problem that emerges from the tests can be completely or partially solved by finding the right mechanism or adjustment. Managers should allocate plenty of time to the testing and refining step.

Communicating the Design

Once an option has been tested, refined, and chosen, the design process is almost complete. However, there is still some work to do. People need to be assigned to the main jobs and the design scanned for clarity. This involves examining each unit, deciding how the top team will be chosen if it is not already in place, and assessing whether the team has enough guidance to start operating.

The key question in this step is about communication. "Are the role definitions, policies, processes, and mechanisms described in a way that will allow unit managers to start work without further guidance?" The temptation in this step is to provide additional detail rather than more powerful communication. The previous step should have resulted in "just enough" design. This step is about helping managers understand what is intended. The roles taxonomy is a useful communication language, but will probably need to be supplemented with process maps and responsibility grids, in order to convey the detailed refinements that have emerged from the tests. If this is necessary, care needs to be taken that the process of articulation does not involve imposing more structure than was intended.

In Chapter 7, we provide an overview of the design process. In Chapter 8, we give a full description of the tests, which are the core around which we have built the process, and of the analyses needed to support them. In Chapter 9, we illustrate the process with a detailed example.

Challenges for Parent Managers

Much of our previous work has focused on the role and justification for the management levels in the corporate hierarchy outside and above the business units. We call these management levels the "corporate parent". Parent managers must discharge certain obligatory or minimum tasks, concerned with due diligence on behalf of shareholders and compliance with relevant legislation and regulations. But their most essential responsibility is to add value. Parent managers need to have a clear added-value rationale for their activities.

In today's complex, interdependent organizations, parent managers face many challenges. They retain or share more responsibilities, are more involved in guiding co-ordination between units, and need to use more complicated and sophisticated performance measures for purposes of control and accountability. Parent managers also have a vital role in creating and maintaining the organizational context in which self-managed networking will thrive. This means establishing clarity in unit roles, being willing to exercise authority when necessary to protect specialist cultures and facilitate difficult links, arbitrating disputes, and encouraging a co-operative, networking culture.

Paradoxically, in order to facilitate networking they often need to play a more hands-on role. With a hands-on parent, the distinction between "business unit" responsibilities and "parent" responsibilities becomes less clear-cut.

In large companies, the parent can include several levels of management, such as groups or divisions, as well as the corporate headquarters. The lower levels of "intermediate" parenting often play a hands-on role, leaving the corporate level to concentrate on obligatory compliance and due diligence tasks, together with a few corporate-wide value-added themes. Parent managers, at both corporate and intermediate levels, are supported by functional departments, in areas such as finance, human resources, marketing, and IT. But these departments sometimes also act as core resource and shared service units, and can undertake tasks that overlap with overlay and project units. Moreover, lead business units can take on some of the responsibilities that would otherwise be performed by the functional departments in the parent. In these structures, the distinction between "the parent" and "the operating units" becomes blurred, and parenting responsibilities are distributed more widely through the organization.

Nevertheless, we believe that it is still important to assess whether and how the parent is adding value. Both the parenting advantage test and the redundant hierarchy test are powerful disciplines for assessing complex design options. With a hands-on parent, playing a more integral role in the organization, upper level managers must be clear about their responsibilities and must have the skills to create as much value as possible. Even if the parent is committed to decentralization, its role in creating the conditions for successful self-managed networking is critical. Value-added parenting is an essential component of a structured network.

In Chapter 6, we provide a full discussion of the role of the parent in complex, interdependent structures.

A New Approach to Organization Design

Our approach to organization design builds on and is compatible with many of the ideas that are emerging about twenty-first century organizations. In Chapter 10, we describe some of these ideas, and show how the concept of the network organization runs through all of them. However, we believe that our approach incorporates several distinctive features that challenge current practices and conventional wisdom.

First, we reject the cynical view that organization design will inevitably be an *ad hoc* process, paying more attention to personalities and power politics than to sound principles and logic. We believe that most managers are keen to adopt a more reasoned approach to organization design, but have been let down by the lack of practical frameworks available. Our framework has been designed around sound underlying principles and leads to a sharply practical suite of tests that bring out the merits of different design options. Armed with the tests, no manager should lack the tools for making principled organizational judgments.

Second, we do not believe that good organization design emerges from a welter of detailed process re-engineering, decision grids, and job descriptions. Senior managers must have a means of standing back and reviewing the overall organization design; they must avoid the trap of being unable to see the wood for the trees. Lower-level managers must have the discretion to fill in the details of their responsibilities as they see fit, rather than being constrained by highly detailed process maps and responsibility manuals. Our approach to enterprise design, using the taxonomy of roles and relationships, provides a means of clarifying design intentions and exploring design options without descending into excessive detail.

Third, we emphasize the value of self-managed networking as the normal way to achieve co-ordination between units. We do not believe that good organization design should call for an extensive use of co-ordination mechanisms. Rather, co-ordination mechanisms should only be designed in if, for some reason, self-managed networking seems likely to fail. What is more, the mechanism chosen should be selected to address the cause of the network failure. For example, there are many co-ordination mechanisms that can be used to share best practices, such as task forces, staff experts, policy manuals, e-mail interest groups, and even a word of advice from the boss. Normally, however, self-managed networking should be sufficient for best practice sharing between commercially motivated units with clear roles. But if the units have insufficient specialist expertise in a specific area, so that networking is unlikely to be a success, there may be a role for a corporate staff expert. The mechanism should only be designed as a response to an identified "difficult links" problem. We regard the default option as self-managed networking, and prefer to design in as few co-ordination mechanisms as possible.

Finally, we see the parent's role in complex network structures as vital. The idea that networks can thrive with no input from upper levels of management is wrong; the centerless corporation is a mirage, not a realistic objective. We fully endorse the elimination of redundant hierarchy, but we see the parent's authority and influence as integral to facilitating the network and enabling linkages that would not be possible through self-managed networking.

In summary, therefore, we acknowledge corporate politics, but believe that organization designs can and should be based primarily on logic and principles. We emphasize clarity of design intentions, but propose a means of achieving it that is not built up from excessive detail. We recognize that some co-ordination processes need to be built into the design, but prefer to leave as much as possible to the network. We are keen to decentralize, but see an essential role for the parent in facilitating and nurturing the decentralized network.

As one manager commented: "I like what you are saying. But it took time for me to get my mind around it, because you are coming at the issues from such a different angle." We are aware that we are putting forward a different way of thinking about organizational design, but we believe that it results in a more powerful and rigorous approach than has previously been available, an approach that provides the key to designing structured networks – organizations with enough, but not too much, structure.

2

The Fit Drivers and Tests

In Chapters 2 and 3, we explain in detail the elements of our design framework (see Figure 2.1). As we have noted, the framework is based on four drivers of fit and five good design principles. We discuss the fit drivers, which establish the criteria for guiding the design, in this chapter. We consider the good design principles in Chapter 3.

In developing the framework, we have concentrated on the manager who is faced with a tough practical design decision. Our purpose has been to provide a framework that builds on well-established and accepted ideas, and creates a clear checklist of essential items to be considered. We recognize that the drivers and principles themselves may seem abstract and conceptual. We have therefore derived from them a matching series of practical tests that can be used to assess any organization or design concept. The tests are introduced in this chapter and in Chapter 3, but described much more fully in Chapters 7–9, where we show how to apply the tests and link them to a process for making design decisions.

The Concept of Fit

Nearly all theories of organization contain a concept of "fit for purpose".[1] It is almost a tautology to say that organizations should be designed in a way that enables them to achieve their

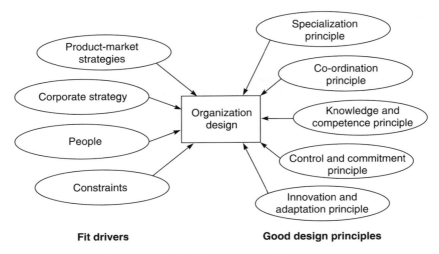

FIGURE 2.1 A Framework for Organization Design

objectives, given the environment that they are operating in. There are some managers and consultants who behave as if there were one best way to design the formal organization. But the weight of academic evidence is against them. All studies show that organization designs need to differ. Attempts to link design type to performance have almost all demonstrated the existence of contingent factors. If the design fits with the contingent factors, the organization performs better than if it does not.

This "fit for purpose" view of organization design was first developed as *structural contingency theory*, and up till the early 1980s it was the dominant strand in organization theory. Structural contingency theory[2] holds that organization structures should be designed to fit with certain contingent factors such as the nature of technology, the size of the organization, and uncertainty in the environment. In the last 20 years, other theories have been put forward, partly because structural contingency theory came to seem too mechanistic, partly because it proved hard to define precise links between contingent variables and organization design choices, and partly because organization theorists were trying to understand more about the informal dimensions of organization.

One alternative is *institutional* theory,[3] which argues that it is the institutional environment that chiefly shapes organizations. Organizational concepts – for example, divisionalization or shared services – are legitimized by influential bodies, institutions, or companies. These concepts then drive design decisions. *Resource dependency theory*,[4] on the other hand, states that organizations are designed so as to "appear" attractive to the holders of resources that are important to them. Design is therefore heavily influenced by perceptions about what resource providers want. Meanwhile, organizational economists, who are behind the development of *agency theory* and *transaction cost theory*,[5] argue that organizations should be designed to reduce agency and transaction costs. But despite the plethora of available theories, at bottom they all agree on the fit concept: organizations, they all claim, will be less successful if their designs do not fit certain contingent variables.

Recognizing this common thread, Lex Donaldson, an influential organization theorist, has argued the case for a unified theory based on the "fit for purpose" concept.[6] His view is that the differences are about which variables should drive design decisions, not whether the "fit for purpose" view should be replaced with an alternative, such as a "one right design" concept. We agree, and in support of Donaldson's ambition have pinpointed four variables that drive organizational fit. These four drivers are the contingent factors, specific to the situation of the individual organization, that we believe matter most. They are therefore the factors that should be used to develop design criteria.

But how have we identified these variables? By drawing on current academic thinking, our own research findings, and experience we have gained doing design work. We would not claim that they break new ground. Rather, they are one practical way of categorizing the contingent factors – a useful categorization rather than an intellectual breakthrough.

To recap, the four drivers of fit – those elements which set the objectives and constraints for the organization designer (see Figure 2.2) – are:

- *product-market strategies*: how the company plans to win in each product-market area it chooses to compete in;
- *corporate strategy*: how the company plans to gain advantage from competing in multiple product-market areas;
- *people*: the skills and attitudes of the individuals who are likely to be available to work within the organization; and
- *constraints*: the legal, institutional, environmental, cultural, and internal factors that limit the choice of design.

We shall now look at each of these in turn.

FIGURE 2.2 Four Drivers of Fit

Product-market Strategies

The design of the organization should make implementation of the company's product-market strategies easier. By "product-market strategy", we mean the strategy for winning and the major operating initiatives that management have planned for each product-market area. For example, a chemical company, such as Dow, competes in the polypropylene product-market area. Its strategy for winning is based on low feedstock costs, the close integration with its hydrocarbon cracker, and high asset utilization, thanks to careful balancing of output streams. Major operating initiatives may include selling a non-integrated asset, improving the links with the refinery business, and adding additional output streams. In contrast, in the polyurethane market area, the strategy is different. The company competes through product innovation and superior technical service to customers. A major operating initiative in this area may be to invest more in product research or improve the IT support to its technical service staff.

We should emphasize that this book is not about developing or critiquing strategy. Instead, we treat strategy as an input to the design process: our objective is to design an organization that will help deliver the strategy.

Different structures direct management attention to different issues. The creation of an organization unit insures that attention will be given to the main responsibilities allocated to the unit. Thus a decision to set up product-based business units rather than customer- or country-based units means that products will get more attention than customer groups or countries. Similarly, setting up a separate unit to provide payroll services to the rest of the company is likely to result in giving this service more management attention than if it was imbedded as a small support department in each business.

In the chemical example described above, management attention needs to be directed to the integration of the polypropylene plant with the cracker. One way of doing this is to put both activities in one management unit or, if they are in separate units, design a powerful integration mechanism. In polyurethane, on the other hand, product research should probably be a separate unit, within the polyurethane division, to give focused attention to the additional investment. It also may need to be linked to corporate research, to insure the investment is well managed. In other words, the strategy should drive the organization design: the design that is chosen needs to give priority attention to the elements that are most critical for the successful implementation of the strategy.

The theory that design should be driven by strategy is far from new. It originated in Alfred Chandler's classic *Strategy and Structure*,[7] a study of diversification and divisionalization in prewar America. He coined the phrase "structure follows strategy" to underline that there is no one definitive best way for companies to structure themselves, and that organizations should evolve to fit their strategies. Subsequently, other academics have pointed out that structure, in its turn, can condition strategy, so that the link between strategy and structure runs in both directions.[8]

It can be argued that companies without clear strategies can choose any organization – "If you don't know where you want to go, it doesn't matter which route you choose". However, even when the strategy is unclear, the organization should still reflect the available sources of advantage and critical success factors of the markets the company is competing in. In addition, the organization needs to be designed to aid the development of strategy. Since the link between organization and strategy is two-way, the designer needs to think about the impact a particular design will have on future strategy choices.

Managers acknowledge the link between structure and strategy, which to some extent guides most organization design choices. In our view, however, organization designs often prove unsatisfactory because managers either do not identify the main priorities of their product-market strategies with sufficient clarity, or else do not give these priorities sufficient weight in the design criteria. Here is one example: in a financial service company, we were discussing a new matrix structure in which the market units were being given equal status with the product units. Previously, the product units dominated the structure, and it was hard to get them to co-ordinate around shared clients. "We want to steal a march on our competitors by being the company which can integrate our product offerings and provide a seamless service," explained the division head. The problem was that the matrix design did not reflect this strategic ambition. The matrix was proposing a balanced relationship between the market units and the product units. But the strategy said that the ability to provide an integrated service for clients was a more important source of advantage than product skills. In other words, the market units should have been given more power than the product units, so that they could provide the necessary integration. Our advice, therefore, is to make explicit the link between a proposed organization design and the intended sources of product-market advantage. Designers who fail to do this make strategy implementation hard. This leads to a practical test – *the market advantage test.*

"Does the design allocate sufficient management attention to the operating priorities and intended sources of advantage in each product-market area?"

Given an existing or proposed design, the test involves the following analyses:

- list each major operating initiative and source of advantage for each product-market segment in which the company plans to compete;
- check whether the units are defined so as to give sufficient attention to each initiative and source of advantage; and
- where the design appears to give too little attention, consider alterations to the design or other changes that will correct the flaw.

Judging whether a design gives sufficient attention is not easy. If the design contains an autonomous unit dedicated to the issue, sufficient attention is evident. For example, if the priority is expansion into Asia and the design includes a business unit dedicated to Asia, run by a senior executive reporting to the chief executive, then there is little doubt that sufficient attention has been allocated to the goal. If, however, the design allocates the responsibility to a unit such as "international sales", which reports in at a low level and has many other competing responsibilities, the attention and authority may be insufficient. More is said about how to make these judgments in Chapter 8.

The value of this test is that it forces managers to be more explicit about operating priorities and sources of advantage. Management attention is a limited resource. Giving more attention to one issue (e.g. products) means giving less attention to another (e.g. functions or countries). The test exposes these conflicts and helps managers to resolve priorities.

Corporate Strategy

In multi-business companies that compete in more than one product-market area, there is a need for a corporate-level strategy as well as product-market strategies. Whereas product-market strategies focus on the product markets and operating functions, the corporate strategy focuses on the priorities for the group as a whole and the activities of the corporate parent. Corporate strategy is about what product-market areas to compete in and how to manage the portfolio of businesses.

The choice of product markets should be driven by the ability of the parent to add value: the company should focus its attention on those market opportunities where it has most to contribute. Decisions about how to manage the portfolio should also be driven by the parent's ability to add value. If the value comes from synergies, the design of the organization will be different from one where the value comes from imposing a standard business model. Corporate strategy is therefore built on the "parenting propositions" of the corporate parent: the sources of value the parent is expecting to add (see box: Corporate Strategy and Parenting Propositions).

Corporate Strategy and Parenting Propositions

The purpose of this box is to insure that readers understand our approach to corporate strategy. It explains what our terms "parent", "parenting advantage", and "parenting proposition" mean.

Corporate strategy addresses two issues: which product-market arenas to compete in, and how to manage the chosen portfolio of businesses. Corporate strategy is therefore about buying and selling businesses, and deciding how much resource to commit to different product or market areas. It is also about how to influence the management teams that run the operating units.

We have been studying corporate strategy for more than 15

years. In the 1980s, the main tool for thinking about these issues was the growth/share matrix, with its language of cash cows, stars, and dogs. It encouraged corporations to be port-folio managers, buying and selling businesses to create "balanced portfolios".

As a result of our research and that of other academics and consultants, a new understanding of corporate strategy has emerged.[9] It recognizes that multi-business companies consist of a parent organization and a number of business units. The parent organization is a middleman sitting between the capital markets and the businesses. As such, it must add value or become a burden on the economic system (see Figure 2.3).

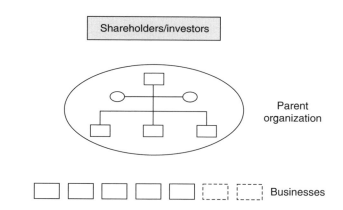

FIGURE 2.3 The Corporate Parent as Middleman

Parent organizations add value by influencing ("parenting") the businesses they own. Based on the needs of the businesses and the skills of the parent managers, parent companies choose to parent different things, enabling them to create "parenting advantage" – that is, they can add more value to a particular type of business than rival parent com-panies. For example, Rio Tinto has skills in mine financing that have enabled the company to add value to a wide-ranging portfolio of mining and minerals businesses; and Unilever has skills at moving product and market information across borders that allow it to add value to a geographically dispersed portfolio of consumer products businesses. The areas of parenting where the corporate level has, or is ambitious to have, special skills are called "parenting propositions".

Parenting propositions are the parental equivalent to sources of competitive advantage at the business level. Parenting propositions are the things parent-level managers can do to win an advantage over their rivals: they are the sources of parenting advantage. The development of a corporate-level strategy, therefore, consists of finding a set of parenting propositions and using them to decide on a list of strategic initiatives, such as buying a business or developing a corporate intranet to promote know-how sharing. We say more about parenting propositions in Chapters 6 and 8.

Different parent companies have different parenting propositions. Charles Allen, chief executive of the UK media company Granada, argues that one of his propositions is his ability to stretch performance: to help managers achieve more than they would if they were working for themselves. Based on a direct and uncomplicated relationship between Allen and the managers running Granada's businesses, this proposition requires a simple organization design with clearly defined divisions and few central staff. In 1998 Granada had only 45 people in its corporate offices.

By contrast, before it merged with Pharmacia, the parenting propositions of Monsanto were about the integration of pharmaceutical, agrochemical, and biotechnology businesses to develop new "life sciences" opportunities. CEO Robert Shapiro therefore designed overlapping responsibilities, management forums, and project groups at the highest level. He wanted to get the senior executives from different businesses to mix in formal and informal ways that would stimulate their creativity and help unearth new opportunities. Monsanto's corporate office contained more than five times as many staff as Granada's.

In previous work, we have written extensively about the differences in the parenting propositions of different companies, and we have shown how these differences can lead to different structures and processes.[10] We have also pointed out that the most successful parent companies have particularly insightful propositions and are especially skilled at implementing them. They have what we call "parenting advantage": they gain an advantage at the corporate level as a result of their choice of parenting propositions and the way they implement them.

This link between corporate strategy and structure is intuitively recognized by managers, who know that organizations can either help or hinder the purposes of top management, and who therefore accept that organization design should take into account the value that top managers are trying to add.

In our work on corporate strategy, however, we have observed that companies frequently do not make their parenting propositions sufficiently clear. In part, this is because parenting theory (the set of concepts that lie behind corporate strategy thinking) is not well understood, and corporate managers have not considered what their parenting propositions are. "Ask not what we do for the businesses," is their implicit position: "Ask what the businesses do for the company." Driven more by the idea of assembling a portfolio of businesses in attractive sectors than a portfolio that will thrive under this particular parent, these managers fail to define the top-down objectives that will guide their design efforts. Even corporate-level managers who do try to add value are often vague about how they will achieve this goal. To remedy this, we propose a *parenting advantage test*:

"Does the design allocate sufficient attention to the intended sources of added-value and strategic initiatives of the corporate parent?"

The test involves the following analyses:

- list the major parenting propositions and parent-level strategic initiatives;
- check whether each proposition and strategic initiative has sufficient attention within the design; and

- where the design appears to give too little attention, consider alterations or other changes that will correct the flaw.

As with the market advantage test, it is not easy to judge whether attention is sufficient. Nevertheless, the test helps managers be more explicit about corporate priorities and parenting propositions, and helps to insure that operating units and layers of the hierarchy are defined in a way that is consistent with rather than contradicts corporate priorities; that the roles and responsibilities of the center and intermediate layers are appropriate; and that parenting processes (e.g. planning, budgeting, synergy management) support the parenting propositions.

The parenting advantage test also helps companies to be more precise in their thinking about the role and added-value of the corporate center. At Cargill, which operates a wide range of businesses including food products and agricultural commodities, a major corporate transformation program identified a number of parenting propositions for the corporate center, including leading a company-wide shift toward providing customer solutions, developing a high performance culture, and promoting sharing of experience and skills between business units. Using the parenting advantage test, it was possible to make these rather general themes much more specific and to translate them into actionable organizational initiatives. For example, the shift to customer solutions was linked to new, more market-focused business unit definitions. The business units were grouped together into "platforms", with a platform management level to promote collaboration opportunities. Peer groups were also established to encourage voluntary co-operation between business units. In addition, the corporate center emphasized behaviors and values that "develop and leverage deep customer knowledge and insights", and emphasized the importance of customer solutions in all their interactions with the business units and platforms. By drawing out the implications of the parenting propositions in this way, Cargill corporate managers were able to make their efforts to create parenting advantage much more tangible. By contrast, companies that fail to apply the parenting advantage test frequently end up with corporate parenting propositions that are too nebulous to create value or which have not been grounded in specific implementation initiatives.

People

The importance of people to the choice of an organization design is not in doubt. Again and again, managers told us that while with the right people you can make almost any design work, the wrong ones will reduce even the best paper design to a shambles. People, the managers who will be available to populate the organization, are thus a fundamental driver of design choices.

The importance of people is partly because of the skills that individuals possess, and hence the responsibilities that they are able to discharge well. It is no good designing a large number of decentralized, profit-accountable business units if there are not enough capable general managers to run them. On the other hand, there may be much to be said for such a structure, irrespective of how well it nominally fits with the strategy, if there exists a large pool of general managers whose skills are not currently being fully exploited. Building the organization with an eye on the available skills is essential. But it is equally important to build around personal preferences and desires, since these determine which responsibilities managers will take on with enthusiasm and which they will resist. A design that calls for close collaboration between managers who are bitter personal rivals is doomed to failure. But if the managers are old friends, with personal trust, mutual respect, and a strong desire to work together, they may be able to do things that would cause friction and frustrations in most normal circumstances.

Despite the evident importance of people, managers often complain that the designs they adopt are thwarted by people problems. This occurs most prominently in acquisitions. How often do companies announce that there has been an unexpected loss of key personnel in the acquired company, or that synergy benefits were smaller than expected, because of personality clashes? Unless the design of the new organization takes account of the people who will make it work, its success will be doubtful at best.

In one company, the CEO wanted to set up a new businesses division to pull together a number of struggling diversification initiatives which he felt were receiving too little attention as part of other units. However, when we started to consider where we could find an individual with experience of natural gas resources, electricity generation, telecoms, waste management, and engineering consultancy to run the new division, we quickly concluded that the design was faulty. In the absence of a suitable internal candidate, hiring an unknown manager to run a portfolio of businesses the CEO did not understand well was too risky a proposition. Instead the CEO sold some of the businesses, left some where they were, and shifted responsibilities for others. He also set up a separate review process to give these businesses some additional attention.

Although managers instinctively know that people should be a key input to organization design, people problems occur all too often. One reason for this is that senior managers become so enamored with a particular design concept that they are inclined to overlook the limitations of their colleagues and subordinates. Because the design looks so well suited to the strategy, they disregard the people issues.

A second reason for people problems is that managers often overestimate the ease with which new skills and attitudes can be acquired, either by hiring new people or by inculcating new aptitudes in the existing management cadre. Our observation is that while both of these options are possible, some jobs are hard to fill through a recruiting process, and some individuals are resistant to change. Limited change may be possible, but not total freedom to remake people in a new image. It is therefore essential to make a realistic appraisal of the strengths and weaknesses of both existing staff and the pool of talent the company can reasonably hope to attract.

This leads to our *people test*:

"Does the design adequately reflect the motivations, strengths, and weaknesses of the available people?"

The test involves analyses such as the following:

- list the senior managers who will be part of the new organ-ization, and assess how committed these senior managers will be to making the organization work;
- list particularly talented individuals and assess whether the design uses their talents to the full; and
- list the job roles that are pivotal (i.e. key to making the organization run smoothly), and judge whether these roles will be easy or difficult to fill with competent managers.

People judgments are never easy. The test involves being clear about who the most talented individuals are and what skills they bring to the new organization. It involves identifying the "influ-ential" managers, on account not only of their current job positions but also of their ability to gain followers within the organization. It also involves examining all the job categories that may be difficult to fill; finding out whether managers with the appropriate skills exist today; and examining whether career paths can be designed so that they continue to exist in the future.

The value of this test is that it insures managers do not overlook the people dimension. Even if the test is limited to the top layer of managers it can be invaluable. It cannot be overemphasized that structures, processes, and roles work best when the people who bring them alive fit the design, or the design fits the people.

Constraints

Constraints represent something of a catch-all category.[11] In it we include a range of factors that can constrain the design choice:
- legal and governmental issues, such as requirements for certain governance processes, legal or ownership structures, and laws, such as health and safety;

- institutional and stakeholder issues, such as the preferences of major shareholders, the requirements of industry associations, or the demands of the capital markets;
- other external issues, such as the local culture, particular pressure groups, or unions; and
- internal issues, such as IT capabilities, internal culture, and organization-wide skills.

We will not devote attention here to all of these items, since in our experience they are only relevant in certain situations. For example, health and safety laws are only relevant to the design of the health and safety function, if at all. A few issues, however, emerge more broadly. The law, as it relates to legal and ownership structures, often limits the choice of structural design. The limitation is rarely of vital importance. It can restrict the ability to create a unit in one country without some joint venture partner. It may prevent the integration of two operations in different countries. Minority holdings in some operations can limit the choices.

A second constraint with broad impact is the historic organization culture and accompanying capabilities. All managers are aware that their corporate culture can limit their choice of organization design. Compare Procter & Gamble and Unilever. Both companies compete head-on in many markets around the world. Unilever, because of its history of dual UK and Dutch nationality, small home market and decentralized structure, developed cultural norms and skills about co-ordinating across borders that are completely different to those of P&G. These differences caused Unilever in the mid-1990s to organize geographically just at the moment when P&G was deciding to reinforce its global product divisions. The differences in culture and skills made it quite rational for two companies with similar market strategies to choose different structural solutions.

Most managers have a strong sense of what will work in their particular environment. If a company has always had problems in persuading shared services to be genuinely responsive to other units' needs, they will be skeptical about extending the role of shared service units in future. If product units and customer units have consistently fought over product development and pricing strategies, it will be necessary for any new organization to pay close attention to how these friction points will be handled. If the relationship between the management teams in Germany and France has always been friendly and co-operative, important co-ordination benefits may be easily achievable without changing boundaries or responsibilities.

In their widely-read book, *Managing Across Borders*, Chris Bartlett and Sumantra Ghoshal use the term "administrative heritage" to refer to a corporation's history, culture, imbedded values, and ways of working.[12] They confirm that, based on their research, the administrative heritage conditions both the choices and the implementation of a company's strategies. Gerry Johnson uses a different term, the "culture web", in his writings, but makes similar points about the pervasive influence of corporate culture.[13]

IT systems are another frequent constraint on design choice. A major UK electricity company wanted to organize into separate business units for engineering, transmission, and supply. The logic for the reorganization was compelling. The utility had been run as an integrated business, but industry deregulation would lay the different parts of the company open to competition. The IT systems, however, could not produce profitability data by business unit. Believing that the move to business units was essential, management made the change despite the IT problems. The result was unfortunate. The new business management teams had no management information. They therefore started out in the new structure using the same functionally-based decision processes as previously. When the IT system finally did deliver the data they needed, they had established their way of working and found it difficult to incorporate the new information. By making the change before the IT systems were ready, the company inadvertently made it harder to switch attention away from functional issues to commercial ones.

Managers are fully aware that constraints can exist. However, they often do not give the issue enough attention early on in the design process. Options can be developed and even selected before the corporate lawyer or IT expert points out the problem. Hence our fourth test, the *feasibility test*:

"Does the design take account of the constraints that may make the proposal unworkable?"

The test involves:

- listing all the potentially important areas of constraint and checking whether the design accommodates them.

The feasibility test can require some tough judgments. In areas such as culture and systems, it can be hard to assess whether a constraint exists, at least until the new design has been tried. Moreover, many constraints can be removed over time. Cultures can be changed, capabilities improved, and sometimes even the law can be altered through successful lobbying. The feasibility test, therefore, requires an assessment of whether there is a problem and how easy it will be to make the changes necessary to implement the new design. The solutions may be small adjustments, delays in implementation, intermediate solutions, or whole new designs.

As with the previous three tests, the purpose of this test is to encourage managers to think about issues that often get only cursory attention. By raising the issue of constraints early in the design process, the feasibility test can substantially reduce the amount of effort that would otherwise be spent on unworkable options.

Review

Our design framework treats the four drivers of fit – product-market strategies, corporate strategies, people, and constraints – as the brief: the challenge is to design an organization that will achieve the strategic objectives given the available people and the relevant constraints. As we will explain in Chapters 7 and 9, the four drivers can also be used to generate design criteria.

Their power derives from their simplicity and completeness: although there are only four factors to consider, between them they incorporate all the important variables that are specific to the situation. The fit drivers are made practically useful through the tests (see Figure 2.4). A design that passes the four tests will be "fit for purpose".

A design that is fit for purpose, however, may not be optimized. In the next chapter, we describe four principles of good design which help managers to create organizations that will function as effectively as possible.

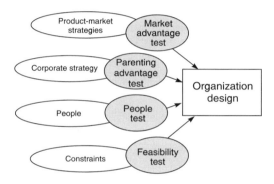

FIGURE 2.4 Fit Drivers and Tests

3

The Good Design Principles and Tests

In addition to the fit drivers discussed in Chapter 2, many more specific rules, guidelines and findings have been put forward on the subject of good organization design.[1] In fact there is a cacophony of advice, much of it complicated, hard to apply and sometimes self-contradictory (see box: How to Group Responsibilities into Units/Departments).[2] As a result, most managers rely on a few homespun rules of thumb, such as that a boss should have no more than six subordinates, or "no man can have two masters".

How to Group Responsibilities into Units/Departments

The list below shows a sample of the advice from a sample of the literature available on a single organization design issue.

- Greater task diversity requires greater departmentalization (Aston Studies)

- The greater the intensity of interaction between activities, the more closely they should be linked (Thompson)

- Functional structures are best for standardization, scale, and task specialization (Galbraith)

- Product structures are best when product characteristics are diverse and rapid product development is important (Galbraith)

- The more power that customers (or other stakeholders) have, the more the organization needs to be structured by customer segment (Galbraith)
- A process structure is best when cycle time and process re-engineering are important (Galbraith)
- A network structure is best when the environment is changing rapidly, product life cycles are short, and markets are fragmented (Hatch)
- Cost centers are best when cost management is important and quantity and mix decisions can be made outside the unit (Jensen)
- Revenue centers are best when revenue maximization is important and quantity and mix decisions can be made outside the unit (Jensen)
- Profit centers are best when the knowledge required to make the product mix, quantity, and quality decisions is "specific" to the unit (Jensen)
- "Expense centers" are the least satisfactory type of unit (Jensen)
- Group by user to maximize responsiveness to marketplace, by activity to utilize and develop people, and by output to improve control (Nadler and Tushman)
- Different ways of grouping lead to different career paths and hence promote different capability development: activity grouping leads to activity professionalism; user grouping leads to general management skills (Nadler and Tushman)

To help managers adopt a less haphazard approach, we have distilled five principles of good organization design. These principles give guidance on how to design organizations that not only take account of the four fit drivers but also address the most difficult challenge managers face in creating organizations that will be as effective as possible in achieving their purposes (Figure 3.1):

- Two principles, the "specialization" principle and the "co-ordination" principle, are primarily concerned with how to group responsibilities into units and what links to establish between them.
- The "knowledge and competence" principle is primarily concerned with which responsibilities to decentralize and what hierarchical levels to set up.
- The "control and commitment" principle is primarily concerned with the process for insuring that managers effectively discharge decentralized responsibilities.
- The "innovation and adaptation" principle is primarily concerned with insuring the organization can change and evolve in the future.

These five good design principles, together with the fit drivers define the underlying ground rules of good organization design. They give managers the guidance they need to create "structured networks".

As with the fit drivers, we have converted the good design principles into tests that can be applied to design proposals. These tests are not only practical ways of applying the principles,

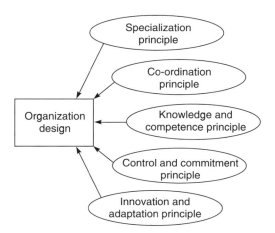

FIGURE 3.1 Five Principles of Good Design

they also capture some important insights that we have developed from our research.[3] While our work on the fit principle does little more than categorize the variables most managers and academics are familiar with, our work on the good design principles goes further. Distilling the mass of current advice into five overriding principles is an important step forward in its own right. But, beyond that, within each test we believe we have made some advances in design thinking.

Specialization, Co-ordination, and Unit Boundaries

When responsibilities are delegated to lower levels of management, a basic issue is how to group the responsibilities: what "management units" to establish. Management units are clusters of responsibilities delegated to a designated manager or management team, and form the basic building blocks of organization design. They can, for example, be departments, functions, divisions, businesses, countries, products, or projects.

The primary influence on how to structure units comes from the product-market strategies. They tell the organization designer where management attention is most needed. But the focus of management attention that follows from creating units has two other consequences. First, it results in the development of specialist skills. As managers give attention to a focused set of responsibilities, they develop skills that relate to those responsibilities. Second, it creates some co-ordination challenges. Whichever way the units are defined, some activities need to be co-ordinated across unit boundaries.

The specialization and co-ordination principles make it clear that there are often trade-offs to be made. The more narrowly defined the units, the more specialization is possible, but the bigger the co-ordination challenge. Alternatively, if the units are defined broadly so that most of the important co-ordination requirements happen within units, the units are unlikely to be optimized for the development of specialist skills. To make complex decisions about unit boundaries, managers need a deep understanding of what specialization and co-ordination is needed, and how design decisions will affect the outcome.

The Specialization Principle

Unit boundaries should be defined to achieve the most important benefits available from specialization.

Managers will develop skills and resources around the responsibilities they are allocated. If the unit is focused on a customer segment, its managers will build up a deep understanding of these customers and design some special ways of meeting their needs. If the focus is on a product, the managers will become expert in the development, manufacture, marketing, and use of the product. If the focus is functional, managers will acquire a deeper understanding of the type of skills and people needed for functional effectiveness. Managers develop these skills because they give priority to a focused set of responsibilities and because they learn from their experience.

The importance of specialization can be traced back as far as the writings of the Scottish economist Adam Smith in 1776. Smith famously used the example of a pin factory,[4] noting that the manufacture of pins was made more efficient by dividing up the responsibility into shaft-making, head-making, and attaching the shaft to the head. By specializing, Smith noted, an organization with 10 employees could make 10 times as many pins as 10 individuals could make on their own. The theme of specialization was further reinforced by Frederick Winslow Taylor in his book, *The Principles of Scientific Management.*[5] His "scientific approach" to management demonstrated that it was possible to improve performance by breaking down each responsibility into its component parts. This made it easier to figure out how each component part could best be executed. More recently the "experience curve", first popularized by the Boston Consulting Group,[6] demonstrated that the cost of producing an item falls by a set percentage every time the accumulated experience of producing it doubles. In other words, when they focus on a specialized activity, managers learn with experience.

The development of specialist skills is a benefit of creating units with a focused set of responsibilities. But there are two sides to this: every structural option has advantages and dis-advantages. If the structure is divided into product units, the organization will develop more product-oriented skills and fewer market, geography, or functional skills. If the structure is organized round functional units, the organization will develop strong functional skills and weaker product skills. No organiz-ation will maximize all dimensions of skill. Every structure is a compromise. As a result, it is important to group responsibilities in ways that will insure the development of those specialist skills that are most important for the organization's success.

The Co-ordination Principle

Units should be defined so that the activities that most need to be co-ordinated fall within unit boundaries.

It is easier to co-ordinate and align activities within a unit than across unit boundaries. Managers of a product unit can easily co-ordinate activities in different markets in support of the product strategy. In a market unit, managers can easily align the func-tional activities to the needs of the customers in the market. If research needs to co-ordinate closely with marketing, this is easier if both research and marketing are in the same unit.

There are three reasons why co-ordination is easier within a unit than across unit boundaries. First, the unit manager has a view of the overall responsibilities and goals of the unit, and can see how all the activities within the unit can work together to achieve these goals. Having an overview of the entire manu-facturing system, the head of a manufacturing function can see how different factories can balance their efforts to achieve the most cost-effective result. In the same way, a business unit general manager can align the different functions such as research, manufacturing, and marketing to serve the customers, making trade-offs between the narrower interests of the individual functions. Because the manager of a unit pays attention to the overall objectives of the unit, he or she is less likely to overlook opportunities for co-ordination and alignment within the unit.

Second, managers in charge of units normally have the authority to insist on co-ordination, even when the members of their teams are reluctant. Even more important than authority, they have powerful currencies with which to persuade individuals to co-operate. The manager can promise promotion or career support; develop a team spirit and identity that rises above the personal interests of individual members; draw on loyalty and obligation: "if you scratch my back I'll scratch yours". The manager can trade off performance in one area for performance in another. Across unit boundaries, many of these incentives for co-operation are not available or are available only in a diluted form.

The third reason is that a manager whose full attention is given to one unit has more time to monitor co-ordination issues and persuade those working in the unit to do what is required.

The advantages of co-ordination within a unit are widely recognized. One of the strongest themes in the literature on organization design is that units should be created where the "intensity of co-ordination needs" is greatest. This idea goes back to James Thompson.[7]

Managers also recognize the importance of forming units as a way of achieving co-ordination and alignment. If there is a need to co-ordinate all the products going to a particular customer group, one reaction is to set up a unit dedicated to that customer group. For example, consumer goods companies have set up "Tesco" or "Wal-Mart" mini-units to pull together and align their various dealings with these influential retailers. Similarly, 3M has an automotive unit whose role is to co-ordinate all 3M's sales to the automotive sector.

Ease of co-ordination is a benefit that comes from forming a unit. But the unit has boundaries, so its creation also has downsides: while some areas of co-ordination fall within units, making alignment easier to achieve, other areas require links across unit boundaries, which makes it harder. As a result, it is important to group responsibilities so that the activities which most need to be co-ordinated fall within unit boundaries.

Specialization and Co-ordination Trade-offs

The specialization and co-ordination principle implies that responsibilities should be grouped into units so as to optimize any trade-offs between the need for specialist skills and the need for co-ordination. This requires the organization designer to review the intended sources of advantage of the chosen strategy, giving particular consideration to the specialist skills and co-ordination benefits that appear most important.

Unfortunately, co-ordination benefits and specialization benefits sometimes suggest different, even conflicting, ways of structuring the units. For example, the promise of specialization benefits may suggest a functional or process structure, because this allows for the development of superior operating skills in each functional area or process. However, co-ordination benefits may point to a market-focused structure, because of the need to persuade different functions to co-ordinate in serving a particular customer group. Alternatively, specialization benefits may suggest setting up units with a narrow market focus to insure closeness to particular segments; whereas co-ordination benefits would indicate much broader units to encourage the sharing of product development costs, sales forces, and other overheads.

This conflict between specialization and co-ordination was investigated in the 1960s by two well-known Harvard academics, Paul Lawrence and Jay Lorsch.[8] In their book, *Organization and Environment*, they pointed out that one of the central dilemmas in designing organizations is the need simultaneously to "integrate" the activities in the organization and provide sufficient "differentiation" between different parts of the organization to match the differences in the environment. Differentiation allows units to specialize. Integration insures that the different parts of the organization work in a co-ordinated way.

It is possible to organize in a way that combines some benefits of both specialization and co-ordination. For example, a broadly defined unit may be established to achieve co-ordination across several market segments. At the same time, more narrowly focused sub-units may be set up within the larger structure to home in on the needs of specific segments. In the same way, functional sub-units may be set up within a broadly defined business to promote the special skills needed in each function. Specialization is possible within more broadly defined units.

However, some of the specialization benefits are likely to be lost. This is because the priorities and skills of the more aggregated, superior unit will influence the sub-units. The needs of the broadly defined business may well prevent the sub-units from developing skills or making decisions that would be optimal for their own activities.

Consider two companies in consumer products (Figure 3.2). One company, called Product Inc, is organized by global product, and, within each product, is sub-divided into country business units. The other company, called Country Inc, is organized by country, and, within each country, is sub-divided into product units. If we examine the organization structure in the USA, both companies have sub-units focused on each of the main product areas. We might therefore expect that both companies would get the same specialization benefits. But the

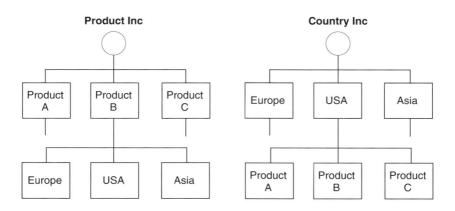

FIGURE 3.2 Product and Country Organizations

units in Product Inc report to global product bosses, whereas the units in Country Inc report to the head of the USA. As a result, the units will develop different priorities. Those in Product Inc will be driven more by the concerns of the global product head and the need to compete for capital and status with other product businesses. They will, therefore, develop more product-related skills. The units in Country Inc will be driven more by the concerns of their country boss, and will thus develop more country-related skills. The differences may be subtle and will depend on the personal skills and priorities of the senior managers concerned, but they need to be taken into account when making the choice about which way to organize.

In theory, managers should choose between competing structures by weighing the specialization and co-ordination benefits. In practice, however, the benefits are hard to measure with any precision, and the choice between alternative structures depends on difficult judgments about what matters most for the company's strategy. Moreover, some skill specialization can be achieved within sub-units, and some co-ordination can be achieved across unit boundaries, whereas other types of specialization or co-ordination will be difficult unless incorporated within a unit.

Given that the specialization and co-ordination principles do not lead directly to clear answers, our advice is to pay particular attention to the "autonomy needs" associated with specialization, and the "difficult links" associated with co-ordination. The concepts of autonomy needs and difficult links are both areas where we believe we have developed new insights that can provide practical guidance. They each yield a test that can be applied to proposed designs.

Autonomy Needs

For a unit to create specialization benefits, it normally develops some special ways of managing. For example, the way the marketing function is managed is different from the way the research function is managed. These differences are not just about the measures used to assess performance, they affect the whole personality of the unit: the sort of people who are hired, the norms of behavior, and the style of leadership. When a unit is integrated into a larger organization, it can be hard to develop and maintain these special ways of managing.

If a unit or a sub-unit is strongly influenced by the layers above, or by sister units, or by its membership of a larger whole, there will be a tendency for the unit to start to behave more like the larger organization. When the unit needs to be managed in a way that is different from the larger organization, it has "autonomy needs": it needs to be protected from possible "contaminating" influences from the larger organization, and it needs freedom to make its own decisions relatively autonomously (see box: Autonomy Needs).

Autonomy Needs

Autonomy needs arise when there is a risk of a unit being "dominated" or "contaminated" by the management approach of the larger organization. This problem occurs mainly where there is insufficient decentralization from the layers above, resulting in some inappropriate influences on a unit. This is a particular danger for sub-units that have been set up within a broader unit, but can also arise where the parent level of management wields strong influence, or when a unit is closely linked to sister units in a way that interferes with the independent running of the unit. If, for example, the unit has to accept standards or policies developed in other units, or to fit in with decisions taken elsewhere, this may inhibit its freedom to develop its own style and strategy. In all of these situations, the unit concerned has to adapt its mode of operations to outside influences. If these changes damage its effectiveness, its autonomy needs have clearly not been met.

For example, many companies have found that their e-ventures need different personnel policies, performance measures, and cultures from their mainstream businesses.

This is often hard to insure unless the venture is separated from the main organization into a new ventures division or even a joint venture with another company. Major structural change is needed to give the venture sufficient autonomy.

There are three reasons why a unit may need autonomy. The first is where the critical success factors of a unit are different from the critical success factors of the rest of the organization. In these circumstances, the objectives, ways of thinking, policies, and norms of behavior of the larger organization may overly influence the managers in the focused unit and prevent it from developing in the way it needs to develop. For example, the human resource policies developed by corporate-level managers may be inappropriate for some specialist units, making it more difficult for these units to hire or retain the type of managers they need.

The second reason for autonomy needs comes from task incompatibility. If you dedicate yourself to one task, you become less good at another, and vice versa. For example, battery maker Duracell chose not to integrate its long-life battery business with its short-life battery operation. Despite the potential for savings in distribution, selling costs, research, overhead functions, and even in marketing, Duracell has kept the businesses separate. Why? "By combining a long-life business with a short-life business, you end up paying less attention to the long-life product. For example, if you give salesmen both products to sell, they will sell many more short-life products than long-life. The reason is that it is an easier sale. Building a long-life business is much harder. It requires dedicated management attention." In other words, the long-life battery business has autonomy needs; the selling tasks in long-life batteries and short-life batteries are incompatible. Other examples of task incompatibility include simultaneously marketing luxury and low-cost products, or manufacturing short-run special products alongside long-run commodity ones.

A similar point lies behind the difficulty that Clayton Christensen observes when companies are faced with "disruptive technologies".[9] These are new technologies that, in the long run, will make existing technologies obsolete and cannibalize the products on which the success of the company was built. Christensen believes that companies will usually suppress the disruptive technology unless a separate, dedicated unit is set up to promote it.

The third reason for autonomy needs comes from the preferences of customers. Customers are often attracted to a product or service because it is distinguished from other products. If the positioning of the two products becomes confused, one product is "contaminated" in the eyes of the customers by another. Take, for example, the luxury sector of the automobile industry. For many years, particularly in Europe, customers viewed cars made by luxury specialists, such as Mercedes or BMW, in a different way from similar cars produced by mass market companies, such as Ford or Toyota. To be a true luxury car, its manufacturer needed to be perceived as a luxury specialist. Companies that tried to move into the luxury sector from their base in the mass market found this perception barrier hard to overcome. The companies that have been most successful are those which set up or acquired separate specialist units, such as Toyota's Lexus or Volkswagen's Audi.

Customer preference is also important in situations where the supplier's independence may be compromised. If the supplier is owned by a competitor, the customer may have concerns about whether the supplier is acting independently. If the supplier can demonstrate sufficient autonomy, this concern is greatly reduced. AT&T spun out its equipment manufacturing business, Lucent, because rival equipment manufacturers were picking up telecoms customers who were reluctant to buy from what they saw as a major competitor.

When a unit has autonomy needs, the influence of other units can "contaminate" or "pollute" its requirement for specialist strategies and ways of managing. The solution is to create mechanisms that insulate the unit from negative influences, while ideally allowing positive influences and coordination. Boundaries between units and autonomy from the layer above are structural mechanisms for providing insulation, but it is also possible to use non-structural mechanisms. For example, appointing a senior manager to run the unit usually gives the unit the status to absorb good influences and reject bad ones. An alternative is to insure that the parent manager has sufficient understanding of the specialist culture the unit needs, and intervenes to protect it when necessary. In Chapter 8 we discuss in more detail different ways of designing solutions.

When a unit needs a high degree of autonomy, as a new e-business unit might, the structure should take this into account. It will be necessary to give the unit power to make decisions in most areas, to allow it to opt out of standard policies or co-ordination committees, and to encourage it to develop its own independent culture and style of operating. All this suggests that the unit needs to be relatively self-contained and insulated from hierarchical and lateral influences. In these circumstances, it will be particularly difficult to achieve both a high level of specialization within the unit and a high level of co-ordination with other units. If, however, a unit has low autonomy needs, and the dangers from domination or contamination are minimal, it will be easier not only to specialize but also to obtain benefits from co-ordination with other units.

We observe that, although managers instinctively understand the need for autonomy, especially those in the unit suffering from domination or contamination, in practice they often underplay the issue in their design decisions. This is somewhat puzzling. The reason may be either that they give too much weight to organizational unity and togetherness (a common human trait), or they overestimate the ability of managers to simultaneously develop specialist skills *and* conform to organization standards. Whatever the reason, it leads us to a practical *specialist cultures test*:

"Do any 'specialist cultures', units with cultures that need to be different from sister units and the layers above, have sufficient protection from the influence of the dominant culture?"

The test involves:

- listing all units with cultures that need to be different from the dominant culture of the company or the division to which they belong;
- assessing whether the specialist culture is in danger of being dominated;
- adding to or changing the design so as to provide more protection where needed; and
- deciding whether any of the risks to the "exposed" specialist cultures are "knock-out" factors.

The purpose of the specialist cultures test is to identify parts of the organization that need more independence than the design currently allows. Normally the design can be adjusted to accommodate the autonomy needs of the unit without making too big a compromise on some other dimension, such as co-ordination. Sometimes, however, adequate solutions prove impossible to develop, in which case the proposed design must be rejected. The risk to the specialist culture eliminates that design option from further consideration: it is a "knock-out" factor.

Judgments about which units require specialist cultures and whether a unit is likely to be dominated require careful thought. However, they need to be made, and the test insures that managers give the issue the scrutiny it warrants.

Difficult Links

On the surface, co-ordinating activity across unit boundaries rather than within units is potentially problematic. However, it is not true that all co-ordination across unit boundaries is doomed to fail. A trading relationship is one example of cross-boundary co-ordination which is easy to achieve. Arm's-length relationships are satisfactory ways of trading between units, provided that there are open-market alternative suppliers and buyers to establish a "fair" comparison transfer price. There are many other types of co-ordination that can and do proceed satisfactorily between separate units. For example, much knowledge sharing, particularly between larger, more experienced units and smaller units, happens spontaneously across unit boundaries. The smaller units seek out the knowledge they need, and the larger unit is flattered by the attention. In other words, much co-ordination between units takes place easily and naturally. Self-managed networking between units is often all that is necessary for effective co-ordination.

At the other extreme, some co-ordination is particularly difficult unless the responsibilities relating to the co-ordination are allocated to a single unified management team. Suppose a number of different units each have sub-scale factories, and there is a need to rationalize them. In this case, co-ordination will be hard to achieve unless there is a powerful authority with the time and expertise to devise solutions, win support, and overcome vested interests. Each unit will want to avoid the pain of making employees redundant and developing new relationships with a different factory, possibly in a different country. Each will argue strongly that its factory should remain open and supply the other units. Factory rationalization needs to be led by a hands-on boss, who can use a combination of authority, incentives, and judgment to bring the relevant managers together, find a good solution, and make it happen. This is easiest within a single unit under unified management.

Difficult links, as we call them, are those co-ordinations that are unlikely to proceed smoothly, or at all, through spontaneous networking between the units concerned. They are difficult because the units will not perceive the co-ordination benefits on their own, they will be unwilling to work together to achieve them, or they will be faced with hard-to-reconcile conflicts of interest. To get the benefits, upper levels of management need to set up a co-ordination mechanism and/or intervene directly. At the extreme, the only solution is to reallocate responsibilities so that the co-ordination is under the control of a single unit.

Difficult Links

Co-ordination between units is important in most organizations. Trading between sister units, peer group meetings to exchange ideas, shared approaches to common customers, shared resources to create economies of scale, and many other forms of co-ordination are common.

In many situations, the benefits can be achieved by spontaneous interactions between the units concerned – what we call self-managed networking. Self-managed networking is little different from collaboration between third parties. The managers in sister units may have more knowledge about each other's operations and closer personal ties of trust or friendship, but the primary motivation is still commercial. If self-managed networking between competent, commercially-driven managers is failing to achieve a potential benefit, the first question to ask, therefore, is why.

In many companies, the corporate context inhibits co-ordination. Misaligned incentives, rivalry between divisional bosses, a culture of secrecy or mutual mistrust can all undermine sensible cross-unit working. A familiar example is a reward system that is based exclusively on unit-specific profitability and gives no credit for other benefits that could flow from collaboration. Where the context includes "synergy killers"[10] of this sort, co-ordination within the company is likely to be more difficult than between third parties. But there is no intrinsic reason for synergy-killers to exist, and organizationally aware corporate parents should be able to adjust the context to remove most of them.

A further cause of co-ordination problems stems from a lack of clarity about the type of relationships that different units are supposed to have with each other. How should the corporate research function work with the business units? How should the market units work with each product unit? How should the corporate service departments work with their users? Organization designers need to specify clearly the intended relationships between units, in order to provide a framework for self-managed networking. This is a topic we will explore in Chapter 5.

Even with a supportive corporate context and clear relationship definitions, there can still be difficulties. The problem may be the result of ignorance about other units and hence about the opportunity for co-ordination. It may stem from different perceptions of the likely costs and benefits. It may be down to personal frictions between managers. More generally, the priority managers give to their own units inevitably reduces the attention they give to the affairs of other units and to the potential for benefits that will accrue to other units.

Sometimes, these difficulties can be resolved in whole or in part by setting up a suitable co-ordination mechanism, such as a transfer pricing system or a co-ordination committee (see Chapter 8 for more details). As an alternative to, or in support of, co-ordination mechanisms, the parent can take initiatives that reduce or eliminate the difficulties. Disseminating information can reduce ignorance about other units. Corporate experts can help align different perceptions of costs and benefits. Moving individuals can calm personal frictions. A strong steer from the boss can bring blinkered unit managers into line. Provided the corporate parent has the skills and resources to see the opportunity and intervene successfully, many difficulties can be eliminated.

But co-ordination mechanisms do not always work, either because the co-ordination is "unworkable" across unit boundaries or because the co-ordination mechanism will yield only a partial solution. Particular problems arise when:

- it is hard to achieve a fair division of the benefits and costs; or
- the basis of collaboration needs frequent reassessment and renegotiation.

A fair division of the benefits or costs is particularly difficult when units have to work with each other and there is no third-party market alternative. For example, in vertically integrated chemical companies the downstream businesses may be constrained to buy from upstream businesses. Agreeing a transfer price, and hence a division of the benefits, will always be extremely difficult if there is no third-party benchmark to refer to.

Difficulties also arise in win/lose situations where parent managers either do not wish to provide incentives to compensate the managers of the losing units for the costs they will incur, or else do not have the power or the currency to provide appropriate compensation. In the example of factory rationalization, some units will be clear losers, while others will gain. In theory, parent managers could compensate the losers for their pain. In practice, the parent managers often lack the appropriate currencies and close knowledge to do so. They may also feel inhibited by their desire not to interfere or micro-manage. Indeed, it is sometimes harder for parent managers to provide adequate compensation within the company than it is for independent units to negotiate adequate compensation in the market.

The second reason why a link can be unworkably difficult arises from the frequency and cost of negotiating an agreement between units. Examples include co-ordination between R&D, manufacturing and marketing in new product development, or co-ordinated marketing strategies between several sub-units selling similar products. If there are many trade-offs to be made and uncertainties that lead to frequent changes in the approach, negotiated agreements between autonomous units may be too costly, slow, or ineffective. Even if parent managers are frequently called on to make arbitration decisions, they are unlikely to have enough detailed knowledge to make wise interventions. Co-ordination between separate units in this situation is likely to lead to sub-optimal outcomes, unless the units are part of a unified management team led by a hands-on general manager.

If the organization design relies on co-ordination between separate units that is likely to be unworkable, it may well be necessary to think again about the design. If the co-ordination is important enough, a different design that groups the activities into a single unit with a responsible general manager may be preferable.

Hands-on general managers can guide linkages in a way that parent managers cannot. They have the detailed knowledge to arrive at an informed judgment about a fair division of the spoils, and the authority to impose it. The sub-units and departments that report to them expect the general manager to push through decisions that are in the interests of the unit as a whole and are less likely to see such decisions as illegitimate interference. Moreover, general managers have more ability to motivate co-operation within the unit.

A further crucial advantage of co-ordination within a unit is that general managers can make the difficult trade-offs much more speedily and effectively within their own heads than through a process of negotiation between separate units. In addition, the general manager's knowledge, perspective, and skills mean that these decisions are likely to be superior and more acceptable to all parties than a multi-partite negotiated outcome or some fiat from the parent.

So the best, and in some cases the only, way to make difficult links is to locate them in a single unit under a responsible general manager.

The benefit of the "difficult links" concept is that it helps with the evaluation of different types of co-ordination. Let us take an example where the choice is between a product organization, a country structure, or a hybrid (some product units and some country units). Designers should start with the strategy. Which dimension is most important to the strategy? Having decided, say, that product skills or product-based economies of scale take highest priority, the designer can test whether a product structure will work by looking at co-ordination issues. Links will be needed, for example, between the product units and the countries. Some may be difficult to achieve. For example, one of the difficult links might be overhead-sharing within each country. Another might be co-ordinating around common customers.

If none of the links is likely to be difficult, there is no need for additional design input. Co-ordination mechanisms and other design solutions are only needed if the designer anticipates difficulties. The challenge then is to design a solution to the difficulty. If a solution is hard to find, the link is likely to be unworkably difficult: it needs to be incorporated within a unit. When this occurs, some significant restructuring of the units may well be necessary.

The difficult links concept is, we believe, an important addition to the repertoire of thinking about organization design (see, for example, the Appendix to this chapter: Difficult Links and Transaction Costs). Most theories do not distinguish between difficult and non-difficult links. They use broad concepts such as "co-ordination intensity" to guide design decisions. Moreover, the emphasis many managers and consultants place on process design and on "synergy" often causes them to make design errors. They develop elaborate co-ordination mechanisms for links that would be better left to self-managed networking, and they expect co-ordination on issues that would be better handled within a single unit.

This leads us to our *difficult links test*:

"Does the organization design call for any 'difficult links', co-ordination benefits that will be hard to achieve on a networking basis, and does it include 'solutions' that will ease the difficulty?"

The test involves:

- listing all the important links between units;
- assessing whether the links are likely to be "difficult";
- where possible, developing "co-ordination solutions" for the difficult links; and
- deciding whether any of the links are "unworkable", and if so whether they constitute a knock-out factor that requires significant structural change.

The purpose of the difficult links test is to make sure that all the important links in the design will work effectively. In practice, the distinction between difficult links and non-difficult links is not always clear-cut. Moreover, a link that is difficult for one company or one combination of managers may be easy for another. Nevertheless, the difficult links concept helps managers to think through which co-ordination issues can be left to networking between units, which can be handled through co-ordination mechanisms, and which need structural solutions.

Taken together, the difficult links and specialist cultures tests form a powerful way of identifying and resolving design dilemmas. In complex designs many important links have to be managed across unit boundaries, and many specialized units have to be closely connected with sister units. These two tests guide managers toward the right balance between independence and interdependence. They indicate powers or rights of appeal that may be needed to protect smaller, more specialized activities; but highlight any associated dangers for cross-unit collaboration. They insure that co-ordination mechanisms and parenting authority are designed where they are needed; but help avoid unnecessary mechanisms or interference where they will undermine the benefits of decentralization or constrain the development of a specialist culture. Learning to work with these two tests is at the heart of learning to design effective "structured networks".

In a large global professional services firm, for example, we were able to use the tests to help resolve the perennial issue of whether to organize around practice areas or local offices. The fit tests had suggested that a practice-based structure would be best for implementing the firm's overall strategy, but there were worries, particularly on the part of local office heads, that such a structure would be catastrophic in terms of local responsiveness. The specialist cultures test was invaluable in focusing attention on specifically which powers the local offices needed to retain in order to be able to motivate local staff and respond well to local clients. The difficult links test identified issues where co-ordination was likely to be important but contentious, and showed where detailed design of co-ordination processes was needed and what the role of senior management in these processes would have to be. The design that emerged from using the tests retained practice areas as the primary dimension, but went a long way towards reassuring the local office heads that their legitimate concerns would be met.

In the box, Autonomy Needs and Difficult Links in IBM, we show how IBM's organization has been designed to take account of both the specialist cultures and the difficult links tests.

Autonomy Needs and Difficult Links in IBM

For many years, IBM was famous for its consensus-based decision-making processes and for its pervasive corporate culture and policies. By the early 1990s, however, these features of IBM's organization were causing serious problems. IBM was not responding sufficiently rapidly and flexibly to challenges from more focused competitors such as Intel, Dell, and Microsoft. But, equally, the different divisions within IBM were not working well together in providing integrated solutions for customers, who were turning to companies such as EDS for help. The first problem was essentially about "autonomy needs", while the second concerned "difficult links" between divisions.

When Lou Gerstner was appointed CEO in 1993, he recognized that IBM's divisions were not free enough to develop their own distinctive cultures and were slowed down by corporate bureaucracy and the need to reach consensus with sister units. He therefore encouraged divisions to be more autonomous, and relaxed unnecessary corporate policies. Units such as the new Center for e-Business Innovation do not conform to traditional IBM ways of operating, are not subject to standard performance measures, and have brought in many new recruits from outside IBM. Gerstner has also pushed for clearer unit responsibilities and fewer consensus decisions. On the other hand, he has established some common global processes that all IBM units must follow in key areas such as customer relationship management, integrated product development, and supply chain management. "What we now have is 'Freedom under the law' ", stated a senior IBM executive. "Different units can go their own ways, providing they conform to a few essential policies and processes." With more autonomy to make decisions, IBM's businesses are competing more successfully against their focused rivals.

More divisional autonomy, however, does not make integrated customer solutions easier: rather, the reverse. Previously, the Components division, the PC division, the Server division, the Software division, and the Sales and Distribution division had not worked well together because they had different, often incompatible, priorities and objectives. With more divisional autonomy, there was a danger that interdivisional conflicts would be exacerbated. Gerstner therefore introduced several new organization design features to overcome the difficulties associated with co-ordinated customer solutions.

First, customer relationship responsibilities were clarified. The primary responsibility for hardware and software sales to large customers would lie with the Sales and Distribution (S&D) division and for services with the newly created Global Services (GS) division. In most cases, the Hardware and Software divisions had to work through the S&D or GS divisions, treating them as internal customers for their products. Furthermore, the S&D division was no longer expected to push IBM products: both S&D and GS divisions were free to use other companies' products, if they were more suitable for creating appropriate customer solutions. The S&D and GS divisions therefore had the authority to put together optimal customer solutions and their performance was measured accordingly.

Second, an Account Planning Process was set up, in which managers from all divisions agreed targets and strategies for each major customer. This process provides a forum for different divisions to express and argue their views. Its purpose is to reach agreement on priorities for the coming year, and therefore to provide a context within which to handle specific enquiries.

Third, the vexed issue of the allocation of costs and revenues between divisions is now handled under a so-called "Fair Shares" transfer pricing process. This process, which is administered by IBM's finance staff, provides a reasonably clear and agreed basis for dividing up the benefits and costs from collaboration between divisions.

Fourth, there are well established processes for divisions to appeal against a decision with which they strongly disagree. If managers in the Server division, for example, believe that a particular account is specially important for them, but think that the account is not getting sufficient priority from Global Services, they can raise the issue at more senior levels. And top managers in each division accept that they will need to arbitrate from time to time.

Last, Gerstner has stressed that IBM divisions must move away from a narrow, silo mentality. They should have freedom, but only within an overriding objective of doing what is best for customers and for IBM overall.

IBM has therefore been able to make the difficult links involved in providing integrated customer solutions more manageable, while at the same time giving more autonomy to units. Its organization allows for the development of more specialist cultures in each unit, but now provides clearer responsibilities for customer solutions, backed up with suitable structure, processes, and hierarchical authority.

The Knowledge and Competence Principle

Responsibilities should be allocated to the person or team best placed to assemble the relevant knowledge and competence at reasonable cost.

A responsibility requires information and competence to implement. Unfortunately, both information and competence can be "sticky": they are often hard or expensive to move from one part of the organization to another. As a result, organizations need to be designed so that responsibilities are allocated to the people who can best execute them.

This might seem to point to centralized decision-making, on the grounds that senior managers are in the best position to make tough judgment calls. In practice, the reverse is usually the case. Managers close to markets and technologies are best placed to make most decisions. This is because knowledge of the markets and technologies is difficult or expensive to transfer in full. It is also because managers lower down in the hierarchy can specialize, developing focused decision-making skills in their own particular markets and technologies.

Some decisions, however, should be the domain of upper levels of management. Traditionally, upper levels focus on strategy and policy while lower levels focus on implementation and operations. The knowledge and competence principle cuts through this administrative view of hierarchy to state that upper levels should focus on those responsibilities where they have a knowledge and competence advantage. The default position is that responsibilities should be decentralized. Only those that are better executed at higher levels are retained.

There is a close link between the knowledge and competence principle and self-managed networking. By decentralizing most responsibilities, the organization designer provides units in the organization with the authority to be self-managing. Units are only constrained for reasons of due diligence control (see next principle), or because higher-level managers can add value.

Decision Rights and Decentralization

The importance of designing structures around knowledge and competence first emerged in the 1970s from academic enquiry by Michael Jensen and others into why the market economy is superior to the planned economy. In a paper entitled "Theory of the Firm,"[11] he and co-writer William Meckling explained that market economies are better mechanisms for achieving alignment between "decision rights" and knowledge. Jensen's term "decision rights" has a similar meaning to our term "responsibilities".

According to Jensen, in a market management, teams possessing knowledge and competence compete to buy decision rights. When a team buys a technology or business, it also buys the right to decide what to do with it: the new owner has acquired "responsibility" for it. The trade in decision rights means that they should end up in the hands of those in the best place to exploit them: managers able to assemble suitable knowledge and competence will create most value from owning the decision right, and will therefore bid more for it.

Within a firm this market mechanism does not operate. A manager who feels less than fully informed or competent to make a decision cannot put that decision up for auction. He can suggest to his boss that the decision should be made by someone else, but, more normally, having been allocated responsibility, the manager will make the decision even if there are others better placed to do so. It is vital, therefore, that the organization designer allocates responsibilities to the precise location in the organization where they can best be executed.

While Jensen was working on the reasons for the success of market economies, other academics were focusing on the resource-based view of the firm.[12] Proponents of this view argued that the firm's resources – skills, knowledge, relationships, assets, brands, market positions, and so on – are the principal cause of differences in performance. Firms with resources appropriate to the marketplace they are addressing will outperform those with fewer or inappropriate resources.

Two of the most important resources are knowledge and competence. As academics have examined these qualities and tried to create models for knowledge management and knowledge creation, they have begun to understand how much competence and knowledge is implicit, intuitive, and embedded in people or routines.[13] In fact, it is embedded knowledge that is the most valuable, because it is difficult for others to copy. But if the knowledge is hard to copy or transfer to other organizations, it is also hard to transfer *within* organizations. Not only is it difficult to move around, it is also unevenly distributed. In design terms, it follows that allocation of responsibilities should follow the "hard-to-move" knowledge and competence, not the other way round. Furthermore, organizations should be deliberately structured to nurture and develop this "hard-to-move" resource. For both reasons, the choice of which responsibilities are decentralized and where responsibilities are decentralized to is vital. The knowledge and competence principle provides the guiding light.

If we take a simple decision like setting a price for a new product, we can see the issue quite clearly. It is important to know what the product cost to manufacture, since this determines the lowest price that can be charged. It would be useful to know which costs are fixed and which are variable. By pricing low, it may be possible to stimulate demand and so reduce the cost of manufacture. It is also important to know how valuable the product is to customers: knowing what they would be prepared to pay if they had no choice provides a price ceiling. It is also useful to have an estimate of the elasticity of demand: how much will customers reduce purchases as the price rises? Finally, it is important to know the price of similar and substitute products, and what reactions competitors are likely to have to any price decision. In other words, there is a great deal of information to assemble.

Assembling the information is not just a matter of collecting facts laid out on paper. Some of the information resides in the mind of individuals in the shape of accumulated experience and understanding. For example, elasticity of demand can be painstakingly assembled into a chart that provides information about the past. But a judgment by an experienced marketing or sales executive who is sensitive to market moods and trends is often more useful. Moreover, arriving at a decision to price at $299 rather than $315 requires competence: competence in assembling the information in a cost-effective way, in weighing and balancing facts, opinions and prejudices, and finally in managing the various individuals who need to contribute to the decision.

Where in the organization structure should this pricing decision be made? At corporate headquarters, where managers with a complete overview can take into account the competitive ramifications, cash-flow factors, and reputation impact on the organization as a whole? Or by a product manager deep down in the organization, who is responsible for getting the product to market?

The hierarchical level is not the only issue. At a single level there may still be a question about which manager or function should take the lead. The decision could equally plausibly be taken by the plant manager who runs the equipment that makes the product, the researcher who designed the product, or the salesman who presents the product on the road.

The answer, of course, is that it all depends – on the people involved and the issues that the decision relates to. Pricing decisions would normally be led by marketing, rather than any other function, and delegated to the level of the business unit, but probably not the individual product manager. Why? Because marketing managers will have developed a competence in making this kind of decision, and because the hardest information to transfer is knowledge about how competitors and customers are likely to react. In other words, the marketing function at the business unit level is often the best place to assemble the inputs and make the judgments required for this decision.

Hierarchies

In practice, a decision initially taken by a business-unit marketing function may be reviewed and discussed by other levels, and even changed as a result. Does this conflict with the knowledge and competence principle? Not if the higher level is reviewing the decision rather than taking control of it. For example, the review may be designed to test the marketing manager's logic. It may bring additional information, opinion, or competence to the attention of the marketing manager. In other words, it may be designed to help the marketing manager without removing the responsibility. In this case, the responsibility still lies with the person best placed to assemble the knowledge and competence. The review thus adds value to the decision process.

If, on the other hand, higher levels wrest decision authority away from the marketing manager, perhaps on the grounds that his decision was unpopular, the decision has been moved to a "less good place". Either the higher level will incur greater costs in assembling the information and competence, or the decision will be made with less of both. Either way, the result is likely to be a less good decision.

The existence of higher level reviews is in itself part of the organization design. By deciding to retain a degree of influence and control, and thus delegate the decision only partly, the higher-level manager is making an important decision. Either he believes that the best point in the organization to make the decisions lies somewhere between the two levels, and the review process is a decision co-ordination mechanism; or he believes that the higher level has important information and competence that the lower level might ignore. The review process then becomes a mechanism for helping with the assembly of information and competence.

The knowledge and competence principle provides a good means of deciding what responsibilities to delegate and to whom. But it can be hard to apply. It is difficult to know for sure which individuals or teams have the most relevant knowledge and competence on which issues. Furthermore, it is all too easy for upper levels to take control of a decision if they are unhappy, inadvertently moving a responsibility to a "less good place" in the organization and undermining the effectiveness of the structure.

While the knowledge and competence principle is broadly understood by most managers, we observe that it often takes second place to other influences. Managers create layers in the structure for a variety of reasons: to reduce spans of control, satisfy career aspirations, develop managers, provide a job for a senior colleague, and so on. When this happens, they may be inappropriately removing responsibilities from the levels below. So it is important to weigh the benefits of, say, satisfying a career ambition against the costs of misallocating some responsibilities. In this case the designer is working with the people driver on the one hand and the knowledge and competence principle on the other.

Managers also have a habit of overestimating their knowledge and competence and underestimating that of their subordinates.[14] This is one reason why the default position should be decentralization rather than centralization of responsibilities, and self-management rather than integrated management. The onus on the designer should be to explain why responsibilities have been retained at higher levels rather than why they have been decentralized. This gives us our *redundant hierarchy test*:

"Are all levels in the hierarchy and all responsibilities retained by higher levels based on a knowledge and competence advantage?"

The test involves the following analyses:

- identify all parenting levels in the structure and define their "parenting propositions";
- for parenting layers with responsibilities not part of defined parenting propositions or with weak propositions, consider alternative propositions or redesign the layer; and
- for parenting layers with defined parenting propositions, consider their skills and resources and assess whether they have or can create a knowledge and competence advantage for the responsibilities they have retained.

The test is the obverse of the principle. Whereas the principle states that responsibilities should be delegated to the people best placed to assemble the relevant knowledge and competence, the test focuses on whether any responsibilities have been retained at higher levels that should have been delegated to lower levels. In practice, it is easier to focus on the responsibilities that have been retained than to examine all those that have been delegated. The default position is that responsibilities should be delegated unless higher levels have a clear knowledge and competence advantage over lower levels.

The power of the redundant hierarchy test is that it forces the organization designer to think carefully about the responsibilities that are not delegated to an operating unit. The test clearly overlaps with the parenting advantage test, but focuses on a different set of issues. The parenting advantage test is about whether the structure gives sufficient attention to the corporate parenting propositions. The redundant hierarchy test is about whether there are too many levels and whether too many responsibilities have been retained at higher levels.

Despite the current fashion for de-layering and corporate break-ups, it is still common to find that corporate hierarchies are not designed to add value. In numerous client situations, we have been able to help corporate managers focus on their value creation role, not their administrative duties or their power bases. Senior positions that have been created primarily to administer corporate planning, resource allocation and reporting processes, or to establish neatly balanced divisional empires with similar reporting spans need to be dismantled in favor of a parent structure that concentrates more clearly on value creation. The redundant hierarchy test forces organization designers to modify or eliminate management layers that would otherwise destroy value.

We believe this test captures an important insight into organization design. Most textbooks acknowledge the importance of decentralization, arguing that decisions should be made "close to the market". Many also point to the problems Alfred Chandler observed of overload at the top when too many responsibilities are centralized. However, none have developed an effective model for deciding precisely what to centralize and what to decentralize. The redundant hierarchy test gives more precision to these decisions. It can also be applied at any level in the organization. It can be used to design the job of a manager of 10 salesmen or the chief executive of a global company.

The Control and Commitment Principle

Units should be formed to facilitate effective, low-cost control and high commitment to appropriate goals.

Effective, Low-Cost Control and High Commitment

When managers decentralize responsibilities, it is essential to be able to assess whether the responsibilities are being well discharged. Otherwise decentralization becomes abdication. Managers who cannot tell whether their subordinates are doing a good job are not able to exercise effective control. They are failing to show "due diligence" in handling their own responsibilities. In other words, the responsibility to exercise effective control is always retained by higher levels. This responsibility uses up some of the organization's scarcest resource – the time of upper-level managers. Hence it is wise to design the units in a way that makes it easy for upper levels to exercise effective control at low cost in time and effort.

The need for effective but low-cost control has been highlighted in an important branch of theoretical economics called agency theory.[15] Agency theory states that whenever a "principal" employs an "agent" to carry out tasks on his behalf, the principal is faced with the problem of aligning the agent's goals with the principal's goals in a cost-effective manner. Alignment depends on establishing suitable target-setting, monitoring, and incentive systems. The snag is that these systems can be costly.

Agency issues are pervasive in decentralized structures. Agency theory asserts that optimal designs involve cost-effective control processes. The search for structures that make effective, low-cost controls possible is a fundamental part of organization design. But the issue is not just about top-down control by those who delegate responsibilities. It is also about the commitment and enthusiasm of those who wield the responsibilities – agency theory from the bottom up, as it were. Principals want manager-agents who will make every effort to accomplish their goals, and whose goals accurately reflect the tasks they have been given. They want managers to strain every sinew to achieve the objectives, not just to do the bare minimum necessary to get by.

Many successful chief executives, such as John Browne at BP and Clive Thompson at Rentokil Initial, emphasize the importance of the motivation of unit managers. They regard creating a "high-performance culture", in which managers throughout the organization are fully committed to the achievement of stretching targets, as a major factor in the success of their companies. For them, the control process is more than a due diligence activity: it is a parenting proposition.

Many things influence managerial commitment, including the process by which targets are agreed and monitored, the extent to which managers support the overall organizational purpose, rewards, and incentives, and the degree to which managers feel they will succeed. The control process needs to be designed to make it easier to generate commitment.

We have combined the requirements for control and commitment into a single principle. This is because both requirements have to do with the effective implementation of decentralized responsibilities. In addition, there are important trade-offs between tighter control and stronger commitment. If the quest for control leads senior managers to draw up detailed goals for every aspect of implementation and monitor results closely and frequently, it leaves those who are supposed to have decentralized responsibilities feeling severely constrained and sensing that their bosses don't trust their competence. Constant detailed checking may create tight control, but it is likely to demotivate managers. For control to be effective, it must allow enough discretion to responsible managers to get on with their jobs and at the same time make them feel that they will be judged by the results they achieve. One business unit manager explained how his boss was closely involved in a decision he was making. "I have probably spent four or five hours discussing this decision, and we have definitely come up with a better answer. But, frankly, I would rather it had been my decision and I had been judged on its results."

Moreover, passionate commitment needs to be channeled towards suitable goals in order to benefit the organization. It is not just about firing up managers to charge ahead, but also about the directions they choose for the charge. The process for generating energy and enthusiasm must be coupled to the process for agreeing targets, otherwise the organization is in danger of lurching forward out of control. As one chief executive said to us: "The biggest mistake I made was as a result of a manager who was in love with his business and got me to fall in love with it, too."

So commitment needs to be coupled with and balanced by control, and vice versa.[16] But an even more fundamental reason for combining control and commitment in a single principle is that they both depend on self-correcting relationships and appropriate performance measures.

Self-correcting Relationships

Control is easiest when units are motivated by self-correcting relationships. Self-correcting relationships mean that, if a unit is not performing well, it will experience strong pressures to improve through its lateral relationships. For example, the relationship between a business unit and its customers is self-correcting. If the business unit gives poor service, poor quality, or poor value for money, customers stop buying and managers are motivated to correct the situation. If the business unit exploits its suppliers, at some point they may terminate the relationship. Again there are strong self-correcting forces at work. In fact, an independent business unit has self-correcting relationships with nearly all of its stakeholders. Even environmentalists can have a self-correcting influence on a business. If the business is creating unnecessary pollution, it will be boycotted by environmentalists, giving managers a strong incentive to change.

An independently quoted company has market relationships with all those it needs to deal with, even its owners. The market provides the self-correcting mechanism. Shareholders, for example, can decide, just like any other stakeholder, to give their loyalty to another company. They sell their shares; the share price declines; and the managers of the company are motivated to do something about it.

A self-contained business unit within a company is similar to an independent company, except for its relationship with its parent. The self-contained business unit is expected to deal with sister units on an arm's-length basis. But the relationship with the parent is different. It is not self-correcting because the parent company is tied to the unit: some of the responsibilities are shared. Of course, the parent can threaten to sell the unit, but this is a last resort.

To make the relationship effective, parent managers need to devise a control process that signals problems and motivates managers to make the necessary corrections. For a self-contained business unit, this is relatively easy. Parents can usually identify a few unit-specific bottom-line measures, such as profit performance, market share, and innovation success. This is because the unit's other relationships are all self-correcting.

However, for a less self-contained unit that has many relationships with other units that are not arm's-length, the problem becomes harder. If units are forced to work together and reach shared decisions, self-correction pressures are reduced. Take, for example, a typical shared service unit. The unit exists to provide lower cost or higher quality services for other units in the company. To insure that the shared service has economies of scale, the other units are obliged to use the service. In order to avoid the costs of internal invoicing and unnecessary accounting, the shared service does not charge for each service offering, but is funded by a levy on sales or personnel. Most of the relationships of this shared service are not self-correcting. The parent of the unit therefore needs a more elaborate and expensive system of measurement and control to insure that the relationship is working well and the shared service unit is providing good value for money.

On the other hand, if the shared service unit is set up independently, so that other units can choose whether or not to use the service, and the service unit can choose whether or not to meet their demands, control is much simpler. The parent can rely on customers of the service unit to police the quality and value for money of its services. The parent can also rely on the service unit to police the reasonableness of the demands of the other units. The relationship between the units is self-correcting. As far as possible, designers should try to establish units that have more, rather than fewer, self-correcting relationships.

Where the self-correcting pressures on a unit are weak, it is necessary to rely more heavily on upper-level parent managers to exercise control and generate commitment. Hierarchical control becomes the main process for insuring that decentralized responsibilities are well discharged.

Performance Measures

What sort of hierarchical control process keeps control costs low and motivation high? There are two kinds. The first kind is based on parent managers with a close understanding of the operations of units reporting to them, and unusual trust and respect from the managers of the units. These parent managers are able to assess the performance of the unit subjectively, based on their feel for its operations, and, because they have the full trust of the managers in the unit, their opinion about what needs improving is given top priority. These parent managers do not need elaborate and costly performance measures and information flows, because they are immersed in the sector and pick up information through their daily activities. They normally have a number of businesses in the same market area, so each piece of information reinforces or builds on their existing knowledge.

Based on our experience, such a degree of "feel" and trust is comparatively rare. Few parent managers benefit from both the level of feel and the degree of trust needed as the basis for a low-cost, high-motivation control process. Most need to rely more on the second kind of control process: one that is built round targets and performance measures. This is not to suggest that the judgment of parent managers is unimportant in most control processes. Rather, we are suggesting that these judgments are normally more effective if they are based on well designed performance measures. In fact, even in situations where high feel and trust exist, most parent managers reinforce their subjective judgments with well-chosen performance measures.

Performance measures need to have a number of qualities. First, they need to be well matched with responsibilities. Objectives and targets should be attainable if, and only if, the allocated responsibilities are being well discharged. Lopsided performance measures that stress certain responsibilities but ignore others do not provide a suitable basis for control or commitment. In addition, it is hard to hold managers strongly accountable for outcomes that depend on activities they do not control. For strong accountability, and hence commitment, the unit's performance targets should reflect what the unit does, not what other units do.

Second, performance measures should be easy to monitor and interpret. These features are dictated by control requirements. Performance measures for which data is hard to collect and difficult to assess demand extra time, cost, and skill from senior managers. Objectively measurable, outcome-oriented, bench-markable measures are normally the easiest to monitor and interpret. If there is some suitable outcome basis of measurement for which relevant benchmarks are available, this simplifies the controller's task. There is less need to be concerned with the detailed operations of the unit and with how the outcomes are being achieved. Equally, few performance measures are preferable to many performance measures for the purposes of control, simplifying the control task and allowing controllers to concentrate their attention on a few "hot buttons". This is something that most managers are, in any case, prone to do, as Robert Simons has pointed out in his book, *Levers of Control.*[17]

It is for this reason that profitability is such a popular performance measure for business units. Profit figures can be assessed on a largely objective basis – provided that accounting conventions have been agreed in advance. They represent a bottom-line outcome that encapsulates the net effect of all the revenue generated and the costs incurred. Furthermore, they are usually easy to benchmark against other units or competitors.

On the other hand, profitability may not be sufficient to assess performance against all of a business unit's responsibilities. Additional measures may be needed to achieve a balance between them. Robert Kaplan has developed this idea into the *balanced business scorecard* concept.[18] Kaplan's point is that a narrow focus on a single goal (e.g. profitability) fails to motivate managers to discharge their responsibilities in a rounded way, and that a mix of performance measures is needed to do this. Precisely what this mix of measures should be is harder to determine, and will vary from company to company and unit to unit.

Without objectively measurable, outcome-oriented performance targets, control usually becomes more costly and difficult, since it has to rest on a detailed sense of how well things are going. To avoid superficiality and error in these judgments, controllers need to be very familiar with the operations they are controlling – running the risk that their monitoring is high-cost and demotivatingly close. If it is impossible to encapsulate a unit's responsibilities in a few objectively measurable, outcome-oriented measures, control will become more problematic. Ultimately, it may be necessary to make trade-offs between the accuracy and comprehensiveness of the performance measures and the simplicity and cost-effectiveness of the control process.

A third set of requirements for performance measures is rooted in commitment considerations. Unit managers prefer to know precisely what they will be held accountable for. "What gets measured, gets done"; but if the measures are clear and objective, there will be even more focus and commitment to what gets done. If, conversely, the performance measures are complicated, imprecise, and subjective, unit managers will quite likely be confused about priorities, less motivated to deliver, and more skeptical about the feedback they receive. The ability to create benchmarks also has an influence on motivation. If managers know that there are other similar operations doing better than they are, they are more likely to raise their game.

Finally, measures need to be economical to collect. For example, it is possible to get an objective, outcome-based measure of employee satisfaction; but it is expensive. The cost of carrying out and interpreting a comprehensive survey of employee opinion every quarter or every year can be prohibitive.

It will certainly be less costly, although also more subjective, for the parent managers to pick up signals from employees when they are visiting the unit for other reasons.[19]

In summary, units should be defined so that they can have performance measures that are relevant to the unit's responsibilities, objectively measurable, outcome-oriented, benchmarkable, few in number, clear, and economical to collect. We will refer to measures with these features as "appropriate" measures. Such measures not only allow senior managers to control cost-effectively without interfering in implementation, but also provide the basis for targets for which unit managers can be held strongly accountable.

Unfortunately, managers frequently fail to pay enough attention to the control and commitment principle. They design units with complex relationships that are not self-correcting; they rely on subjective judgments of performance when parent managers do not have sufficient feel or enough trust; they also adopt inappropriate performance measurement systems that fail to achieve effective control and demotivate subordinates. As a result, it is hard to hold the units accountable for their performance. Hence the *accountability* test:

"Does the design facilitate the creation of a control process for each unit that is appropriate to the unit's responsibilities, economical to implement, and motivating for the managers in the unit?"

The test involves the following analyses:

- for each unit, are there any factors that hinder the creation of an effective control process?
  - does the unit have any lateral relationships that are not self-correcting?
  - are there any important dimensions of performance that cannot be assessed with "appropriate" measures?
  - does the parent have sufficient feel and status to rely on more subjective, informal controls?
- for each factor, look for refinements and adjustments to the design, such as changes to unit responsibilities, design of

lateral relationships, improvements to the skill of the parent, or choice of performance measures, which will make it easier to create an effective control process; and

- if refinements and adjustments cannot be found, the test may be a knock-out, and an alternative design may need to be chosen.

As with the other tests, difficult judgments are involved. When are the controls too costly or too demotivating? When are performance measures insufficiently aligned with the responsibilities of the unit? When does the parent manager have sufficient feel? Clearly there are no right or wrong answers. However, the test insures that attention is given to these critical design issues. Some units are easy to control and motivate, for example, a self-contained business unit. Some units are inherently difficult to control and motivate, for example, a corporate research function or a unit that has many interdependencies with other units. The organization designer should avoid creating units that are difficult to control and motivate unless the next level up is particularly skilled at coping with the problem.

The value of the test is that it underlines what is needed for control and commitment. It encourages the organization designer to create units that can be controlled with simple, objective accountabilities. In companies with matrix structures, unit accountability is almost always weaker than in companies without matrix structures. Shell is only one of many companies that have moved away from matrix structures with tied relationships, shared decisions, and collective responsibilities in order to create stronger unit-specific accountabilities and clearer performance measures. When the design creates units that will be hard to hold to account, managers should think twice. They need to consider redesigning unit responsibilities, reporting relationships, and performance measures to allow tighter control, more commitment, and clearer accountabilities.

Few complex designs, however, fully satisfy the accountability test. In addition, control requirements in complex structures place more demands on parent managers.[20] The test exposes these issues, making sure that any disadvantages of inappropriate or higher cost control and lower motivation are taken into consideration when structural choices are made.

The Innovation and Adaptation Principle

Organizations should be structured so that they can innovate and adapt as uncertainties become clarified and environments change.

Organizations need to adapt. In the first place, the design at any one time is the encapsulation of judgments managers have made – judgments about strategy, people, the relative importance of different specialization and co-ordination benefits, which teams are best able to assemble relevant knowledge and competence, and how to lower control costs and raise commitment. These judgments are made in the face of uncertainty. Some of them will prove to be wrong, requiring corresponding changes in the design. The need for change will be particularly strong if the design is developed at a time when there is no clear strategy. As more understanding develops or as views about strategy change, the strategy itself may change, calling for different priorities.

A second reason for change is the need to adapt to a changing environment. Even if the initial judgments are correct, they need to evolve as the environment changes: the importance of a market focus can diminish as a result of product innovation; the value of a functional focus can decline as functional skills become less scarce – the need for a separate unit for Mexico changes if consumer tastes in Mexico come to resemble more closely those of the USA.

A third reason for change is that managers learn new skills and change their attitudes over time. Equally, new managers may be brought into the organization from outside. Given the importance we place on the fit between the design and the people, any change in senior management is likely to require adjustments to the design.

The fourth, and perhaps most important, reason why organizations need to be adaptable is to encourage and accommodate strategic innovation. Old strategies must evolve as new strategic opportunities emerge. In fact, many of the best strategies are the result of bottom-up discoveries, of learning by doing. The most famous example in the academic literature is Honda's entry into the US motorcycle market. Initially the company had no clear strategy, but believed that its products would sell well because the handlebars were shaped like the eyebrows of Buddha. After several false starts, and prompted by a project undertaken by an MBA student at UCLA, Honda's managers found that more interest was generated by the 50 cc models they were using to ride around Los Angeles to get to work than the bigger models they had intended to market. Unable to sell their larger bikes, they were forced to sell the smaller models to generate cash flow. Eventually, the new strategy led to a highly successful market entry.

The academic literature refers to these bottom-up, evolved strategies as "emergent strategy" that arises out of "autonomous strategic actions" by managers in the field.[21] It is important to design the organization to be receptive to this sort of learning by doing.

Sources of Rigidity and Flexibility

There are three ways in which organization structures can hinder innovation and adaptation. Structures can create power bases that resist change. They can create relational complexity that makes it hard to change one thing without affecting all the others. And they can be so tightly specified that they prevent innovation and adaptation from taking place at all.

Structures create power bases and define status differences. Given human nature, these become hard to change, particularly at the top. Managers defend their autonomy and resist interference by other managers. Moreover, the problems of rigidity get worse the longer a particular structure has been in place. Precedents develop, turf wars are fought and won or lost, and gradually the organization stops challenging the status quo. Decisions about which units should report to the chief executive and which managers should be part of the "executive" should be taken with a view to adaptation. Will these appointments lead to power bases that could create awkward rigidities in the future?

Structures can also create complex relationships that are difficult to redesign. If the structure involves many co-ordination mechanisms, overlapping responsibilities, and interdependencies, it can be hard to change one part without redesigning the whole organization. On the other hand, if the structure consists of units that operate in a largely arm's-length way with other units, one part of the structure can be changed with little impact on the other units. "Modular" structures with "plug-and-play" units are less rigid than "web" structures with many carefully designed connections. When managers design co-ordination mechanisms they are introducing complexity. They should consider whether these design elements could limit future flexibility.

A third cause of rigidity can be the way the design is specified. If units are tightly specified – "marketing large bikes in the USA" – they can become straitjackets that limit flexibility and experimentation. If units are given a clear focus, but flexibility in the way they address the focus – "Honda in the USA" – they have more opportunity to find innovative solutions. In the same way, if processes are tightly specified, there is little room for innovation or for individuals to adapt to evolving circumstances.

Finally, if there are no resources or processes for pursuing new ideas, particularly ones that cut across the existing unit structure, innovation outside the existing strategy will be discouraged. When managers are specifying the details of the design, they need to consider the impact they may have on innovation. They must also make some explicit design decisions aimed at focusing attention on developing strategies and new ways of working that would not come from the existing units.

Of course, the most important source of rigidity is the way managers think. If managers have an open-minded approach to strategy, encourage experiments and recognize that the responsibilities they have today may change tomorrow, there will be few obstacles to change. If, on the other hand, managers have set views, resist change, and consider the latest reorganization to be the last, then nothing in the design will increase the organization's ability to respond.

Unfortunately, we have observed that managers pay too little attention to the need for change and innovation when designing their organizations. In part, this is because the design problem is hard enough without the added complication of change and innovation. It is also because they underestimate the need for change. This leads us to our last test, the *flexibility test*:

"Will the design help the development of new strategies and be flexible enough to adapt to future changes?"

The analyses involved in this test are:

- identify mechanisms that exist for strategic innovation and decide whether they are sufficient, given uncertainties about the current strategy; and
- list the areas of uncertainty in the current design and areas of likely change in the markets, technologies, and competitive environment, and consider whether the organization will be able to adapt if necessary.

As with the previous tests, tough judgments are needed. There are tools for assessing areas of likely change, such as scenario and trends analysis, but there are no tools for judging how the organization will respond to these changes. Managers must rely on their knowledge of the people and their feel for how the organization will react. Comparisons are particularly valuable, since it is easier to decide which of two different structures is likely to be more flexible than to grade a single structure. The value of the test is that it insures attention is paid to an issue that is often overlooked.

We worked with one company that was considering setting up an international division to be responsible for all its operations outside the UK. The purpose was to smooth the transition to a more fully global structure, which was expected to be established in a few years' time. The UK operations would have been headed by the CEO's heir apparent and the intentional division by the only other executive on the main corporate board. Using the flexibility test, we were able to point out that the head of the international division, once appointed, was not likely to be in favor of the move to full globalization, since the global structure would not include a position of comparable power and status for him. There was a strong possibility that he would slow down the move to a global structure. The flexibility test alerted the company to a source of rigidity that was intrinsic to the proposed structure, and forced a reconsideration of its merits.

The Good Design Tests

In this chapter we have discussed and synthesized the guidance on good organization design that we could find in the literature and in the minds of managers. We have also added some important insights that we have developed through our research and consulting work. The result is a list of five good design principles that point us to five tests of good design (see Figure 3.3). It is worth summarizing what is new or counter-intuitive in these tests.

Whereas most writers emphasize the value of interdependence, the specialist cultures test emphasizes the value of autonomy. For example, the idea of the boundaryless organization[22] is built on a presumption that boundaries create problems. By contrast, we believe that boundaries are often valuable and important. They provide the opportunity for the development of specialist cultures and the competencies that go with them. Boundaries, of course, do create problems, so they need to be designed with care. By combining the specialist cultures test with the difficult links test, designers can find the right balance.

The difficult links test points out that not all links are difficult. Most writers argue that designers should develop coordination processes for all cross-unit links. We believe that most links can be handled through self-managed networking.

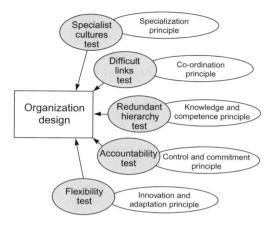

FIGURE 3.3 Five Good Design Tests

Co-ordination mechanisms are only needed for links that would otherwise be "difficult". Moreover, using the difficult links concept in practice has led us to the conclusion that some links are so difficult that no co-ordination mechanisms will be effective: such links require structural solutions.

The redundant hierarchy test presumes that higher levels should only retain responsibilities if they have a knowledge and competence advantage over lower levels. This fits with the current trend in writing about hierarchies. However, our concept of "knowledge and competence advantage" gives intellectual substance to an otherwise pragmatic call for more decentralization. It provides a way of identifying and eliminating layers of management that are likely to end up destroying value. It provides a means of auditing those responsibilities that have been retained at higher levels to see if further decentralization or centralization is appropriate.

The accountability test focuses on control processes that minimize cost and maximize motivation. This is in line with agency theory. However, we believe that our concept of designing units with as many self-correcting relationships as possible is novel. We emphasize the cost and potentially demotivating aspect of controls, and point out that the burden on the parent is greatly reduced if objective, outcome-oriented, benchmarkable measures can be used to assess performance.

Finally, the flexibility test develops a theme that is at the center of much current work on organizations. We do not claim to have advanced on current thinking, but we believe that the test provides a practical way of bringing the need for innovation and adaptation to the attention of managers.

In this chapter we have not explained the tests fully enough for managers to make practical use of them. We provide this detail in Chapters 7–9. But first we want to describe the results of our research with different types of organization, which gives further grounding for the principles and tests (Chapter 4), provide guidance on how to specify organization designs (Chapter 5), and review the role of the parent in complex structures (Chapter 6). We can then return to the task of selecting and testing an organization design.

Appendix

Difficult Links and Transaction Costs

One of the most fruitful ideas in theoretical economics over the last two decades has been the concept of "transaction costs". Pioneered by Oliver Williamson,[23] transaction costs theory explains economic structures in terms of how the costs of carrying out transactions can be minimized.

For example, in a situation where a company had made a major investment in a specialized facility to supply components that are only used by a single customer, transactions between the supplier and the customer will be difficult and costly. Both the supplier and the customer are dependent on each other, and there is no third-party market to establish a "fair" price for transactions between them. It is likely that there will be long, costly, and ultimately unsatisfactory negotiations between them in order for them to work together. In these circumstances, Williamson argues that transaction costs will be reduced by vertical integration, so that the transaction is "internalized" within a single firm rather than carried out on a market basis. Where "market failures" of this sort occur, the answer is to remove the transaction from the market and locate it within a corporate hierarchy. Transaction costs thinking has proved powerful in explaining the boundaries between firms and markets.

The concept of difficult links that we have advanced takes transaction costs thinking a stage further. It implies that internalizing a transaction within a firm may not be sufficient. If the transaction takes place between separate units within the firm, and if the transaction is "difficult," there may also need to be a satisfactory co-ordination solution to allow the transaction to proceed satisfactorily. In the most difficult cases, it may even be necessary for the transaction to be internalized within a single unit in the firm.

Given the realities of power and legitimacy in companies, "hierarchy failures", in which parent managers are unable or unwilling to reduce transaction costs by creating co-ordination solutions for difficult links between units, are not uncommon. In these circumstances, the transaction, or co-ordination, will only proceed satisfactorily if it takes place within a single unit under unified general management. The crucial step is not so much, as Williamson argues, moving the transaction from the market to the corporate hierarchy as moving it from separate units to a single unit with a responsible general manager.

4

Simple and Complex Structures

During the last 30 years, many companies have adopted corporate structures based on self-contained, profit-responsible business units. When these units are largely autonomous and have little overlap with each other, they are often referred to as strategic business units (SBUs). In terms of the design principles discussed in Chapter 2 and 3, simple structures based on SBUs have attractions. But they also have some limitations and drawbacks. To address these drawbacks, an increasing number of companies have set up structures with more interdependencies between units.

Interdependent structures can give attention to more dimensions of focus than simple, SBU-based structures, since there is more overlap and sharing of responsibilities between units. But such structures give less autonomy to units and call for more complex accountabilities and relationships between units.

In this chapter, we lay out the results of our research into the advantages and disadvantages associated with simple, SBU-based structures and complex, interdependent structures, shown schematically in Figure 4.1. We recognise that most companies' structures lie somewhere between the extremes represented in Figure 4.1. "Pure" cases are rare. Nevertheless, some companies, such as BP, GE, and Hewlett-Packard, are clearly closer to the simple end of the spectrum, whereas others, such as ABB, Citibank, and Monsanto, are closer to the complex end of the scale.

By comparing simple and complex structures, we highlight

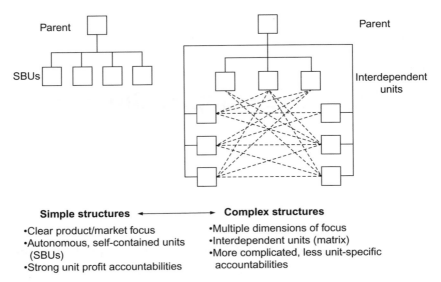

FIGURE 4.1 Simple and Complex Structures

the important management challenges at both ends of the spectrum. These challenges influenced our formulation of the good design tests, which we described in Chapter 3. In fact, the tests provide a good summary of the advantages and disadvantages of simple and complex structures, helping to bring out important design choices and trade-offs. In particular, we argue that, although interdependent structures may be needed in companies whose strategies call for multiple dimensions of focus, they can easily encounter problems of excessive complexity and lack of clarity. To work well, complex structures should encourage decentralized decision-making and unit autonomy wherever possible, and should strive to make managers clear about their intended responsibilities and relationships with other units. The aim should be what we call a structured network, not a traditional matrix organization.

SBU-based Structures

Terms such as a strategic business unit (SBU) or self-contained business are widely but somewhat imprecisely used in descriptions of corporate structures. We shall use the term SBU to refer to units with the following characteristics:

- market-focused: responsible for serving specified customer segments;
- autonomous: having a general manager (or management team) with substantial autonomy to make decisions that impact the results of the unit; and
- profit-accountable: generating revenues and costs from serving the target segments, and hence able to measure profitability, for which the SBU's management is held accountable.

Units with these characteristics have a clear focus on their target markets, unequivocal decentralization of responsibilities to minimize unproductive interference from outside the unit, and strong accountability for performance.

Market-focused

SBUs are market-focused. Hence, management attention should be dedicated to creating products and services that are tailored to the specific requirements of their target segments. The SBU also has responsibility for putting together a value chain that will effectively deliver these products and services. This encourages the development of the special skills and resources needed to serve the target markets well, especially in those components of the value chain that the business is carrying out itself. It also leads to co-ordination and alignment of all the components of the value chain in profitably serving the needs of the target segments (see Figure 4.2). If there are important sources of competitive advantage that stem from focusing on the target segments, establishing an SBU to serve them makes sense.

EMAP, the UK publishing company, believes strongly in setting up small, market-focused SBUs to address the different segments of the consumer magazine market. "It's all about backing small, creative teams, in decentralized units. Every magazine has to be targeted at, and understand, the lifestyle of its specific readers," stated a senior company manager. The corporate center is kept small (around 30 people in total), and there is little

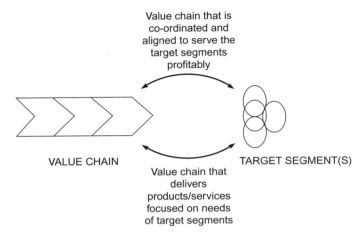

FIGURE 4.2 Market-focused SBUs

sharing of services or resources between units: "This provides plenty of motivation to the units to come up with products that will maximize the growth opportunities in each segment".

An SBU-based structure is also a good way of insuring that corporate policies and standards do not stifle managers and prevent them from providing differentiated products for market segments whose needs differ. Despite the economies of scale in the automotive industry, it makes sense for volume producers such as Ford to maintain the separate identities of acquired subsidiaries such as Jaguar and Volvo, in order to encourage them to retain their distinctive market positionings.

Autonomous

SBUs are largely autonomous in the decisions that they take. This means that, on most issues, the SBU's managers are free to make decisions without consulting or accepting advice from senior managers or sister units, and have sufficient power over resources to implement decisions. The SBU structure represents a strong form of decentralization. Few responsibilities are shared with other units or reserved for higher levels of management.

Organization designers give autonomy to SBUs because they believe that the SBU managers are in the best position to make the detailed decisions and trade-offs required to optimize performance in their target markets. Autonomy allows them to act quickly and decisively. It also reduces interference from senior managers, who are less knowledgable about the specifics of the business, and it avoids the need for consensus-building and compromises with other units, whose influence might slow down or contaminate[1] decisions.

In contrast to many financial services companies that emphasize the importance of cross-selling and customer relationship management, GE Capital Services (GECS) has adopted a structure with 28 SBUs, each with a separate product focus. For example, GE Card Services provides credit and card-related services for retailers and consumers, GE Aviation Services is the world's largest aircraft leasing firm, and GE Structured Finance Group provides specialized financial products and services associated with large and complex transactions. Each of the businesses operates independently, and there is no attempt to impose integrated customer solutions involving several of the businesses or to cross-subsidize one business at the expense of another. In this way, each SBU is free to concentrate exclusively on its own market. This has helped GECS to build up a formidably successful collection of businesses focused on different financial services niches.

Other companies that have used SBU structures specifically to insulate a business from other corporate influences include BA for its low-cost Go[2] subsidiary and Toyota for Lexus. By granting a high level of autonomy to these businesses, their corporate parents hoped to encourage them to adopt strategies that would otherwise have been constrained by wider corporate influences.

Within autonomous SBUs, general managers typically exercise considerable power. They are expected to take a close interest in all aspects of their businesses, and are empowered to make decisions and trade-offs, overrule lower-level managers, and push through implementation. As pointed out in Chapter 3, they should have the detailed knowledge to make well-judged decisions, and they have a wide variety of currencies and incentives with which to motivate their staff to implement them. This is especially important in achieving co-ordination benefits from "difficult links" between functions or sub-units within the SBU.

But the other side of autonomy is accountability. It is for this reason that "feet to the fire" (being strongly accountable) is part and parcel of an SBU manager's job. Since SBU managers have extensive decentralized power to make decisions, they can be held strongly accountable for delivering results. Conversely, if senior managers wish to hold SBU managers strongly accountable for results, they need to give them autonomy to make the decisions they see as necessary to deliver. Strong accountability means that SBU managers face major personal incentives, in terms of career and compensation, closely linked to the performance of their units.

Profit-accountable

The ability to measure profitability is implied by the dual responsibility of an SBU for serving target customers (revenues) and for the value chain components needed to serve them (costs). The results of the SBU can therefore be summarized in bottom-line profit numbers (revenues minus costs).

The existence of a bottom-line profit for an SBU is, however, much more than an accounting identity. It is important for purposes of accountability, performance measurement, and control. Profitability is a largely objective and measurable goal[3] that, in one figure, sums up how well the unit is performing. Admittedly, it may not capture all relevant aspects of performance: trade-offs between short-term profits and long-term business building are notoriously neglected.[4] But it does provide a simple overall performance measure for which SBU managers can be held accountable. Bottom-line profitability encapsulates the net result of an SBU's market relationships, and is well suited for purposes of control, since senior management can monitor it without needing a detailed understanding of how all the responsibilities delegated to the unit have been carried out.

Profitability also provides a clear and motivating target for SBU managers. They know how their performance is being measured, and have the autonomy to be held strongly account-able for the results they achieve. Furthermore, they know that the results of the SBU are typically visible to senior manage-ment. Success will be noticed and rewarded; failure, with all its consequences, will be equally evident. SBU heads have good reason to be highly motivated and committed to achieving their profit targets. A shortfall in budgeted profitability is an immediate warning signal to SBU managers to embark on corrective action, if possible before the shortfall has been noticed by the senior managers to whom they report.

A large part of BP's turnaround in performance since the early 1990s can be put down to the establishment of a "perform-ance culture", in which the company has been divided into a large number of relatively small, autonomous, profit-accountable business units. The management team of each unit agrees a stretching annual "performance contract" with John Browne, the chief executive, and is then held strongly to account for delivering on its contract. These performance contracts give individual managers a great sense of personal responsibility, coupled with transparency of performance to top management. This has unleashed a new energy and commitment, and led to greatly improved results (see box: BP's Performance Contracts and Peer Groups later in this chapter for further details).

Simple Structures

SBU-based structures provide a simple way of organizing. The SBUs are largely self-contained, and parent-level managers decentralize most decisions to the SBUs. Relationships between SBUs are handled on an arm's-length basis. The structure makes for clear responsibilities and leads to rapid decision-making, with SBU managers handling the vast majority of issues on a self-managing basis.

Management Challenges for SBU-based Structures

Although SBU-based structures have some important advantages, they also give rise to some management challenges, including:

- selecting an appropriate market focus for SBUs;
- achieving co-ordination between SBUs;
- avoiding SBU silos;
- parenting SBUs; and
- adapting SBUs to changed circumstances.

Selecting an Appropriate Market Focus

The choice of target segments and value chain responsibilities as the focus for the SBUs, sometimes called business unit definition or design,[5] has a major impact on competitive advantage. Different business unit design choices yield different opportunities for the development of special competences and resources and for alignment and co-ordination. SBUs that focus in one way will build up certain advantages, but will sacrifice advantages that could have been achieved from a different focus. Deciding what market focus will allow an SBU to develop the competences, resources, and co-ordination opportunities that are most vital for competitive advantage is a crucial choice, and one that can be hard to make. The choice between a product and a geographical focus, for example, is fundamental. For many years, Shell was organized around autonomous country-based operating companies. This encouraged strong local knowledge and contacts, but made it more difficult to plan investment in facilities on a regional or global basis. With global scale economies becoming increasingly important, especially in commodity chemicals, the nationally-based operating company structure became less and less appropriate. In 1998, Shell Chemicals moved to a structure with product-based global businesses.

Similar issues arise concerning e-commerce opportunities. Most major retailers, for example, have launched some form of e-commerce activities. But should these be managed as part of a broader SBU, which includes the traditional retail channel, or as a new separate SBU? There may well be benefits through shared purchasing scale, common product range knowledge, and logistics efficiencies from a broader focus that combines both e-commerce and traditional channels. But there are also benefits from a narrower focus, in which a dedicated management team with appropriate skills concentrates exclusively on maximizing the e-commerce opportunities, without having to worry about co-ordination with the established retail channel or about cannibalization. The right choice of focus depends on some difficult trade-off judgments, and is often far from clear.

Selecting the right focus for an SBU requires clear thinking about the sources of competitive advantage and the ability to identify which source of advantage should receive the most attention. This is particularly difficult when there are a variety of important sources of advantage. In these circumstances, as we shall argue later in the chapter, there may be no SBU-based structure that will pass the market advantage test.

Achieving Co-ordination

Many managers believe that achieving co-ordination between autonomous SBUs is bound to be hard. However, even SBUs that are designed to be largely self-contained quite often choose to collaborate. For example, one SBU may supply inputs for another, and different SBUs may all share a common call center or distribution system, or may choose to standardize communications around a company-wide intranet.

Collaboration between SBUs need not inhibit their autonomy provided that the SBUs work together on the basis of mutual self-interest. For example, if there are benefits in terms of costs and service levels from a shared call center, commercial considerations may well lead the SBUs to co-operate voluntarily in establishing and running it. A "deal" of this sort between sister units is in principle no different from a deal with external third-party trading partners. If no mutually acceptable terms can be agreed, there will be no deal. The business units remain free to make their own decisions about whether and how to collaborate.

In order for co-operation based on mutual self-interest to flourish, senior managers need to insure that there are no impediments that will prevent SBUs from voluntarily collaborating. In previous research,[6] we have found that, unfortunately, many companies have a variety of "synergy killers" in their culture, which makes co-operation between sister units harder than with third parties. These synergy killers include rivalry and infighting between SBU heads, who actively discourage "working with the enemy"; misaligned incentives, which fail to support sensible, commercially-justified co-operation; and mistrust of senior managers, especially if they are liable to override agreements reached between sister units for what they see as some greater corporate good. Corporate managers need to clear away these synergy killers, so that internal co-operation becomes no harder than external collaboration. Ideally, they should go further and create enough family feeling that sister units will actively try to help each other, for example through first refusal trading rights or sharing best practices.

Given the right corporate context, mutual self-interest can guide much of the collaboration that is needed between SBUs. Cargill, like BP, has established a series of "peer groups", forums that bring together the managers of different business units to explore mutually beneficial co-ordination and sharing. It is these peer groups, rather than upper levels of management, that drive most of the co-ordination that is needed.[7] Similarly, Mars has for many years enshrined a Mutuality Principle as one of the cornerstones of its distinctive corporate culture. The Mutuality Principle requires Mars units to work together for mutual benefit in the interests of the firm as a whole.

But there are some limits to what can be achieved through mutual self-interest. Particular problems arise for the sorts of co-ordination opportunities which we referred to as "difficult links" in Chapter 3. Due to the autonomy of SBUs, it is often hard for parent managers to create strong co-ordination mechanisms or to intervene with sufficient authority to push through difficult links. In these situations, either the link will not happen, or else the structure must be redesigned to incorporate it within an SBU. An SBU-based structure is unlikely to be suitable if many difficult links between the SBUs are needed in order to execute the corporate strategy successfully.

Avoiding SBU Silos

While SBUs provide advantages in terms of unit autonomy, accountability, and commitment, they are frequently also accused of generating organizational silos: groups of managers so dedicated to their allocated focus that they become blinkered and unco-operative. Such managers are so concerned about preserving their "baronial" autonomy that they are excessively resistant to any influence from elsewhere in the group. They feel so accountable for the results of their own SBUs that they become parochial and ignore their impact on other parts of the group. And they are so committed to short-term profitability targets that they fail to pay sufficient attention to wider performance measures.

The extent of silo risks depends on the nature of SBU accountabilities and incentives. Parent managers can pump up the dangers by tolerating barons, and rewarding SBU managers exclusively for parochial, unit-specific profit performance. They can mitigate the dangers by emphasizing that SBU boundaries should not be impermeable (GE's boundarylessness), and by making clear to SBU managers that they should aim at agreed SBU targets, but not be blinkered by them. In particular, they need to establish accountabilities that incorporate profitability, but also stress other performance measures that will provide a more balanced view of how well the SBU is doing.

To some degree, the risks of silo thinking are intrinsic to SBU-based structures. But much depends on the way that parent managers and SBU managers interpret the nature of SBU autonomy and accountability. The box: BP's Performance Contracts and Peer Groups, shows how a suitable balance can be struck.

BP's Performance Contracts and Peer Groups

In 1990, BP, one of the world's leading oil companies, embarked on a "culture change" program. During the 1980s, the company had a large and influential corporate head office, and a complicated matrix organization based on geography and product streams. The company's performance was moderate, and the culture did not stress tight personal accountability for results. The culture change program, launched under Bob Horton and continued by David Simon and John Browne, his successors in the chief executive role, was designed to bring about a shift to a more decentralized, empowered, and high performance culture.

As part of the change, BP has reorganized around four business streams (Exploration and Production, Downstream Oil, Chemicals, and Gas) and has de-emphasized regional and country management. Each business stream consists of numerous separate profit-responsible business units. In total, there are nearly 100 business units. The business units are defined around BP's major assets and "in terms of the market and the competitors: large enough to compete effectively in their markets, but small enough for the management and employees to identify with." The business unit definitions are kept under constant review, and are frequently adjusted to create a better alignment between the organization structure and BP's market opportunities.

As far as possible, decisions have been pushed down to the managers running these "human scale" business units. The corporate center has been radically downsized, and now concentrates only on a small number of major strategy issues, on creating the high performance culture, and on knowledge sharing between the businesses.

The business streams' managements are kept very small and regarded as part of the corporate center. In this way, there are in principle only two levels in the company: the corporate center and the business units. As one director put it: "the business units are the vital delivery units within the company."

The essence of the new high-performance culture is a process of performance contracting between the business units and the corporate chief executive. The performance contracts are intended to set stretching targets ("business unit managers will not know at the beginning of the year how they will be able to achieve them"). They emphasize financial performance, but can include other non-financial targets. The contract is a clear one-page formal document, signed off by both the business unit and the corporate center, and followed up with disciplined monthly monitoring. "The key has been to build around managers who were able and willing to work well within this performance culture." Between 1993 and 1998, BP's total headcount fell from 135 000 to 50 000.

The other main innovation in the change process has been the use of peer groups. Peer groups were first set up in 1992 in the Exploration and Production business stream to make the business units less silo-focused and more collaborative. Over time, they have become increasingly important for know-ledge sharing and performance delivery and have been adopted throughout the company. Peer groups are now formed around related business units in areas such as refining, retail, or oil fields at similar life cycle stages. They provide a forum to share information and work together on common problems in a constructive but challenging environ-ment and have underpinned the performance management process. All business unit leaders present their performance contract to a rigorous "peer review process" and ask for help from their colleagues through an intensive peer coaching process called "peer review". While individuals own their own performance contracts, the peer groups have provided powerful collective commitment to stretch performance challenges, and have been invaluable in finding ways to achieve them. Peer processes are now well rooted in all parts of BP and are used widely by functional networks and by groups of managers from different business units who meet to tackle complex group-wide issues.[8]

When David Simon was chief executive, he used the mnemonic "PRT" – Performance, Reputation, Teamwork – to communicate the goals of the change program. PRT goals, which are still implicit in the way the company operates, made clear that, while performance was vital, it should not be at the expense of reputation or teamwork. Managers who delivered on their contracts through a narrow, silo focus on their business units would not be rewarded. To succeed, it was necessary both to attain business unit targets and to work together with other units to help them to succeed. This is why the peer groups provide a vital complement to the performance contracts.

Parenting

In earlier chapters, we introduced the concept of the corporate parent and outlined its role. In SBU-based structures, the parent needs to play a relatively hands-off role, since the SBUs are designed to be both self-contained and autonomous. Taken to extremes, this can lead to questions about whether the parent is necessary at all.

Even in decentralized, SBU-based structures, the parent's main purpose should be to add value. There are many examples of parents in SBU-based structures that add considerable value, including Virgin with its powerful brand, Emerson with its Best Cost Producer program, and Granada with its stretch performance targets.[9] Nevertheless, parents in SBU-based structures must be careful not to intervene too extensively. It is fundamental to the SBU concept that business unit managers should be strongly accountable for the results they achieve, and any tendency for parent managers to assume too much power and influence weakens the autonomy, and hence the accountability, of the SBUs. For this reason alone, parents in SBU-based structures need to remain relatively hands-off. This is not incompatible with selective influence that adds high value, but it can sometimes inhibit parents from exercising influence that would otherwise have added value. For example, parent managers with a strong commitment to SBU autonomy are not likely to promote company-wide synergies.[10]

If the parent does make attempts to add value, there is also a danger that the parent's influence will be value-destroying, not value-creating. With decentralized, self-contained SBUs, the parent will typically be relatively distant, and will lack detailed knowledge about the businesses. Well-intentioned attempts to add value and exercise control can easily degenerate into misguided interference and unproductive second-guessing, unless the parent concentrates only on a few key issues where it has a real contribution to make.

The difficulty of adding value to separate SBUs has led to serious questioning about the rationale for many multi-business groups. During the last decade, break-up strategies, which imply that the parent does not have a real value-added role, have become increasingly common for diversified, decentralized groups.

Adapting to Change

SBU-based structures are not inherently inflexible. SBU managers have considerable discretion about how to carry out their responsibilities. They can modify the precise scope of their market focus, and decide what value chain activities they will carry out in-house or outsource. This allows the details of SBU responsibilities to evolve in response to circumstances.

Parent managers can also flex SBU-based structures by redefining the SBUs. Indeed, in their book, *Competing on the Edge*,[11] Shona Brown and Kathleen Eisenhardt argue that small, focused SBUs can offer a high degree of structural adaptability, provided that senior managers in the parent are willing to implement frequent redefinitions of the product-market segments for which each SBU is responsible. This process of organizational change, which Brown and Eisenhardt call "patching", allows SBU-based structures to adapt to changes in the market environment and the sources of competitive advantage. Companies like HP and 3M have coped with rapidly changing markets by constant patching. On a visit to HP, we were shown no fewer than eleven organization charts, which documented the series of patching changes made to HP's structure during the previous two years.

In principle, there is therefore no reason for SBU-based structures to become rigid and impervious to change. There is, however, a risk that in practice silo thinking sets in and reduces flexibility. SBU managers may feel protective about their territory and resist changes to it. Attempts by the parent to patch the SBUs may be seen as illegitimate interference with SBU auto-nomy, and as unwelcome attacks on the power and status of SBU managers. Not many companies would be able to introduce as many changes to SBU definitions as HP did without provoking strong resistance from SBU managers. So the adaptability of SBUs is conditional on the attitudes of SBU managers, and their personal willingness to accept change. Patching will only work well in companies where the SBU managers are prepared to support it.

Advantages and Disadvantages of SBU-based Structures

In Table 4.1 we summarize the advantages and drawbacks of SBU-based structures, and show how they relate to the tests described in Chapters 2 and 3.[12] In many cases, the dis-advantages are the "dark side" of precisely those features that lead to the advantages.

The market focus of SBUs allows them to score well in terms of the *market advantage test*, provided that their chosen markets focus them on the most important sources of competitive advantage. But SBU-based structures are less capable of creating a focus on markets or sources of advantage that cut across SBUs.

SBU autonomy discourages parent managers from getting closely involved in SBU operations. In terms of the *parenting advantage test*, this is positive, in so far as it reduces unnecessary detailed interference; but it is negative if it inhibits parent managers from adding as much value as they could.

SBUs provide exciting opportunities for independent, entrepreneurially-minded general managers to develop and use their skills. This can be an advantage in terms of the *people test*. But it can also be a disadvantage for a company with a shortage of managers with the appropriate competencies.

TABLE 4.1 The Advantages and Disadvantages of SBU-based Structures

Tests	Advantages	Disadvantages
Market advantage	Entrepreneurial decisions that focus on the needs of the target markets	Less easy to develop skills and resources for markets or activities that cut across SBUs
Parenting advantage	Parent managers discouraged from detailed interference	Parent managers inhibited, even where they could add value
People	General managers have opportunities to develop and use entrepreneurial skills	Depends on availability of entrepreneurial managers
Specialist cultures	Autonomy gives insulation from pressures that might compromise or contaminate	Insulation may lead to baronial behaviour
Difficult links	General manager with authority to co-ordinate all the activities in the SBU	Hard to co-ordinate across different SBUs
Redundant hierarchy	Strong form of decentralization	Parent managers may not add much value
Accountability	Self-correcting relationships, and sufficient autonomy to be strongly accountable for performance. Bottom-line profitability measures that do not require detailed knowledge by the parent	Strong accountability can lead to parochialism. Bottom-line profitability measures reduce emphasis on other important measures
Flexibility	Design of SBUs can evolve, and can be "patched" to cope with change	SBU "barons" may resist changes to preserve power and status

The autonomy of SBUs means that they are well insulated from pressures that might otherwise compromise or contaminate their strategies. As a result, they meet the *specialist cultures test* well. But the downside is that SBUs' insulation may result in "baronial" behavior, an unwillingness to co-operate with sister units, and a rejection of all influence from the parent. This not only damages competitiveness but also creates bad relationships within the company.

The hands-on authority of SBU general managers makes it possible for SBUs to implement difficult co-ordination links for activities within the SBU. But SBUs only collaborate based on mutual self-interest, which limits what can be achieved through networking between SBUs. As a result, they run into problems with the *difficult links test* for co-ordination across SBUs.

SBUs represent a strong form of decentralization, in which the vast majority of decisions are taken on a self-managed basis by SBU managers, who should have the greatest knowledge of their businesses. This is an advantage. However, parent managers are discouraged from intervening, which can raise issues in terms of the *redundant hierarchy test*.

The profit-accountability of SBUs means that there should be strong pressures to self-correct for failing SBUs. SBUs have sufficient autonomy to be held strongly accountable for their performance, which can be simply measured in terms of a bottom-line target. SBUs therefore rate well in terms of the *accountability test*. However, strong accountability can lead to exclusive concern with SBU results, and hence parochialism, silo thinking, and excessive competition with sister units. Also, if profitability is seen as the key performance measure, there may be insufficient emphasis on other important measures of performance.

Lastly, SBUs can adapt to change through self-managed evolution in the details of their market focus and value chain design, and through a process of patching, in which the market focus of the SBU is constantly reviewed and adjusted by senior parent managers. These are reasons why SBUs can pass the *flexibility test*. But there may also be resistance to change if SBU management teams dig in their heels in an attempt to preserve their power and status.

SBU-based structures therefore provide several advantages. But they also have disadvantages, which have resulted in a move away from SBU-based structures amongst many leading companies during the last decade. These companies have been searching for structures that will preserve most of the benefits of SBUs, but be more suitable for the competitive challenges they face.

Interdependent Structures

Often, an SBU-based structure is not the right organization design. If a company requires multiple dimensions of focus in order to pursue a variety of sources of competitive advantage, there will be no satisfactory way to design self-contained business units. A more complex structure, incorporating a wider range of overlapping and mutually interdependent units, will be needed.[13]

Multiple Dimensions of Focus

For many companies, there are focus benefits associated with serving differently defined target market segments. In corporate banking, for example (see box: Citibank's Organization Structure for Global Relationship Banking), there are good reasons for focusing around "products", such as structured lending or foreign exchange, in which specialist expertise can be built. But there are also arguments for focusing around customer groupings, such as industry sectors, for which integrated financial solutions can be developed, or around local geographical markets, in which a network of contacts, a reputation, and a physical presence can be established. Several dimensions of focus are each important.

In these circumstances, self-contained SBUs are likely to miss some valuable focus benefits. The most common solution is to set up co-ordination mechanisms, such as integration teams, to address secondary dimensions of focus.[14] But, as we argued in

Chapter 3, even if there are co-ordination mechanisms in place to encourage the business units to collaborate, their main energies will still be devoted to their primary focus. Product-bases business units will not pay as much attention to customer solutions or local presence; customer-based business units will not focus sufficiently on developing specialist expertise in the key individual products; and geographically-based business units will overlook the potential of global products and global customers. Whatever basis of business unit definition is chosen, organization designers may need to set up other dedicated units with different dimensions of market focus in order to insure that some managers are giving primary attention to the cut-across segments.

In corporate banking, Citibank decided in the mid-1990s to define the main business units around customers, but to maintain product and geographical units as well. The customer units and the other units had overlapping market focuses, and had to work together in serving their respective target markets. We refer to units with a market focus that cuts across the main business units as "overlay" units, and will discuss them more fully in Chapter 5.

Similar issues arise if there are benefits associated with more and less aggregated ways of defining target markets. Citibank not only faced dilemmas about whether to focus its business units on products, customers, or geographies, but it also had to decide whether, for example, customer-focused industry sector units should be broadly defined (e.g. manufacturing) or narrowly defined (e.g. semiconductors) and whether geographical units should cover large regional groupings or small local areas. Often, organization designers want to get the benefits of leverage from a broad scope as well as the benefits of focus from a narrow scope.

To achieve focus both on more and less aggregated market segments, the main businesses can be defined broadly, but more narrowly focused profit-responsible sub-units, which report to the main businesses, can also be set up. These "sub-businesses", as we call them, achieve additional focus benefits by giving dedicated management attention to the needs of their specific target segments. Again, we will discuss sub-businesses more fully in the next chapter.

Focus benefits can also accrue from specializing on value chain components or tasks that are relevant in the target markets of several business units. Shared sales activities, a common IT infrastructure, or new product development can all provide such opportunities. Again, co-ordination mechanisms between separate business units may lead to some of these benefits. But if the potential benefits are substantial, there is often a need for cut-across units with a focused management team to achieve them fully. These units, which we refer to as "core resource", "shared service" and "project" units, are intended to reap economies of scale and specialization that would not have been achieved if the business units had each been responsible for their own activities in these areas. In Citibank, the product units and the customer units all draw on the shared infrastructure units, in the belief that this will create superior cost competitiveness. But the result is less self-contained business units, and more sharing and interdependence between units. We will have more to say about core resource, shared service, and project units in Chapter 5.

Interdependent structures, therefore, can include a variety of overlapping units, each of which may have a different sort of focus. The wider the range of important focus benefits available, the more likely it is that companies will need to adopt inter-dependent structures rather than structures with a single dominant dimension of focus (see Figure 4.3).

Citibank's Organization Structure for Global Relationship Banking

Citibank's Global Relationship Banking Group's mission is to "serve global customers globally, delivering the global promise locally." It concentrates on about 1700 key global customers, and aims to be the leading provider of financial services for customers who value a bank with a global network and global capabilities. Its product platforms include

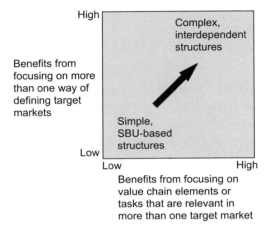

FIGURE 4.3 Focus Benefits and Interdependent Structures

cash management and trade services, custody and clearing services, debt capital raising, foreign exchange (FX), structured products, equities, and mergers and acquisitions (M&A). It has grown out of Citibank's corporate banking business, but now works closely with Salomon Smith Barney, which was part of Travelers Group prior to its merger with Citicorp to become Citigroup,

Until 1996, the Corporate Banking Group's main line of reporting was geographical. Each major region (and some countries) was a relatively self-contained business, with its own customer and product specialists and infrastructure, and responsible for profit from its regional operations. Citicorp's objective, however, was not only to develop a strong local reputation, franchise, and set of relationships, but also to use its international reach to reinforce many of these relationships. This called for co-ordination between the regional and local management teams. An important step was the establishment in the early 1990s of informal regional customer interest groups around industry sectors, such as automotive or telecoms, which created networks that fostered business development and co-ordination.

In 1996, following a strategy review led by John Reed,

Citicorp's chief executive, a radical reorganization was introduced to de-emphasize local country management and to give more focus to global customer relationships. Corporate Banking was split into the Global Relationship Bank (GRB) and the Emerging Markets (EM). The main line of reporting in the GRB was through global industry heads, who were responsible for the aggregate profitability of global customer relationships in their industry, while the EM retained a geographical structure. The product platforms were given a global remit, and reported to the head of the GRB. Country management retained responsibility for day-to-day contact with customers in their areas within the strategic direction set by the global industry heads, and for some elements of infrastructure. But a move began towards a greater sharing of infrastructure, such as IT, on a wider regional or global basis. The purpose of the reorganization was to align the structure more closely with the strategy, to give more attention to global customer relationships, and to give more authority to global industry heads and relationship managers to deliver distinctive value propositions to their customers.

The new organization, shown in Figure 4.4, included customer-based units (e.g. Telecoms, Commercial Banks), product units (e.g. Global FX, Structured Finance), regional and national units (e.g. US South East, Italy, Latin America), and infrastructure units (e.g. Human Resources, Operations and Technology). All these units had to work together to implement the strategy, but the main drive lay with the customer dimension, with the other units playing supporting roles. The new structure decisively shifted the balance of power away from local managements and towards global relationship managers, but created a much more complex web of interdependencies to manage.

In 1997, the structure was modified again, this time to give more autonomy to the global product units. A separate, profit-responsible products organization (Global Products) was broken out from the GRB. Global Products reported directly to the head of Global Corporate Banking, served

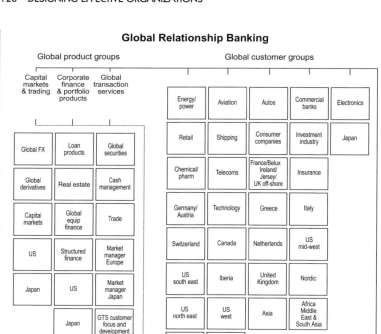

FIGURE 4.4 The GRB Structure (1995)

both the GRB and EM, and also had primary responsibility for the increasingly global shared infrastructure. But the GRB retained responsibility for customer relationships and profitability. In this way, the product units had more power and responsibility for focusing on global products, while the GRB continued to maintain a focus on customer groups. This recognized both the importance of strong customer relationships and of top quality products, but required constant co-ordination between the GRB and Global Products. Subsequently, further modifications to the structure have been made to integrate Citibank and Salomon Smith Barney more closely.

Citibank has, therefore, evolved a complex, interdependent structure because it sees important focus benefits in four different dimensions:

- customers: why the GRB exists, and vital to the strategy;
- products: prerequisite for, and often driver of, good sustainable customer relationships. Also, can be major profit generators, but not as effectively without a strong customer relationship;
- countries: purely local presence now less important (except in EM), but still need to recognize that local perspectives, contacts, and service matter; and
- infrastructure: globally cost-effective infrastructure is increasingly important for success.

No self-contained SBU structure can possibly achieve focus in all these dimensions. This is why, given its strategy, Citibank has decided to adopt a complex structure in corporate banking.

Overlapping Responsibilities

In interdependent structures, the units' responsibilities will be less self-contained and more overlapping. The business units cannot act like SBUs. They must work in parallel with the overlay units and co-ordinate the efforts of the sub-businesses in order to present a coherent face to the market. They must also draw on the core resource and shared service units in order to deliver their product or service offerings, and collaborate with the project units. Units are therefore less autonomous, and there is a need for collaboration between them.

Multinationals, such as ABB or Unilever, all tend to have global product-based units and local geographical units. In this way, they seek to blend the benefits of global integration and local responsiveness. But aggressively independent behavior on the part of either the product units or the local units causes friction and, ultimately, chaos. The benefits only come through if the units are able and willing to collaborate harmoniously. The structure calls for and promotes collaboration, not independence.

Some chief executives, such as Bob Shapiro at Monsanto (see box: Monsanto: A Life Sciences Company), have even argued that overlapping unit responsibilities help managers to see opportunities for sharing and co-operation, and make them more willing to work together to achieve synergies that benefit the group.

Monsanto: A Life Sciences Company

During the 1990s, Monsanto embarked on a determined effort to transform itself from a diversified chemical company into an integrated life sciences company. The vision was to concentrate on businesses concerned with human health, in which new developments in biotechnology and genomics could be utilized. Under the leadership of Bob Shapiro, the chief executive, Monsanto exited a number of chemical businesses, and moved away from a structure with 13 self-contained SBUs to a more interdependent structure, involving five sector teams (Pharmaceuticals, Agriculture, Nutrition and Consumer Products, Health and Wellness, and Sustainable Development), with cut-across teams for selected core capabilities, shared service "foundations", key processes, and global co-ordination. The various teams were co-ordinated at the corporate level by a 12-member Life Sciences Business Team (see Figure 4.5). In Shapiro's view, "the old ideology of separate SBUs was no longer appropriate for a Life Sciences company."

The sectors were the customer-facing business units. Each sector had "two-in-a-box" leadership, with responsibility shared between a marketing executive and a technical manager. There were also sector teams, which acted like closely involved boards of directors, with "non-executive" representatives from other parts of the company. Pharmaceuticals ("satisfying unmet medical needs through biopharmaceutical innovation") and Agriculture ("transforming the way food and fiber is produced while contributing to health, wellness, and nutrition") were the main sources of sales and profits. Nutrition ("healthy eating"), Sustainable Development ("being part of the solution to sustainability") and Health and Wellness ("improving the quality of life") were more concerned with exploring future potential in the expanding field of life sciences.

The Core Capabilities teams covered areas such as information technology, knowledge management, manufacturing, and science/technology. They were intended to execute some of the fundamentals of the company, such as invention and operations, and share ideas and enable learning across the company. The Foundation teams covered shared services, in areas such as procurement, finance, and people. They provided support for other parts of the company. The Process Hubs included, for example, budgeting, communications, mergers and acquisitions, and strategy development. Their purpose was to strengthen key processes and share learning

FIGURE 4.5 The Organization of Monsanto as a Life Sciences Company

throughout Monsanto. The Global team was concerned with spotting global opportunities and helping the sectors to work smoothly in different economies and cultures.

All these teams had representatives from other parts of the company on their management boards, in addition to the senior executives working in the team. For example, the head of Knowledge Management also sat on the Pharmaceutical sector team and on the Global team. The overlapping structure involved frequent meetings for senior managers, but Shapiro believed that these were essential for cross-company integration: "If a manager is spending more than 50% of his time on running his own unit, then he is doing the wrong sort of job."

The structure was intended to create a variety of focuses for management attention, and to force managers to think about evolving opportunities that cut across traditional business boundaries. Shapiro was searching for a "new organizational paradigm, with more connections and networking across the whole company, and relying more on team accountability and trust and less on controls." He recognized that ambiguity and redundancy were part of the approach, but believed they were a price worth paying to achieve interdependence and flexibility. Given the rapid pace of developments in biotechnology, together with uncertainty about the rate at which new life sciences businesses would grow, Monsanto's structure was designed to allow a rapid response to opportunities as they opened up. Shared and overlapping responsibilities, and cross-working between units, were supposed to prevent opportunities being overlooked and to make sure that learning was spread widely throughout the company. Successful initiatives would be recognized and supported, while less successful initiatives would wither. This Darwinian process was seen as the best way to cope with the opportunities and the uncertainties in life sciences.

Many managers in Monsanto were excited by Shapiro's vision, and made strenuous efforts to work within the new structure. But others felt that its complexities and inefficiencies in decision-making were hard to tolerate. This view was particularly prevalent amongst older managers who had grown up within the previous SBU-based culture. It was widely accepted that the pay-off from this new approach would not come for several years, and would depend on transforming patterns of management within the company. As one manager put it in 1998, when Monsanto's stock price was riding high, "Food-Health-Hope is Monsanto's corporate motto: the share price is based mainly on the latter."

Eventually, however, the negative public reactions to GM crops severely damaged Monsanto's Life Sciences strategy, and the company was forced to merge with Pharmacia and Upjohn in 2000. It remains unclear, therefore, whether the structure put in place by Shapiro, probably the most complex and overlapping that we encountered in our research, would, in due course, have achieved its objectives or not.

Overlapping responsibilities also call for the parent to play a more active role in guiding interdependencies and arbitrating disputes. Even if the product units and the country units normally co-operate harmoniously, there will always be some contentious issues. The parent needs either a clear process for resolving these conflicts or a willingness to get involved as arbitrator.

Shared Accountabilities

More sharing of responsibilities means that it is harder to hold individual units strongly accountable for their own results. Because units have to work together, interdependent structures can rely less on individual unit self-correction. And because units' results depend not only on their own efforts but also on how well units work together, they are less unequivocally masters of their own destinies. Shared accountabilities are needed, which recognize that managers should not be exclusively concerned with the results of their own units, but should also be trying to help other units to achieve their goals as well.

In interdependent structures, performance measures need to be designed to take account both of the different responsibilities of each unit and of the contribution that each unit makes to other units and to overall group results. Bottom-line profitability is not a suitable performance measure, since different types of unit each need different performance measures.

Complex Structures

The basic features of interdependent structures are multiple dimensions of focus, overlapping units with extensive collaboration between them, and shared accountabilities. Such structures are fundamentally more complex than SBU-based structures. Dealing with this complexity gives rise to a number of issues, which we will discuss in the following section.

Management Challenges for Interdependent Structures

Interdependent structures offer key advantages over SBU-based structures in terms of a wider range of focus benefits and better sharing of responsibilities. But they also pose significant management challenges:

- selecting a primary dimension of focus;
- managing with less unit autonomy;
- achieving more extensive co-ordination across unit boundaries;
- working with more complex accountabilities;
- playing a more demanding parenting role; and
- adapting to change.

These factors will now be discussed in turn.

Selecting a Primary Dimension of Focus

The fundamental drawback in multidimensional structures has always been that decision-making has been too slow and complex. If there is a balance of power between different dimensions, so that decisions require consensus amongst a variety of different units, there are usually endless wrangles about what to do, with acrimonious disputes between the protagonists. Strategy implementation then becomes ponderous and ineffective. We have found no remaining advocates of "balanced" matrix structures, in which most decisions are shared between units.

With interdependent structures, it is important to decide which units will have the main authority, the final word, on which decisions. Consultation and co-ordination between units may be desirable and necessary, but a clear process for resolving disputes and arriving at decisions in a timely way is also needed. This also clarifies accountability for the results of the decision. In Booz Allen and Hamilton, for example, the respective powers and accountabilities of global practice areas, client relationship teams, regional management levels, and local offices have been clearly laid out in a decision grid for all the most important and contentious decisions, such as partner election proposals and capacity management.

As a background for clarifying respective responsibilities, it is essential to determine which dimension in the structure will, in general, represent the primary line of reporting, with lead responsibility for most decisions. This creates a default responsibility for any decisions not explicitly allocated to other units. In ABB, which spent many years advocating a matrix structure with shared responsibilities between product-based business areas and geographical regions, the global product units have now become the primary organizational dimensions, with the most power. Regional and country management units have been de-emphasized, although they retain certain specific powers. By selecting a primary dimension of focus, decisions and accountabilities have been made clearer and less complex.

Selecting the primary dimension raises similar issues concerning the main sources of competitive advantage to decisions about how to define the market focus of SBUs, discussed earlier in this chapter. We will return to this issue in Chapters 7–9.

Managing with Less Unit Autonomy

In interdependent structures, units are designed to be less autonomous. They share more responsibilities and have less power to make unilateral decisions. A common complaint from operating unit managers is that this leads to insufficient independence for some units and a slower, more complex decision process.

To avoid paralyzing complexity in the decision process, companies with interdependent structures need to clarify who is responsible for what, and how shared decisions will be taken. Wherever possible, consensus decisions should be avoided, and each unit should know its own role. A major thrust behind Shell's transformation program in the late 1990s was to move away from its traditional matrix of shared responsibilities to a situation in which units were clearer about their specific responsibilities and had less need to seek consensus with each other. Business streams and their global "product" businesses still had to work with local and regional operating companies and with corporate functions, but their respective roles were clearer. Although consultation between units was still needed, there were fewer decisions made on a consensus basis.

Interdependent structures are liable to create particular problems for smaller units that have "autonomy needs" (see Chapter 3). The lack of autonomy of the smaller unit, together with strong influence from elsewhere in the group, often mean that it is inhibited from developing its own skills and ways of working and becomes dominated. For example, in one company in our research, we were regaled with the problems of an industrial products sub-business which never felt able to break away from the mindsets – and resource allocation priorities – of the larger consumer products business in which it was imbedded. These "specialist culture" problems (discussed further in Chapter 8) are a particular hazard in interdependent structures.

Problems related to suppression of specialist cultures and complexity in the decision process can be reduced by laying out roles and responsibilities clearly. Often, the problem stems less from intentional domination of a specialist culture and more from a lack of clarity about how its role differs. Some degree of protection for specialist cultures can be achieved by giving them power over certain key decisions and by allocating a ring-fenced budget to them. It is also possible to design the critical processes through which different units work together in ways that take account of specialist culture interests (e.g. representatives on key committees, designed in opportunities for consultation, appeals processes). Last, senior management can encourage respect for differences by appointing high status managers to specialist culture units, sponsoring appropriate differences, perhaps through a high-level mentor in the parent, and counteracting any tendencies to uniformity and standardization for its own sake. In the box, How Citibank Makes its Structure Work, we discuss the ways in which Citibank attempts, with considerable success, to avoid the suppression of specialist cultures.

Nevertheless, organization designers need to recognize that interdependent structures cannot afford as much autonomy to units as SBU-based structures, and there will always be some risk that units which require separateness in order to thrive will be held back. In the consumer products company discussed earlier, it eventually proved necessary to set up the industrial products sub-business as a separate SBU, reporting directly to the chief executive, to give it the autonomy it needed.

How Citibank Makes its Structure Work

The interdependencies in the Citibank structure mean that it presents tough management challenges. However, the structure fits Citibank's strategy and culture, and its working has been improved and refined over the last six years. It now functions smoothly and, more importantly, is delivering for Citibank's customers. How has Citibank overcome the challenges it faces?

Suppression of specialist cultures

Citibank recognizes that there are bound to be some tensions between the global product groups, the global customer groups, and the national managements. The priorities and approaches of these units will differ, so that views about the level of resource to devote to a local customer, for example, will sometimes lead to disagreements. In principle, the customer groups and the product groups now have equal status, but the local country dimension has less power, and can be overruled. But Citibank has designed processes for escalating disputes to upper management levels if they cannot be resolved between the managers involved. The dispute resolution process is a fallback option, to be used sparingly, but it prevents local management from feeling, and being, dominated. In this way, differences in view can be aired and can lead to a more balanced resolution. "Disagreements create a positive and dynamic tension: they are only unhealthy if they are allowed to fester," claimed one GRB manager.

The GRB's culture and values also stress that the customer comes first. Whatever formal authority different units may have, the most important thing is front-line innovation and service delivery for the customer. This means that even though the global product and customer groups have primary responsibility, they recognize that management located close to the customer is vital in responding to customer needs and delivering Citibank services.

Difficult links

Recognizing that there are some difficult links between units on issues such as customer priorities, pricing, and cross-selling, the GRB has set up some detailed co-ordination mechanisms with clearly defined unit roles and responsibilities. One particularly important mechanism is the global relationship account planning process, which involves all units that need to collaborate in serving the client. The respective roles of each unit and each manager in this process have been laid out in process maps and decision grids. Although these process maps and decision grids are not now used on a regular, day-to-day basis, they were valuable at the outset in helping managers to understand both how they were supposed to work together and how the planning process was meant to operate.

The co-ordination mechanisms are backed up by the willingness of senior management to arbitrate disputes: "We have to be willing to resolve disagreements. It doesn't happen frequently, but we probably get involved in about 3–5% of the issues that come up." Citibank's co-operative, customer-comes-first culture is also a helpful background factor.

Accountabilities

Citibank places emphasis on the importance of a sophisti-cated Balanced Business Scorecard (BBS) approach to objective setting and rewards. The BBS is an integral part of the planning process. It establishes a range of objectives and performance measures, for units and for individual managers, covering factors such as customer satisfaction, share of customer "wallet", product rankings in comparison to com-petitors, and profitability. These targets are derived from the unit's strategy and form the basis of personal evaluations and bonuses.

Role of the parent

GRB senior managers play a hands-on parenting role in corporate banking. They set the overall GRB strategy, main-tain a close watch on the performance of all of the inter-dependent units in the GRB, and are willing to get directly involved in establishing priorities, guiding co-ordination, and arbitrating disputes. Their role is essential to the success of the structure.

The corporate headquarters in Citigroup is much more distant and hands-off. It does not concern itself with the detailed issues handled by the GRB management, and is more concerned with overall portfolio development, M&A, and corporate affairs.

Summary

Citibank's complex structure in corporate banking works well. But it has evolved over several years, during which senior managers have refined both the structure and the planning and decision-making processes to achieve a suitable balance between the interdependent units. It also depends on a clear strategy, based around serving global customers, and a culture in which managers are strongly focused on their customers and willing to invest time and effort in working together to implement the strategy.

Achieving More Extensive Co-ordination across Unit Boundaries

With the move away from self-contained SBUs, co-ordination across units becomes more extensive and necessary. Furthermore, because collaboration is designed into the structure as an essential feature, co-operation cannot be left purely on a voluntary, mutual self-interest basis. Product units and overlay units cannot simply agree to differ on how to approach a given customer; business units and shared resource units have to reach agreement on how to prioritize the use of the resources. Without co-ordination between units, the whole structure will grind to a halt.

But co-ordination across unit boundaries is never so easy as within unit boundaries. Thus, although interdependent structures are set up to achieve links and collaboration between units, they face the risk that some of these links will not be delivered, especially if the link concerned is a difficult one. Monsanto found it hard to get its Pharmaceuticals sector to devote resources to the development of neutraceuticals, in conjunction with the Nutrition sector, rather than to the development of its own highly profitable drugs. It also proved difficult to advance cut-across themes, such as knowledge management and global development, since the executives in charge of these teams had no real authority to make things happen.

These risks can be mitigated by stating clearly what type of relationship is sought between different units. If the intentions and ground rules for collaboration are understood, it is more likely that conflicts will be avoided. For example, if shared service units know that they should treat other units as "customers" and should respond as far as possible to their requirements, or if overlay units know that they must work through persuasion to convince business units to co-ordinate with them, these understandings create a context in which individual unit managers are more likely to see how they should collaborate. Better co-ordination is a further benefit that Booz Allen and Hamilton gains from laying out explicitly the respective roles and responsibilities of its geographical offices, industry practices, and functional specialisms. This helps partners and staff to appreciate what type of relationships they should have with their colleagues elsewhere in the firm.

Ideally, most areas of collaboration can be left to informal networking between managers rather than dictated by senior management. Tightly prescribed top-down collaboration processes make interdependent structures rigid, bureaucratic, and cumbersome, all the well-known disadvantages of hierarchical matrix structures. Freedom to network within agreed roles and relationships allows a much more flexible and responsive approach to collaboration, provided that managers work together in the right spirit. A networking culture in which managers know how they should relate to each other, develop strong personal relationships, and enjoy working together is a vital component of successful interdependent structures.

But informal networking is not always sufficient. It is sometimes necessary for top management to specify in detail how some critical collaboration processes are going to work, to retain responsibility and authority for certain areas of collaboration, and to use the incentives available to them to motivate collaboration. We return to this topic in Chapters 7 and 8.

Even if clear relationships, a networking culture, and well-designed collaboration processes are in place, organization designers must recognize that extensive co-ordination across unit boundaries will almost certainly slow down decision making. Furthermore, there may be some unworkably difficult links that will only be fully achieved in a structure in which there is a single responsible general manager with hands-on authority, where everyone works together as members of a unified team.

Working with More Complex Accountabilities

There are several reasons why accountabilities are more complex in interdependent structures:

- tied, interdependent relationships mean that units are less exposed to market disciplines, and so make self-correction less likely;
- performance measures are needed for groups of units as well as for individual units, in order to reflect the contribution that each unit makes to other units' performance;
- unit profitability is a less powerful and less generally relevant performance measure, since not all units have revenue generating external customers;
- there is more need for "input" measures and subjective performance assessments, since suitable bottom-line "output" measures are harder to find; and
- less unit autonomy means weaker accountability for unit performance.

Self-correction, based around simple, objectively measurable, output-based performance measures, is harder and control is more complicated, time consuming and costly. What is more, unit managers have more nebulous targets to go for. Managers in several companies with interdependent structures complained that it was too easy for many units to underperform without coming under any real pressure. Control was too loose and commitment too weak.

These problems can be reduced by minimizing tied relationships and shared responsibilities where possible, in order to promote self-correcting control. ABB, for example, has set up its shared services as quasi-business units. But there is a limit to what is possible if the design has tied interdependencies built into it.

It is also necessary to think through the cost-effectiveness and motivational impact of the performance measures for each unit. The measures must be usable by upper levels, given the knowledge and time constraints they face. They must also be clear enough and align sufficiently well with the unit's respons-ibilities to be motivational. As Citibank has found, a range of balanced scorecard measures will usually be needed, attuned to the responsibilities of the unit. Some form of compromise between sophistication and simplicity is likely to emerge. Given the interdependence between units, performance assessment processes should incorporate peer group evaluations and com-parisons, and should make use of 360° feedback. What business academic/writer William Ouchi calls a "clan culture" (all-for-one, one-for-all: motivation through shared values and sense of purpose rather than through specific goals) may be useful to reinforce specific performance measures.[15] But self-correcting control, with simple, objective, low-cost performance measures and high-powered incentives related to unit-specific goals will always be more difficult in interdependent structures.

Playing a More Demanding Parenting Role

In interdependent structures, a more demanding and integral role for the parent is part of the design. The parent must be more involved in deciding how responsibilities should be shared, in providing protection for specialist cultures, and in guiding co-ordination between units. It faces a more demanding control task, and it may choose to retain more responsibilities than in SBU-based structures.

The nature of parenting in complex, interdependent struc-tures is a major topic that we take up in Chapter 6. Here, we simply observe that while the parent has more opportunities to add value, it can also undermine the structure by failing to fulfill the demands placed upon it.

Adapting to Change

In some respects, interdependent structures provide more opportunities for adaptation to change than do SBU-based structures. The extent of each unit's responsibilities, the basis of sharing responsibilities, and the relationships between the units can all be modified in evolutionary ways, without calling for a wholesale revision of the structure. For example, an informal committee with responsibility for co-ordinating all the business units' relationships with certain key customers can be given added authority by establishing it as an overlay unit, or the balance of power between units concerning specific decisions, such as pricing, can be shifted by giving the final say-so to an overlay unit which previously could only offer advice. In Unilever, we were told about some product-based overlay units that had been set up in South America as a first step in a possible change away from geographical business units to product-based business units. Unilever was able to shift the balance of power towards the product dimension, without a radical change in design, and then to see how well the modified structure worked. Companies such as Citibank, Shell, and Unilever are constantly adjusting the details of their organization designs in an attempt to learn from experience and reflect new requirements.

However, it is hard to force the pace of evolutionary redesign of this sort. Thinking through the knock-on effects of proposed changes and laying out new roles and relationships requires careful planning. Individuals need to understand and buy in to the changes, and must learn to work with new responsibilities and processes. All this takes time, especially if there are some managers who oppose the changes and are intent on sabotaging them. Evolutionary redesign is possible, but by no means easy to implement.

More radical redesign, in which the whole basis of responsibility groupings is changed, is also more complicated for interdependent structures than for SBU-based structures. Typically, SBUs are more modular, and so can be "patched" into new groupings without requiring a whole new set of relationships between units to be developed. The units in interdependent structures are less self-contained, and so new designs need to put in place all the complex relationships between the units as well. It is much easier for GECS to set up a new SBU, or disaggregate or amalgamate SBUs, than it is for Citibank to plan and implement the sort of changes described in the box on pages 118–121. And Monsanto underestimated how long it would take for managers to become comfortable with its new structure.

Advantages and Disadvantages of Interdependent Structures

Table 4.2 summarizes the advantages and disadvantages of interdependent structures, and relates them to our tests.[16] The contrast with SBU-based structures is evident.

Interdependent structures come into their own when ambitious multi-focal strategies are necessary to pursue several different important sources of competitive advantage. In such situations, interdependent structures are likely to be needed to pass the *market advantage test*. The drawback is that such structures lead to slower, more complex decision-making, which reduces the effectiveness of strategy implementation.

Interdependent structures provide more opportunities for the parent to add value, a potential advantage in terms of the *parenting advantage test*. However, the demands on the parent are more onerous, and are by no means always adequately met.

The *people test* is challenging for interdependent structures. Such structures are attractive for managers with good networking skills, who like to work in a collegial context. But many managers take time to acquire the networking skills required, and some will always prefer the clarity of a simpler structure.

The *specialist cultures test* is often a stumbling block for interdependent structures, since units are not autonomous. This means that smaller, less powerful units can easily be dominated or suppressed by other units. Conversely, however, the structure

TABLE 4.2 The Advantages and Disadvantages of Interdependent Structures

Tests	Advantages	Disadvantages
Market advantage	Multiple focuses possible	Slower, more complex decision process
Parenting advantage	More opportunities for parent managers to add value	More demands on parent managers, more danger of value destruction
People	Attractive to managers with networking skills	Depends on availability of managers with networking skills
Specialist cultures	Promotes collaboration, not independence	Suppression of specialist cultures possible
Difficult links	Pursuit of synergies through networking between units	Some cross-boundary links may be unworkably difficult
Redundant hierarchy	Essential role for parent	More skills needed to play the parenting role: less unit self-management
Accountability	More sense of collective accountability	Less self-correction, less strong commitment to unit-specific goals, more complex, costly, time consuming performance measures
Flexibility	Evolutionary fine-tuning of responsibilities possible	Harder to change responsibilities quickly or radically

has the advantage of promoting collaboration between units, and has less risk of baronial independence.

The *difficult links test* is especially important for inter-dependent structures. With more need for co-operation between units, extensive networking between units, supported by suitable co-ordination mechanisms and processes, is needed to pursue synergies between units. But it is essential to recognize that some cross-boundary links will be too difficult, and will not be work-able on a networking basis. This sets limits on what can be achieved.

In interdependent structures, the parent's role is integral and essential. The danger of failing the *redundant hierarchy test* should therefore be lessened. But parent managers do not always have the skills needed to play their role well, so they may destroy more value than they add. Also, complex structures often have multiple parenting levels, not all of which can be justified, and the importance of the parent reduces the scope for self-managed decisions within the units.

In terms of the *accountability test*, interdependent structures have some disadvantages. They include more tied relationships, which reduce self-correction; they require more complex, costly and time consuming performance measures; and they are less con-ducive to strong commitment to unit-specific goals. These are serious problems. But there can also be some advantages. Ideally, there can be a greater sense of collective accountability, based on a wider-ranging and more sophisticated set of performance measures.

Finally, interdependent structures satisfy the *flexibility test*, to the extent that they can achieve evolutionary fine-tuning of responsibilities. But they are less satisfactory where adaptation requires rapid or radical change.

Complexity and Clarity

The balance of advantages and disadvantages of interdependent structures brings out two underlying issues: the danger of excessive complexity, and the need for clarity.

Complexity

Interdependent structures present a number of managerial challenges and are never easy to implement well. The complexity of decision-making, responsibility allocations, cross-unit working, and collective accountabilities can lead to indecisiveness, ambiguity, slowness, and high costs. Many managers feel deeply uncomfortable in complex structures, and much prefer the clear responsibilities and accountabilities of SBU-based structures.

It makes sense, therefore, for organization designers to opt for simple, SBU-based structures, *unless* strong and explicit strategic reasons dictate a more complex alternative. Interdependent structures are essential for some multi-focal strategies, but they are inferior to SBU-based structures if a single dimension of focus dominates the strategy. It may even sometimes make sense to choose a simpler structure, and accept that some opportunities for achieving competitive advantage will be foregone. The onus of proof should be on organization designers who advocate a complex, interdependent design to demonstrate why it is needed.

This is not to say that interdependent structures cannot work well. Rather, the choice of structure should reflect the corporate strategy to achieve advantage. Both GECS and Citibank compete in the corporate banking market. While Citibank has adopted a complex structure with extensive interdependencies, GECS has chosen a simple, SBU-based structure. Is Citibank's complex structure really needed, given that GECS (and other competitors) are structured more simply?

The key questions for Citibank to answer in making this assessment are:

- Are competitors with simpler structures, such as GECS, more or less successful than us?
- Does our strategy dictate a complex structure, whereas other companies' strategies allow a simple structure?

- If our strategy does call for a complex structure, is it paying off in terms of our competitive position and performance?

In terms of financial performance, market value, and reputation, both GECS and Citibank are among the industry leaders. It is evidently possible to be successful with either a simple or a complex structure.

In the box on page 117, we analyzed the reasons why Citibank has chosen its current structure. Because its strategy to achieve competitive advantage rests on its global customer relationships and shared global infrastructure, it is pushed towards an interdependent structure. GECS, whose strategy does not depend on these sources of advantage, can afford to adopt a simpler structure. The structural differences reflect underlying strategy differences.

And, for Citibank, its strategy does seem to be working. Because it has a unique position in terms of global coverage and relationships, and because it has learnt to handle the challenges of complex structures, it is now reaping the reward in its markets.

Citibank's complex structural design therefore seems to be justified. But this does not imply that GECS's structure is wrong. Given GECS's strategy, a simple structure makes sense. Nor does it imply that other financial institutions with complex structures in corporate banking have made the right decision. Many of them have achieved little advantage from their complexity, since the costs involved have not been repaid in terms of greater competitiveness and superior profitability. These companies' complex structures are not justified. And even for Citibank, it remains useful to ask questions about how much extra complexity and cost is truly essential for its strategy.

Ashby's law of requisite complexity suggests that any system needs to be sufficiently complex to deal with its environment.[17] But we believe that it is equally important to remember that organizations should be no more complex than is necessary. This is an underlying theme that is relevant in the application of all our design tests.[18] The default position should always favor decentralization, self-management, and networking solutions, not complex designed-in matrix structures, co-ordination mechanisms, and management processes. Additional structure, mechanisms, and processes should only be created if they are specifically needed to pass the design tests. In this way, structured networks can replace excessively complex matrices as the means of implementing strategies that call for multiple dimensions of focus.

Clarity

A major impediment to the working of interdependent structures is lack of clarity on the part of managers about how they are intended to operate. They know that they have certain responsibilities and that they must collaborate with other units in discharging them. But they are often unsure about what sort of relationships they should have with other units, how major decisions will be handled, what the relative balance of power will be, and how their performance will be evaluated.

"We are going to set up a new unit with responsibility for . . ., and you will be in charge of it," say the organization designers. Their intention is to give more attention to the responsibility in question, but they fail to say what powers the new unit will have and how it is supposed to relate to other units with overlapping responsibilities. Confusion, frustration, and friction result from underspecifying unit roles in interdependent structures.

On the other hand, many of the drawbacks of interdependent structures are mitigated when managers are clear about their roles. Provided they know what their main responsibilities and accountabilities are, and understand the spirit in which they are meant to work with their bosses and colleagues, they will usually be more capable of handling the organizational challenges they face. Clarity on these issues allows the chaos of the traditional matrix structure to be replaced with the power of a largely self-managing network.

The importance of clarity in organization design as a

precondition for self-managed networking is a major theme of the next chapter. In it, we offer a taxonomy of unit roles that is helpful in achieving the clarity required.

5

A Taxonomy of Unit Roles

In the last chapter, we argued that clarity is an important feature of good organizational designs, particularly in complex, interdependent structures. If the extent of different units' responsibilities, or how they are supposed to work together in discharging their responsibilities, is not clear, the structure will become mired in ambiguity and disputes.

In this chapter, we assess the trade-offs between too little and too much detail in achieving design clarity. We put forward the concept of unit "roles", which convey the main responsibilities, relationships, and accountabilities of units, as a practical means of clarifying design intentions, and we propose a taxonomy of unit roles, which we believe can greatly assist organization designers in specifying design options.

Clarity, Detail, and Design Intentions

If managers are not clear about their respective responsibilities in an organization design, it is unlikely to work well. There will be conflict about who should take the lead on what activities, wrangling about the decision process in areas of shared responsibility, and a danger that some important tasks will fall between the cracks and be ignored. In complex, interdependent structures, these problems are particularly damaging. Networks without clarity can easily lead to confusion.

We worked with one professional service firm which was extending the range of its services and establishing an international network of offices. Individual partners had been asked to lead specific practice areas, such as information systems, and regions, such as Asia. But the front-line of the firm remained client teams, assembled for particular projects by the relevant client relationship partners. The nature of the responsibilities of the practice areas and the regions was left somewhat vague, and the extent of the power and authority of their leaders in dealing with the client relationship partners was unclear. Although most partners recognized the need to try to manage both the practice area and the regional dimension, there was widespread dissatisfaction with the new structure because it led to constant friction between client relationship partners, practice area leaders, and regional heads, together with higher management overheads and slower decisions. Furthermore, there were complaints that the practice areas and the regions were not proving effective in enhancing the firm's capabilities in these dimensions and were not being held to account for these shortcomings. Lack of clarity in roles and responsibilities was undermining an organization whose basic concept was generally agreed to be sound.

The obvious answer to a lack of clarity in organization design seems to be to specify responsibilities in more detail. Make clear the respective responsibilities of practice areas and regions, lay out the processes by which client relationship partners, practice areas, and regions should jointly agree on priorities, establish the roles of firm-wide regional management, and so on. Laying out responsibilities in more detail is often helpful: indeed, one chief executive told us that the most important lesson he had learned from trying to design and implement a network structure was the need to provide a more detailed blueprint at the outset. But there is a limit to how much detail the organization designer can, or should, attempt to impose.

As all practicing managers know, weighty manuals that lay out exactly who is responsible for what are seldom used or even useful. There may be some valuable discussion about roles and responsibilities in the process of developing the manual; but once the manual has been produced, it is usually filed away and forgotten. It does not become an essential reference guide for shaping decisions, and any managers who try to use it for such purposes are branded as bureaucrats, who are more concerned with following procedures than with getting the job done. We asked many companies with complex structures whether they used responsibility charts and manuals to guide day-to-day decisions, and almost invariably met with a negative response.

There are good reasons for this apparently Luddite attitude to responsibility manuals. First, no manual, however detailed, can anticipate all eventualities. Decisions will be required on issues that the manual did not (and could not) foresee, and for which no clear responsibilities and procedures therefore exist. Unpredictable developments in markets and technologies, new communication techniques, shifts in the political or regulatory context, and changes in the climate of public opinion can all present new challenges for a company. And, on a more mundane level, detailed issues are constantly coming up that do not quite fit within predefined processes or responsibility allocations. A manual laying out the respective responsibilities of the two authors of this book would have required almost daily revision over the course of the last three years!

So responsibility manuals cannot be comprehensive. Worse still, attempts to make them comprehensive render them less user-friendly. Their length increases, the "ifs" and "buts" proliferate, and their intelligibility and usability for the average manager decline. The quest for a comprehensive responsibility manual is not only vain but counterproductive.

A second, and even stronger, reason for avoiding excessively detailed responsibility allocations is to allow flexibility for lower levels of management to decide how they will work together as circumstances evolve. The knowledge and competence principle suggests that, on most detailed issues, lower-level managers will be better placed than senior managers to take decisions. This applies to the process by which decisions should be reached as much as to the content of decisions. The adaptability principle also implies that all organizations need to be able to alter responsibilities as circumstances change. A flexible structure, in which lower levels can evolve and change their respective responsibilities and relationships to take account of new circumstances and individual learning, is therefore much preferable to a rigid and cumbersome design in which management try to mandate and fix every responsibility from the top down. Many organization experts[1] now argue strongly that companies need to move away from excessive reliance on hierarchically imposed structures and systems, and empower front-line managers to make their own decisions in accordance with a broader sense of corporate purpose.

The organization designer is therefore confronted by a dilemma. Clarity about the way the organization is intended to work is vital. But it is neither feasible nor desirable to design an organization in great detail from the top down. How can organization designers make clear their intentions without descending into excessive detail?

What to Specify

From our research, we have concluded that the most important things for organization designers to make explicit are the basic purpose or role of each unit and the types of relationships it should expect to have with other units. An important contribution to clarifying design intentions can be made by specifying, for each unit,

- its broad area of responsibility;
- the nature of its intended reporting relationship to upper levels of management;
- the nature of its intended horizontal relationships with other units in the company; and
- its main accountabilities.

Although it may also be necessary to spell out some of the key decision processes in more detail (see Chapters 7 and 8), specifying broad responsibilities, relationships, and account-abilities provides a context and orientation within which unit managers can, in most situations, work out detailed decisions for themselves on a self-managed basis.

Broad Responsibilities

Unit responsibilities need to be specified in a way that makes the broad remit clear, but leaves most of the details to be determined by the unit. A product group, for example, needs to know what sort of products and markets are, and are not, within its respons-ibility. An Automotive Components Group, for example, should know that breakdown services are not in its remit, but that it has discretion about whether to compete in shock absorbers as well as brake pads, and can make its own decisions about the specific shock absorber product range to offer. Similarly, an European Manufacturing unit is clearly charged with running the manu-facturing facilities in Europe, but can have a high level of discretion about the processes and equipment to adopt, and even about the overall European plant configuration.

It is also useful to specify what sort of responsibility the unit has. Is it a market-focused responsibility, including both revenue generation and associated costs in serving the target markets? If so, the unit can be a profit center, whose role is to decide how to serve its target markets. Or is it an activity-focused respons-ibility, with no external customers, in which case it becomes a cost center whose role is to carry out the activity as cost-effectively as possible.

In addition, the unit needs to know what sort of resources and authority it will have to carry out its responsibilities. Broadly, what resources will be included within the unit? How much freedom will the unit's management team have to make decisions, and on what key decisions will the unit have "final word" authority? Units need to be clear about their main areas of responsibility, and about the extent of the authority they have in carrying out these responsibilities.

Reporting Relationships

It is also important to specify to whom units will report, and the nature of this reporting relationship. It is in the nature of reporting relationships that the senior manager (or managers) to whom the unit reports have ultimate authority to appoint and reward the unit's general manager, to approve the unit's budget, plans, and major investments, to monitor performance, and to intervene in exceptional circumstances or crises. Upper levels cannot delegate these responsibilities, which are necessary for them to exercise due diligence control. But they may also reserve a range of other responsibilities and powers, and exercise more or less influence on the unit.

The details of the reserve powers and responsibilities retained and of the influence that upper levels will exercise do not need to be spelled out as part of the organization design; but the extent of the unit's intended autonomy from hierarchical influence should be made clear.

In our research, we have encountered a variety of levels of influence by upper levels on the units that report to them. At one end of the spectrum, business unit general managers are normally closely involved in the decisions made by the main operating functions reporting to them. They usually expect to be consulted, and to have the final word, on important decisions within the R&D, operations, sales, and marketing functions in the business. They exercise strong influence because they are responsible for integrating the efforts of all the functions to achieve the business's overall goals.

At the other end of the spectrum, some corporate parents adopt a very hands-off role with respect to the units reporting to them. They are involved in few issues beyond those necessary for due diligence, do not expect to be informed of the units' decisions, and exercise little influence on them. They prefer the units to have a high level of autonomy, believing that the parent does not have enough knowledge to intervene productively, except on a limited set of issues. Richard Branson interferes little in the operations of Virgin's businesses, except on issues concerned with overall brand positioning.

Other corporate parents are more involved. In order to add value, they believe they need to have a more hands-on relationship with the units reporting to them. Hands-on parents recognize that the managers reporting to them are primarily responsible for the affairs of their units, but they reserve more powers for the parent and they exercise more active influence on a wider range of topics. In Chapter 4, we described the hands-on parenting styles of Citicorp and Monsanto.

There are therefore many possible reporting relationships, ranging from a closely involved general manager, through a hands-on parent, to a hands-off parent. There are, of course, many variations along this centralization/decentralization spectrum and many detailed differences in which responsibilities are delegated or retained. But specifying the type of reporting relationship that is expected is important, since it helps to clarify how much freedom of action the unit will have.[2]

Lateral Relationships

Lateral relationships between sister units are even more varied than reporting relationships. But in interdependent structures it is important for units to have a sense of what sort of relationships they are meant to have with other units. In part, this concerns relative power and influence in key shared decisions, but it also concerns the spirit of collaboration that should prevail, and the extent to which collaboration is optional or mandatory.

In our research, we found five main types of lateral relationship, in each of which the basis of collaboration was fundamentally different:

- mutual self-interest;
- pressure group/principal;
- service provider/client;
- resource owner/user;
- team.

Mutual self-interest relationships are similar to third-party, market relationships. Sister units work together if both parties see an interest in doing so, but are free not to collaborate if they do not. Customer–supplier relationships, for example, where both sides are free to do business outside the company, can be governed by mutual self-interest. In companies with a strong family feeling, there may be a cultural pressure to collaborate, and hence a desire to discover mutual interest in doing so, but the basic principle of voluntary decisions by all parties to work together remains. Mutual self-interest relationships create self-managing quasi-market pressure on units to satisfy each other's commercial objectives, since otherwise the units will not collaborate.

Pressure group/principal relationships exist where one unit has the final word on a decision, but the other unit is expected to exert its influence on the outcome. The unit acting as a pressure group advocates its perspective vigorously and seeks to persuade the unit with ultimate authority, the principal, of its view, but is expected to buy in to and support whatever is finally decided. The principal unit has an obligation to listen to the pressure group unit and to try to satisfy it, but has the right to make its own decision. The principal has the final word. As we shall argue later in the chapter, overlay units and project units typically have pressure group/principal relationships with the business units with which they collaborate.

In service provider/client relationships, the service provider must aim to be responsive to the client's stated requirements, subject to any overriding corporate guidelines. In other words, the service provider must treat other units as its customers, endeavoring to win their business through the quality, responsiveness, and cost-effectiveness of its service offering. The client unit's obligation is to state its requirements clearly, and to make it as easy as possible for the service provider to satisfy them. In some companies, both sides are free to walk away if they cannot reach agreement, in which case the relationship moves towards mutual self-interest. In other companies, there are more constraints. Clients can only cease to use the service provider if specified conditions are met, such as giving due notice, obtaining external prices that are x% lower, and so on. Sometimes client units are mandated by corporate management to work together with the in-house service providers. But even with tied relationships of this sort, the service provider has an obligation to strive to satisfy the client units.

The resource owner/user relationship is similar to the service provider/client relationship, but has some important differences. The resource owner must not only respond to users' stated requirements, but also develop and nurture the resource on behalf of the company. With scarce and valuable resources such as skilled researchers or software programmers, the resource owner's first duty is to strengthen the depth and quality of the resource and to insure it is used as productively as possible. This may imply prioritizing different users' requests, rather than attempting to respond to all demands. Similarly, user units must recognize that they are bidding for the resource, and cannot always expect to have all their bids fully met. Furthermore, user units are likely to be constrained to work with the in-house resource owner, except in special circumstances. Resource owners therefore need to strike a delicate balance between responsiveness to their users and attention to wider corporate priorities.

In team relationships, all units must collaborate to realize the goals of the larger, upper-level unit of which they are part. Team members must strive to learn enough about each other's concerns that they can arrive at a consensus about the best collective way forward. This is a costly decision process, unless the team has a clear leader, who is empowered to impose a decision on the team. In any case, all the team members are eventually expected to align themselves with the decisions of the team. Thus all the function heads within a business unit should work together, under the direction of the business unit general manager, to achieve the business unit's objectives. The function heads must ultimately put the business unit's needs ahead of their functions' needs, must attempt to reach consensus with other members of the team about how to work together, and, if necessary, must accept that the business unit general manager has the authority to resolve disputes and impose a way forward.

The value of these five archetypal relationships lies in their ability to capture the intended orientation of each unit towards other units. There are, of course, subtle variations within each type of relationship. For example, the nature of the discretion of resource owner units to override user requests varies widely. Furthermore, units' main relationships may be complemented by different secondary relationships on specific issues: for example, an overlay unit which normally acts as a pressure group may have the final authority on a few issues. However, we believe that the five relationships we have described provide a simple but powerful means of specifying the majority of intended lateral relationships in interdependent structures.

We accept that, in many companies, there are examples of corrupted relationships in which, for example, business units make no attempt to listen to overlay units, service providers are impervious to client requests, and sub-units within a business fight each other rather than collaborating as a team. But these are dysfunctional relationships that have gone wrong, not ones that have been intentionally designed into an organization.

Understanding intended lateral relationships helps a unit to work out for itself how it should handle specific collaboration issues with other units. The intended relationship provides guidance on how each unit should conduct itself, without imposing detailed process design.

Main Accountabilities

The final component of a unit's role concerns its main accountabilities. What key performance measures will be used? Will they emphasize bottom-line profitability, or will they focus on other goals? Will they be unit-specific or more widely drawn? How accountable will unit managers be, in terms of close monitoring, powerful incentives, and tight control?

The importance of a unit's accountabilities is amply demonstrated by the control and commitment principle: it is the "what-gets-measured-gets-done" aspect of performance measures that is vital. The nature of a unit's main accountabilities helps managers to decide what priorities they should give to different tasks on their "to do" lists, and therefore shapes the way in which they discharge their responsibilities. A business unit manager who is held tightly to account for annual unit profit performance will pay little attention to collaboration that does not have an immediate benefit to his unit's profit. An overlay unit that is measured on sales growth will see its role differently from one that is measured on profitability. So a unit's main accountabilities give further essential context for interpreting decentralized responsibilities.

Specifying Design Intentions

The organization designer needs to lay out in broad terms what the unit is supposed to be doing (broad responsibilities), how it is supposed to work with other units (reporting and lateral relationships), and how its performance will be assessed (main accountabilities). This leaves the unit's management to work out most of the details as it confronts specific situations and develops a *modus vivendi* with its boss and with other units. But it provides sufficient specification to allow the unit management to make sensible decisions that are compatible with the organization designer's intentions.

Clarity about broad responsibilities, relationships, and accountabilities does not prevent all organizational conflict and confusion. Difficult people, who disagree with the organization design or are dissatisfied with their personal positions within it, may try to flaunt the intentions behind the design. Difficult decisions, where managers can legitimately disagree about the extent of their units' responsibilities, their relative power and influence, and how they should therefore work together, may still arise. But, provided managers are willing to accept the designer's intentions, clarity about these key issues does resolve most disputes and is essential for avoiding the sort of chaos that so often bedevils interdependent structures.

A Taxonomy of Unit Roles

Although many different combinations of responsibilities, relationships, and accountabilities are theoretically possible, we have found in practice that most units conform to one of a relatively small number of roles. Each role represents a basically different combination of responsibilities, relationships, and accountabilities. Corresponding to these combinations, we have devised a taxonomy of eight different unit roles:

- business units;
- business functions;
- overlay units;
- sub-businesses;
- core resource units;
- shared service units;
- project units; and
- parent units.

In the following sections, we lay out the key features of each type of unit, and show how they can be used in describing organization designs.

We believe that the taxonomy provides a useful common language for describing and analyzing organization designs. Even more importantly, it gives managers practical and useful building blocks with which to design and specify decentralized responsibilities.

The roles we propose are intended to highlight fundamental differences in purpose between units. They convey essential information about responsibilities, relationships, and accountabilities, but at a generic level. The specific responsibilities, relationships, and accountabilities for each business unit will differ, as they will for all unit types. Also, the roles are "ideal" prototypes, and we accept that there are shades of gray between them. In concept, for example, the distinction between a core resource unit and a shared service unit is clear. But in reality there may be some units that have intermediate features, and thus are hard to classify. Nevertheless we believe that the value of our taxonomy as a framework for researching and designing organizations outweighs any potential dangers of oversimplification.

Business Units

Business units are fundamental building blocks in corporate structures. They are set up to achieve focus benefits in serving selected target product/market segments. Ideally, the target markets should be chosen so that the business units create a focus of management attention on those things that are most important in achieving competitive advantage. As such, the business units represent the primary dimensions of focus in the organization. Table 5.1 summarizes the role of business units.

Business units have a relatively high level of autonomy over decisions about precisely which customers fall within their product/market scope, and about how to serve their target segments. They are responsible for maximizing the value that can be created from serving these markets.

Business units report to parent managers, who leave most decisions to the business's management. The parent may be more or less hands-on, with more or fewer reserved powers, but in any

TABLE 5.1 The Role of Business Units

Purpose	To achieve benefits from focusing on product/market segments that are most important for competitive advantage
Responsibilities	To develop specialist skills and align value chain activities to serve the target product/market segments
Reporting relationships	Reports to parent that gives substantial autonomy on day-to-day decisions, but less than for SBU
Lateral relationships	Mutual self-interest with other business units; interdependent with other types of units
Accountability	Strong accountability for bottom-line performance, including profitability, but less accountability than SBUs

case the business will expect little interference on day-to-day issues.

Business units' relationships with other units are generally guided by a mutual self-interest orientation. However, the nature of the relationship also depends on the role of the other unit or units concerned, as we shall see later in this chapter.

Last, accountability emphasizes unit-specific performance. Business unit managers are held strongly accountable for the bottom-line performance, and particularly the profitability, of their units.

In Chapter 4, we discussed SBUs extensively. SBUs are business units with a high degree of self-containment and autonomy. In interdependent structures, business units are less self-contained, since their responsibilities will in many areas overlap with other units. This means that the business units have to work more collaboratively with other units to achieve their goals, and the parent is likely to be more involved than with SBUs. Since they experience more influence on decisions from both lateral and hierarchical relationships, business units in interdependent structures are not as free to make unilateral decisions about how to serve their target markets. But, by the same token, they cannot be held as strongly accountable for unit profitability as SBUs, since they have a lower level of autonomy. With a more interdependent structure, Shell, for instance, has found it difficult to establish the strong accountability for performance contracts that has been instituted at BP.

Business Functions

Within the business units, there is usually a functional structure.[3] For example, there may be a logistics function, an operations function, a sales function, and a development function. Each of these functional units is set up to focus on specific value chain activities. Business functions' responsibilities are to achieve functional excellence and cost-effectiveness, in a way that contributes to the overall success of the business unit. Table 5.2 summarizes the role of business functions.

TABLE 5.2 The Role of Business Functions

Purpose	To achieve benefits from focusing on important functions (value chain activities) within the business unit
Responsibilities	To carry out the functional activities cost-effectively, and in a way that contributes to the business unit's success
Reporting relationships	Reports to business unit general manager who has ultimate authority over decisions
Lateral relationships	Works with other functions as part of business unit management team
Accountability	For functional effectiveness and for contributing to business unit performance

The design of the functional units within the business units, including the extent of their decentralized powers, is normally left to the business unit general manager to whom they report. The general manager may well retain responsibility in key areas, and is likely to have an influence on most major functional decisions. For example, the general manager will help to shape the marketing strategy and will be involved in major IT investment choices. General managers need to be close enough to functional decisions for their guidance to be positive and beneficial.

Business functions are intended to work together as part of a unified team, led by the general manager, to develop and implement the business unit's strategy. The power and influence of the general manager means that it should be easier to push through collaboration between functions, even where there are difficulties to be overcome. For example, the general manager can insist that product designers take account of manufacturing implications, and can make sure that those who don't make little career progress.

Given the nature of these reporting and lateral relationships, business functions, such as sales or R&D, do not have much autonomy. It is not possible for the sales force or staff in research labs to go their own separate ways. This implies that individual functions are less free to establish their own distinctive specialist cultures, and we encountered several business units in which one function, for example manufacturing, felt stifled by a business unit culture that was dominated by other functions (e.g. innovation and marketing). This is a danger against which business unit general managers need to guard.

In terms of accountability, function-specific measures of performance are not sufficient, since they may not capture the vital importance of the contribution that the function makes to overall business unit results. For example, it is obviously wrong to penalize the sales function for underachieving its revenue targets, if it has been asked to cut back severely on advertising spend in order to help meet the business's profit goal. Simple, output-oriented, unit-specific measures of performance are not appropriate for business functions. Fortunately, however, the business unit general manager is likely to have enough knowledge about what is going on in all the functions to be able to make holistic judgments about their performance.

To work well, business functions depend on the knowledge and competence of the influential business unit general managers to whom they report. In large, complicated business units, there can be a danger of overloading the general manager. If so, it may be desirable to break up the business unit into a number of smaller businesses or sub-businesses.

Overlay Units

The purpose of setting up an overlay unit is to create a focus of management attention on product-market segments that may not be given sufficient emphasis by the business units. The overlay unit is intended to achieve focus benefits for product-market groupings that cut across the product markets the business units have been set up to serve. Table 5.3 summarizes the role of overlay units.

Overlay units resemble business units in the nature of their responsibilities. They are also market-focused, with responsibility for selected product market segments. But the segments for which the overlay units are responsible represent an alternative dimen-

TABLE 5.3 The Role of Overlay Units

Purpose	To achieve additional product/market focus benefits
Responsibilities	To develop specialist skills and influence value chain activities for serving target product/market segments, defined along different dimensions from business units
Reporting relationships	Reports to parent that gives substantial autonomy on day-to-day decisions, but may sometimes need to arbitrate disputes with business units
Lateral relationships	Acts as a pressure group on behalf of the overlay's target product/market segments
Accountability	For success in serving target product/market segments, usually including profitability, but not strongly accountable due to low autonomy

sion of focus. If the business units are focused on countries or regions, the overlays may focus on product groups or channels. If the business units are designed around products or technologies, the overlays may target customer groupings or even major accounts. The overlay units are intended to create additional dimensions of focus, and thus to develop sources of competitive advantage that the main business units are likely to neglect.

Overlays are common in professional service firms, where focus benefits may be sought around practice specialisms, customer groupings, and geographical regions. In McKinsey and The Boston Consulting Group, the primary line of reporting and the business units are defined geographically, in terms of local offices or regions. However, there are also overlay units concerned with practice areas, such as value-based management or organization development, and with customer groupings, such as healthcare or financial services. In Booz Allen and Hamilton, where the primary business units are defined in terms of customer groupings, around global industry specialisms, the geographical regions and the practice areas are the overlays. WPP, the marketing services group, has overlays to pull together its advertising, market research, PR, and other services for specific industry sectors: a unit called The Common Health, for example, concentrates on healthcare customers. Equally, a number of consumer products companies, such as Unilever and 3M, whose business units are defined around products, have set up overlay units to focus on their relationships with key retail customers, such as Wal-Mart or Carrefour.

Overlays cut across the main reporting line. They may need to work with several business units or can fall within a single business unit. In Mars, the European Snackfoods business is organized around a series of national sub-businesses. The main product for these sub-businesses is chocolate confectionery, but they also sell ice cream. Ice cream, however, also has a dedicated management team with a pan-European responsibility that cuts across the sub-businesses. A Mars manager suggested that we should refer to this as an "underlay" unit, rather than an overlay unit, since it is within the European Snackfoods business.

The extent of the influence that overlay units have over the value chain activities necessary to serve their target markets varies. The overlay can be made more powerful by giving it a budget to spend and authority over certain decisions. But overlays inevitably have smaller budgets and final responsibility for fewer decisions than business units.

In its lateral relationships with other units, the overlay is essentially acting as a pressure group on behalf of its target product-market segments. It should be pressing hard to accumulate resources and influence decisions in ways that will improve the service offered to its target segments and enhance their profitability. Good overlay managers are endlessly energetic in promoting their unit's causes.

But overlays must ultimately accept that decisions on most issues rest with other units, especially the business units that they cut across. The business units have some obligation to listen to the overlays, to take their proposals seriously, and to try to reach a mutually agreeable consensus. They cannot simply dismiss overlay concerns. Since the overlays have been set up by top management to promote additional dimensions of focus, they have some right of appeal to senior managers on important and contested issues. Senior management may intervene to support the overlay if the business unit is acting unreasonably, but on most issues the business units have the final word. Mars ice cream unit must work with and through the snackfoods business in order to be successful. It is part of the definition of an overlay that it is less self-contained than a business unit, and there is always some danger that overlays will become dominated specialist cultures.

As with business units, overlays report to a parent level of management that is not normally involved in day-to-day decisions, but the parent may occasionally need to arbitrate disputes between the overlay and other units. In executing its responsibilities, the overlay can lobby the parent as well as other units it is trying to influence. The parent must make sure that the overlay's views are heard and taken into account, while recognizing that the business units remain the primary decision-makers. This is not an easy balance to preserve.

Overlays can usually measure the profitability with which their target markets are being served. The revenue from these markets can be tracked and it is possible to assess the costs associated with serving them. But parent managers do not always choose to measure overlay profitability, partly because it may involve tricky cost allocations between business units and overlays, and partly because profitability is a less appropriate performance measure for overlays. With less autonomy to set and implement strategies for their target segments, bottom-line profit may not be the best measure of their performance. In fact, it may even be undesirable for overlay managers to push too hard to maximize profitability, if this results in a reduction in the profitability of the business units. In some companies, targets such as sales volume or customer satisfaction rather than profitability are used to motivate and control overlay managers.

Overlay units typically do not rate well in terms of the accountability test. It is often hard to find simple, output-oriented performance measures that encapsulate how well they are doing, and they cannot be held tightly to account for their performance, because they have limited autonomy and are constrained to work through sister units.

Last, it is worth observing that overlays can be a source of flexibility in organization designs. By shifting the relative power of overlays and business units, gradual adaptation to new circumstances can occur. The process may begin with the creation of an informal network between product group managers to consider their common interests in serving a shared customer, such as Tesco. Then an overlay unit can be created, with a dedicated management team, but little power and a low budget. Then the powers of the overlay, in areas such as discount policy, distribution, or sales representation, can be slowly enhanced. Ultimately, the whole basis of business unit definition can be redesigned around customers rather than products. Overlays create the potential for evolutionary change in organization designs.

Sub-businesses

Sub-businesses provide a means of combining the benefits of a broader and a narrower business unit focus. They give additional focus benefits, around more narrowly defined, disaggregated product-market segments than the business units. For example, if there are strong reasons for creating the main business units at the level of the product group, but also specialization benefits available for specific product lines, it may be worth creating separate profit centers for each product line, reporting to the main product group business unit. These profit centers, or sub-business units, can concentrate on developing special skills and aligning resources for their respective product lines in a more dedicated way than the wider product group, while reporting to the product group's general manager as part of the product group's management team. Table 5.4 summarizes the role of sub-businesses.

As with business units, the responsibilities of sub-business units are defined in terms of a market focus. The sub-businesses are set up within the business units, with the same type of focus, but at a greater level of disaggregation. For example, if the business concerned is a national division, the sub-businesses may be set up for local regions or areas. In its US drinks operations,

TABLE 5.4 The Role of Sub-businesses

Purpose	To combine the benefits of broader and narrower market focus
Responsibilities	To develop specialist skills and influence value chain activities to serve selected product/market segments, defined at a more disaggregated level than the business units
Reporting relationships	Reports to business unit general manager, who has ultimate authority over decisions, but who delegates some independence to sub-business on matters exclusively concerned with their target segments
Lateral relationships	Collaborates with other sub-businesses as part of the business unit team, while promoting the interests of the sub-business's target product/market segments (quasi-team)
Accountability	For bottom-line performance, including profitability, but not strongly accountable due to low autonomy

Diageo set up a new, locally-focused sub-business structure in 1999. As Jim Grover, director of corporate strategy, explained:

"We recognised that, with a much warmer climate and a huge Latin American community, the drinking preferences in Florida and the South Eastern States are quite different from New England or the Mid-West. So you need a different product mix and different marketing campaigns. We decided that the best way to develop and implement strategies focused on these different markets was to disaggregate the overall US business into several separate regionally-focused profit-responsible sub-businesses."

The sub-businesses have some influence over how to serve their target markets, and have sole responsibility for some activities. But they report to the business units, which typically retain responsibility for key decisions and shared resources. A common role for sub-businesses is to take the lead on sales and marketing tactics, while drawing on shared research, product development, and even manufacturing at the business unit level.

In Rentokil Initial, the business units are national divisions, responsible for different service lines such as pest control, tropical plants, or security. Within these divisions, there are separate profit-responsible sub-businesses at the local branch level.[4] The division retains responsibility for most major decisions, such as the services to offer, pricing, and investment in systems support. But the branch management is free to recruit, train, and motivate branch staff, and to market and deliver services within the local territory.

The decision to set up, to reorganize, or to disband sub-businesses is usually made by the business unit, which chooses to delegate some of its responsibilities down to a lower level. The sub-businesses recognize that the general manager of the business unit will remain in close contact with their affairs and may decide to intervene to align individual sub-business decisions with the interests of the wider business unit. Sub-businesses should neither have nor expect the extent of discretion and autonomy enjoyed by business units.

Sub-business unit managers form part of the business unit's management team. They typically meet regularly, under the leadership of the business unit general manager, to co-ordinate and align decisions across all the sub-businesses. Each sub-business is expected to fight its own corner and argue for decisions that will benefit its specific market focus. Sub-businesses need to have sufficient independence to pursue the focus benefits they have been set up to achieve, but it is even more important for all the sub-businesses to work together and accept decisions taken in the interests of the wider business unit as a whole. Sub-businesses that are too aggressively independent cause problems for the business unit general manager, who should have the authority to bring them firmly back into line when necessary. Branch managers in Rentokil Initial must conform to divisional policies and decisions and share ideas with their colleagues, as well as trying to come top of the branch performance league table. In relationships between sub-businesses, there is a need for collaboration and teamwork is well as self-interest and independence. This is a variant on a team relationship, which we refer to as a "quasi-team" relationship.

Given their relationship with the business unit general manager, there is a risk that sub-businesses will lack the autonomy to defend their special interests and priorities against standardization pressures from the business unit level. But, conversely, it should be more possible to achieve difficult links between sub-businesses as a result of the influence and authority of the general manager to whom they all report.

Profitability is a key performance measure for sub-businesses: indeed the sub-businesses within a business are often referred to as "profit centers". But sub-businesses are less accountable for performance than business units. Their performance is likely to be as strongly affected by business unit decisions as by sub-business decisions – possibly more so. Their lack of discretion means that parent managers and business unit managers cannot hold them as tightly to account for the results they achieve. But sub-businesses can be judged based on the relative performance of other comparable sub-units. In Rentokil, profitability league tables allow the performance of each branch to be benchmarked. Clive Thompson, the chief executive, maintains that good branch managers can make more than a 100% difference to branch profitability. Given a relevant peer group, even sub-units with quite low discretion can be rewarded for and motivated by their performance and profitability.

By setting up a sub-business, the organization designer encourages lower-level managers to feel more autonomous and profit-responsible. Sub-business managers should be acting entrepreneurially to maximize their opportunities, not just implementing decisions taken higher up. But sub-business managers must also be good team players, contributing to overall business results and working within policies set by the business management. This is not easy, and an understanding of the role intended for the sub-business is essential in doing so.

Core Resource Units

The purpose of a core resource unit is to focus management attention on selected resources that are key to competitive advantage in several business units. For example, many companies have corporate or divisional R&D units that work on behalf of several businesses, in the belief that these units are the best way to develop and leverage certain scarce and valuable research competences in the interests of the company as a whole. Table 5.5 summarizes the role of core resource units.

Core resource units are responsible for nurturing resources, and for prioritizing and allocating the use of these resources on behalf of the group. In pharmaceutical companies, such as AstraZeneca or Pfizer, corporate R&D acts as a core resource unit. Likewise, the competence teams at Monsanto (see box on page 122 in Chapter 4) are core resource units. In 3M, there are core resource units for different technology platforms, such as adhesives, fiber optics, and films. We have also encountered core resource units for IT, manufacturing, sales, distribution, and e-business. The management teams of core resource units are charged with developing the resource in question into a source of advantage for the company. They are responsible for recruiting the right people, developing their skills, and investing in the support necessary to achieve competitive superiority. Bringing the resources together into a single unit makes it easier to

TABLE 5.5 The Role of Core Resource Units

Purpose	To achieve benefits from focusing on selected resources, competences, or activities that are key to competitive advantage for several business units
Responsibilities	To develop the resources into a source of advantage for the company, and to allocate the resources in accordance with corporate priorities
Reporting relationships	Reports to parent that gives some autonomy in decisions about how to develop and allocate resources, but is influential about corporate needs and priorities
Lateral relationships	Acts as a resource provider to other user units
Accountability	For the development and utilization of the core resource, and for its contribution to the company as a whole

achieve critical mass and economies of scale, and to develop the specialist skills and culture needed.

Core resource units have to determine priorities for the use of their scarce resources. If the unit does not have enough skilled people or budget to respond to all the requests on it, how should the resources be allocated? In making these judgments, the core resource unit needs to develop a view on corporate priorities for the utilization of its resources. Indeed, part of the reason for setting up a separate unit is to encourage it to make its own independent judgment of priorities.

Core resource units report to a parent level of management. The parent gives the core resource some autonomy to make decisions about the development and use of the resources. But it also needs to have considerable influence on decisions, both to inject its own views on corporate priorities and to resolve any disputes between the core resource unit and other units. The parent therefore needs to be relatively hands-on in its relation-ship with the unit. This can be a challenge, since it requires the parent to get to grips with some difficult, often technically complex trade-offs and judgments: it is never easy for the chief executive of a pharmaceutical company, for example, to inter-vene wisely in the determination of research priorities. But core resource units with hands-off parents are liable to become too insulated from the commercial needs of the rest of the company, too driven by their own special interests.

Resource users will normally be expected to work with the core resource units. Ideally, the core resource unit will guide other units on how to make the best use of the resource. Hence the resource owner/user relationship is critical. If it works well, the core resource unit will be respected for its ability to provide top-quality resource and for its judgments about when and how to use the resource. If it works badly, the core resource unit will be seen as arrogant and insular, with little interest in helping the businesses to succeed. At the extreme, the core resource unit becomes a fiercely independent "empire", impervious to the needs of other units and unwilling to change or adapt to new demands placed upon it. There is plenty of room for conflict between core resource units and other units, which is why clarity on the role of core resource units and the availability of a knowledgable hands-on parent to arbitrate is so important.

Core resource units are accountable for the quality and cost-effectiveness of the competences and resources they provide. These are typically difficult to assess. Objective, output-based measures need to be supplemented with a more holistic and subjective judgment about the contribution of the core resource unit to the company as a whole. 3M's technology platforms not only need to deliver a measurable flow of new products to the marketplace: they also need to maintain leading-edge skills in the technology. The latter goal is harder to measure or bench-mark and, again, calls for some well-informed, close contact between the parent and the core resource unit.

For some companies, core resource units provide a vital means of focusing on critical activities that cut across business units. As Hein Schreuder, director of corporate strategy for DSM, put it:

"We recognize that different customer groups have different needs. But it is critical to competitive advantage for us to have an integrated approach to certain key technologies, especially in biotechnology. For us, this is a basic premise in organization design, and means that we will not fragment our resources in these technologies across several business units."

But core resource units create special demands on the parent and involve some potentially difficult links with other units. Organization designers need to lay out the role of core resource units carefully to get the best out of them.

Shared Service Units

The purpose of a shared service unit is to achieve benefits from focusing attention on services that are needed by several other units in the company. This purpose is similar to the purpose of core resource units, but the crucial difference is that shared service units do not provide services that are key to competitive advantage. As with core resource units, the reason for establishing a shared service unit is to achieve economies of scale and benefits of specialization that might be lost if the services were not provided centrally by a dedicated unit; but the services are unlikely to provide an important competitive edge. Table 5.6 summarizes the role of shared service units.

Shared service units are responsible for providing their services to meet the needs of other units cost-effectively and responsively. They should be driven by what their "customers" want, rather than by their own views of how best to nurture and allocate their resources. The services may be standard, process-driven, transactional activities, such as payroll or payments processing, or they may be more sophisticated, professionally-driven, expert services, such as applications software development or business intelligence. Provided that they are responsive to customer needs, shared service units have discretion over how to provide their services.

Shared service units report to a parent level of management. The corporate parent, whose priorities usually lie elsewhere, is not likely to intervene much, unless there are obvious problems with the shared service. There may, however, be some corporate guidelines and policies concerning things such as service level agreements, transfer prices, and the freedom or otherwise of

TABLE 5.6 The Role of Shared Service Units

Purpose	To achieve benefits from focusing on selected services that are needed by several units
Responsibilities	To provide services to meet the needs of other units cost-effectively and responsively
Reporting relationships	Reports to parent that gives substantial autonomy on decisions about how to provide services, but subject to corporate policies and guidelines
Lateral relationships	Acts as a shared service provider to other "customer" units
Accountability	For "customer" satisfaction and unit costs of services (and profitability, if set up on quasi-market basis)

business units to opt out of using shared service units. Furthermore, there may be a shared services head within the parent, who takes a much more hands-on interest in the affairs of the shared service units.

The key to the success of shared service units lies in their lateral relationships with other units. The shared service units should see themselves as winning the business of their customers in other units, and other units should deal with the shared service units basically as if they were third-party suppliers. In some companies, the shared service units are set up as quasi-business units, aiming to make a profit from serving their in-house customers in competition with external suppliers. Other companies prefer a closer relationship between shared service units and their customers, in which there is less reliance on time-consuming contract negotiations and less freedom for customer units to outsource their requirements. In either case, however, the shared service units need to understand and accept their obligation to treat their users as valued customers, and the users need to make clear what they expect of the shared services. Under these circumstances, collaboration between shared service units and other units should proceed smoothly.

Shared service units are accountable for customer "satisfaction" and for unit costs. Both these goals can be measured relatively easily. A further check on performance is provided by the service and cost levels available from third parties. Indeed, if the shared service unit is set up as a quasi-business, it can also be held accountable for its profitability. However, profitability should not be the main performance measure, because it is more important for the unit to give good service to its customers than to maximize its profits from them.

Shared service units, therefore, can have relatively simple relationships and accountabilities, and so encounter few of the typical problems of complex interdependent units. Indeed, companies with a structure based on self-contained SBUs, such as GE Capital, are often comfortable setting up shared service units, since they need not compromise the simplicity of the structure or the accountability of the SBUs.

In the past, many companies have been concerned about whether their shared services were really cost-effective and responsive. Functional heads have often run shared services as parts of their departmental empires rather than as client-responsive services for the businesses, and business managers have complained that their needs were disregarded and that better and more cost-effective services could be bought in from third-party providers. Many corporate chief executives have therefore sought to reduce the size and scope of shared services, mainly by outsourcing.

More recently, the trend to cut back on shared services has begun to reverse. Increased pressure on cost competitiveness, the drive for service improvements, and new technology applications are making companies think again about the potential benefits to be gained from centralized services, particularly if the shared services are provided by organizationally distinct units, separated out from other functional or departmental activities, and run by someone in a dedicated role. Such units are very different from traditional corporate center functions, with a much more dedicated, customer-responsive, and performance-driven approach. Many proponents of shared services, among them ABB, Dupont, and Shell, believe that the benefits of shared services only emerge under this type of approach.

The rationale for the renewed enthusiasm for shared services is that, as dedicated units, they are capable of yielding large performance improvements; for example, 20–50% cost savings, together with improvements in service levels, are quoted by some supporters of shared service units.[5] The main source of these performance improvements seems to be the focused management attention that shared service units can give to activities that were previously neglected or poorly managed. For example, Ciba Specialty Chemicals was able to achieve a 50% headcount reduction in its new Business Support Centers (finance and IT), while achieving faster and more error-free reporting on increased volumes of sales.

It is therefore not so much a matter of centralizing a service to reap economies of scale as creating a shared service unit with a clear role. If the services are just one part of the responsibilities of a function head, who may well be much more interested in advising the CEO and setting corporate functional policies than in service provision, they will not get the dedicated attention they need. Equally, if the services are imposed on the businesses with little attempt to benchmark them against outside providers, to take account of business needs, or to measure their performance, they are not likely to be customer-responsive or cost-effective. Shared services that are insulated from market pressures and are low-status, low-attention parts of monolithic departmental empires remain good candidates for downsizing or outsourcing. But shared service units with a clear and dedicated role can work much more effectively.

Project Units

Project units are set up to achieve benefits from focusing on specific tasks or projects that cut across other units. For example, a new product development that involves several businesses and a core R&D resource unit, or a major turnkey project that draws on the products and services of several businesses may be handled by setting up a dedicated project unit with its own management team. The projects usually have a finite duration, so that the life of the project unit is time limited. Table 5.7 summarizes the role of project units.

The responsibilities of project units relate to the tasks for which they were set up. Canon, for example, is renowned for its use of project units of different types to work on different stages of new product developments.[6] ABB has made extensive use of dedicated units to create an integrated approach to major construction projects, such as new airports or hydro-electric dams.[7] Professional service firms invariably set up project units to handle specific client assignments. Tasks that cut across other units may benefit from dedicated project unit attention if they are sufficiently important.

The powers of project units depend on how "heavyweight" senior management wishes to make them. Project units with full-time managers assigned to them, large budgets, the ability to

TABLE 5.7 The Role of Project Units

Purpose	To achieve benefits from focusing on specific tasks or projects that cut across other units – normally time-limited
Responsibilities	For carrying out the specified task or project. Extent of power over resources depends on status of project unit
Reporting relationships	Reports to parent, that may give varying levels of independence to project unit in how it carries out its tasks
Lateral relationships	Acts as a pressure group on behalf of the project. Influence depends on status, but usually relies on co-operation of units from which team is drawn and with which team works
Accountability	For project delivery and performance

override other units on at least some decisions such as pricing or customer contact, and the wholehearted support of top management represent significant formal additions to the organization structure. By contrast, projects with no full-time staff, little authority, and a circumscribed task are better seen as more informal mechanisms for getting different units to work together than as separate organizational units. Heavyweight project units usually report to a parent manager, who may be more or less involved in the unit's work, depending on personal skills and interests.

Rather like overlay units, project units normally work with other units in a pressure group/principal relationship. The extent of their power and influence in these relationships depends on how much support they have from top management, but they usually have to rely on the co-operation and goodwill of other units from which the project team is drawn and with which the project unit works. There are therefore limits to what project units can accomplish if they find themselves at cross-purposes with other units. Canon's new product development teams work well, because all units recognize the benefits that will accrue to themselves and to the company from collaborating freely with them.

Project teams usually have clear performance measures focusing on project delivery. But they must avoid damaging the performance of other units by being over-committed to their goals, and their accountability is weakened by their limited discretion over resources. For these reasons, control by upper levels is not easy.

There is obviously a gray area between strong co-ordinating mechanisms and formal project units, but our research suggests that organization designers need to be aware of the potential benefits of setting up dedicated project units with full-time managers to handle important issues that cut across other units, and which might otherwise receive insufficient attention. The use of project units can also provide a flexible means of refocusing the organization's resources on new opportunities as they emerge.

Parent Units

We reviewed the nature of parent units in SBU-based and interdependent structures in Chapter 4, and we will devote the whole of Chapter 6 to a full account of the more challenging role of the parent in complex structures. This will include discussion of intermediate parents at group or division levels, as well as corporate-level parents. We will not therefore dwell on the role of parent units in this chapter.

Table 5.8, however, summarizes the role of corporate-level parent units, noting that they are responsible for obligatory parenting and added-value activities. At the corporate level, there is no upper management level to which the parent reports,

TABLE 5.8 The Role of Corporate-level Parent Units

Purpose	To achieve focus benefits on corporate-level tasks
Responsibilities	To carry out obligatory corporate parent tasks, and to influence and add value to other units
Reporting relationships	Ultimately reports to board, which decentralizes extensively to the parent
Lateral relationships	Mutual self-interest, with joint venture and alliance partners
Accountability	For the bottom-line performance and profitability of the corporation as a whole

although the board acts to some extent in this capacity. Equally, the corporate parent has no other units at the same level with which to establish lateral relationships, except through joint ventures and alliances with other companies. In terms of accountability, the parent is responsible for the results and profitability of the whole group. We will explain the nature of the parenting role much more fully in Chapter 6.

Summary of Unit Roles

Table 5.9 provides an overview of the eight different types of unit we have described. It is evident that each type of unit will

TABLE 5.9 A Taxonomy of Unit Roles

Type of unit		Type of responsibility	Relationships Reporting	Lateral	Main accountabilities
Parent	◉	Obligatory and added-value parenting	Board/parent	Mutual self-interest	Corporate bottom line
Core resource unit	⚡	Resource-focused	Hands-on parent/unit	Resource owner/user	Resource development and utilization
Shared service unit	⊂	Service-focused	Parent/unit	Service provider/ client	Service cost-effectiveness
Project unit	○	Project-focused	Parent/unit	Pressure group/ principal	Project delivery
Overlay unit	▷·	Market-focused (cut-across)	Parent/unit	Pressure group/ principal	Effectiveness in serving target segments
Business unit	▨	Market-focused	Parent/unit	Mutual self-interest	Bottom line (strong)
Sub-business	□	Market-focused (disaggregated)	General manager/unit	Quasi-team	Bottom line
Business function	⊃	Functional	General manager/ function	Team	Functional effectiveness and contribution

see its responsibilities and relationships differently, and so will make different decisions about how to implement them.

Figure 5.1 shows the different unit types on a conventional organization chart, conveying the differences in role by using different symbols for each unit type. But the lines and boxes emphasize the traditional hierarchical view too strongly. We have therefore developed a new, less familiar display (see Figure 5.2). We believe that this display is more helpful, since it implies a new way of thinking about organization design and a new emphasis on clear role distinctions.

Some organizational arrangements can be hard to classify between the eight roles. For example, if the chief executive has asked a manager to lead a task force to develop a new strategy for serving large customers who buy from several businesses, is this an overlay, a project unit, or simply a co-ordination mechanism? Or, if the corporate human resources department spends most of its time administering the careers of internationally mobile managers, is it a core resource unit (developing and allocating a

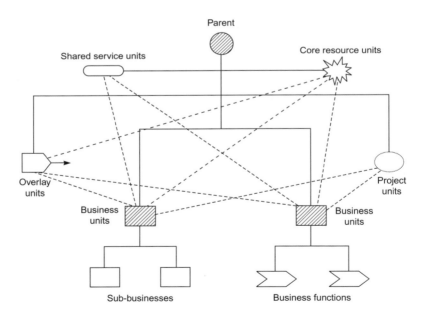

FIGURE 5.1 A Traditional Organization Chart Showing Different Roles

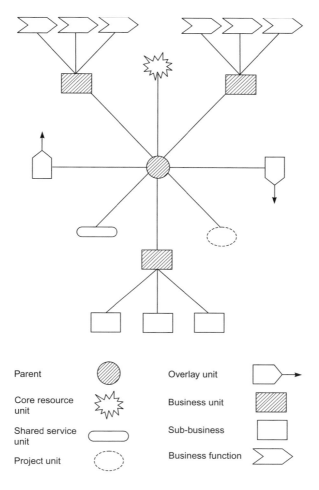

FIGURE 5.2 A New Display Bringing Out Different Roles

key human resource), a shared service unit (providing a service to the businesses in which the managers work), or part of the parent (adding value to the businesses by influencing the quality of their human resources)? With more information about precisely how these units are intended to work, we could no doubt form a judgment about how best to classify them. Is the task force time limited, does it have any profit responsibility, and does its manager work full-time? Does the HR department have its own agenda for the international management cadre, or is it simply responding to the administrative needs of the businesses, or is it briefing the CEO on top appointments and career development? Questions of this sort will help to pin down a unit's true role.

But we should also recognize that there can be some gray areas that are intrinsically difficult to classify. It may be that the major client task force falls somewhere between an overlay, a project unit, and a co-ordination mechanism, or that while the corporate HR department has some of the features of a core resource unit, it has others that resemble a shared service unit or a parent support unit. In these cases, none of the role labels completely fits the situation.

Nevertheless, the differences between unit types are clear in principle, and in the vast majority of cases there is little problem in how to classify units, provided the nature of their intended responsibilities is understood. Indeed, the value of the taxonomy is precisely to convey the intentions of the organization designer.

Specifying Organization Designs

We have found that the taxonomy has great value in allowing clearer specifications of how organization designs are intended to work. Proposals to set up new units and modify the organization chart are often made without clarifying sufficiently how the new units are supposed to operate. For example, a retail group may set up a central category management unit to co-ordinate across its different retail businesses, but without stating explicitly how it should work. How broadly should the new category management team see its responsibilities, and over what decisions, if any, will it have final authority? How should it relate to the retail business units, which have previously had primary profit accountability? How involved will corporate managers be in influencing the decisions they face? What key performance indicators will be used to judge its performance? All too often, answers to these vital questions remain vague, leading to confusion. Discussions about which role the unit is meant to play forces organization designers to resolve these ambiguities.

If the category management unit is intended to be an overlay, it will have to work through influence and pressure on the retail business units, except on any specific decisions that the organizational designers allocate to it. Primary profit accountability then remains with the retail businesses, and the category management unit will have a different accountability that may include category profitability but could also emphasize, for example, category market share. If, however, the category management unit is supposed to be a business unit, or a support unit for the parent, this will have different implications. The roles language helps to clarify how the unit should operate, without attempting to delve into all the details.

The need for a more precise language for specifying organization designs is brought out by the ambiguities inherent in many commonly used organization terms. For example, a "product group" can be, in terms of our taxonomy, a business unit, a sub-business, an overlay, or a parent unit. The same is true of "country units". Equally, a "corporate research unit" can be a core resource unit, a shared service unit, a project unit, or a functional department supporting the parent. Organization designs specified using these terms almost inevitably give rise to confusions, unless the roles of the units are more clearly defined.

Clarity about roles is particularly important in interdependent structures. The term "matrix structure" can be applied to many different types of structures and relationships, and different companies use it very differently. When Shell moved to a business stream structure in 1997, it claimed to have abandoned its matrix organization; but it retained local country organizations and shared manufacturing. Responsibilities may have been less overlapping and consensus less necessary, but the organization remained multi-dimensional and interdependent. Labeling the organization as a matrix (or not) is not helpful, because it gives no useful information about how the different dimensions should work together. Laying out the roles of the different units is helpful, because it makes clear how they should all interpret their responsibilities and relate to each other. In the box below we show how our roles taxonomy can be used to clarify the changes in organization at Citibank described in Chapter 4.

Using the Roles Taxonomy to Describe the Citibank Structure

The 1996 restructuring of Citibank's Global Corporate Banking Group created a complex, interdependent structure: "Matrix management gone mad," as one manager described it. Yet there was sound strategic logic behind the changes. The challenge was to communicate the different roles of the units that were set up and the intended relationships between them. Citibank addressed this challenge by setting out job descriptions for the main positions, defining a number of management processes (including working through decision grids to agree the roles of different individuals and units in these processes), and prescribing some key behaviors.

Over time, and after a further organizational change in 1997, Citibank managers have learned how to operate within the new structure, and are now comfortable with it. However, we believe that use of the taxonomy to describe the new structure could have made clear the intended nature of the new structure more rapidly and more effectively.

Table 5.10 summarizes the roles of different units before and after the reorganizations. The taxonomy brings out some key points:

- Before 1996, regions and countries were the main business units, with primary responsibility for serving customers and generating profits.
- After 1996, customer groupings become the business units, with the most authority. But they must collaborate with all the other units to serve their customers effectively and profitably.

TABLE 5.10 Changing Unit Roles in Global Corporate Banking

Units	Pre 1996	1996–1997	Post 1997
Countries/ regions	Business units	Overlays	Overlays
Customers/ industries	(Informal networks)	Business units (global)	Business units (global)
Products	Sub-businesses (local)	Core resource units (global)	Business units (global)
Infrastructure	Business functions (local)	Shared service units*	Shared service units*

* Progressive movement away from local to regional to global

- After 1996, countries and regions continue to be focused on local presence, but, as overlays, must accept that on global product- and customer-related issues they have to work through influence (as local pressure groups) rather than having the final word. They therefore have less strong accountability for local profitability, and more obligation to work within global customer and product strategies.

- After 1996, the infrastructure units' role shifts from being part of a local business unit team to supporting the global customer and product units. As shared service units, they should respond to "customer" needs, coming from the customer and product units, and aim to deliver their services to them as cost-effectively as possible.

- The product units initially cease to be sub-businesses, subject to the authority of regional business unit heads, and become global core resource units, developing and providing products that are vital for the success of the global customer business units. After 1997, their role is further strengthened by making them business units, with equal status, authority, and profit responsibility to the customer units. This recognizes that both the customer and product dimensions of market focus are critical, but requires the "back-end" product businesses to work with the "front-end" customer businesses and find ways of resolving conflicts of interest or priorities between them to the advantage of the group as a whole.

The roles taxonomy could have provided an efficient short-hand for communicating the intent behind the organizational changes, and given managers guidance on how they should behave in discharging their responsibilities. This would have provided a useful context for helping managers to understand the basis of the new organization. There would still have been a need to define some critical processes, such as relationship planning and Balanced Business Scorecard reviews, but the foundations of the design would have been clear.

The taxonomy is also useful for comparing and contrasting different possible design options. For example, so-called "front-back" structures are becoming more popular.[8] In front-back structures, separate back-end product or technology units go to market through one or more front-end customer units which sell the products of some or all of the back-end units. Companies that have adopted front-back structures include Tetrapak, Acer, Procter and Gamble, and, of course, Citibank. But the front-back label can cover many different possibilities (see Figure 5.3). The roles taxonomy helps to bring out differences between possible front-back structures, and clarifies the range of design options available. Without such clarification, there is a danger of misunderstandings about how the front-end and the back-end should work together.

In Chapters 7, 8, and 9, we will show how design concepts based around the taxonomy can be tested and refined, adding further details on key responsibilities, relationships, and accountabilities as needed to pass the design tests. In particular, we will

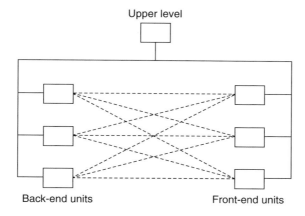

Back-end	Front-end	Upper level
Overlay	Business unit	Parent
Core resource	Business unit	Parent
Shared service	Business unit	Parent
Business unit	Overlay	Parent
Business unit	Core resource	Parent
Business unit	Shared service	Parent
Business unit	Business unit	Parent
Business function	Sub-business	Business unit
Underlay	Sub-business	Business unit
Sub-business	Underlay	Business unit
Sub-business	Business function	Business unit

FIGURE 5.3 Front-end and Back-end Units: Possible Options

explain how to decide which co-ordination mechanisms and other management processes need to be specified, in order to create sufficient but not too much detail in the design. We will also show how the taxonomy can be used as part of a process for developing and choosing between design options. But, first, we turn in Chapter 6 to a more detailed discussion of the role of the parent in complex structures.

6

Parenting In Complex Structures

As we explained in the foreword, we embarked on the research that led to this book in order to explore the relevance of Ashridge's parenting concepts in complex, interdependent corporate structures.

In our book, *Corporate-Level Strategy*, we concentrated on the role of the management levels in the corporate hierarchy outside and above the business units.[1] We called these management levels the "corporate parent". We noted that corporate parents inevitably destroy some value by incurring overhead costs, slowing down decisions, and making some ill-judged interventions, and that many corporate parents do not add enough value to compensate for this. In these companies, the net effect of the corporate parent's activities is negative, and it would be better to break up the group. We therefore argued that, to justify their existence, parent managers in multi-business companies need to have, and be able to articulate, a clear added-value rationale for their activities. This is a necessary component of any valid corporate strategy.

Most managers and corporate strategy experts now accept the need for the parent to add value, at least in SBU-based structures. In these structures, the SBUs are, by definition, self-contained and could therefore operate independently without a corporate parent. Spin-offs, buy-outs, or de-mergers are very real possibilities, and the parent can only defend the continued existence of the group with an added-value logic: the group should remain together if and only if the parent adds value to the SBUs. But the situation is rather different in more interdependent structures.

In interdependent structures, there is more overlap and sharing of responsibilities. Business units and other types of unit must collaborate with each other, and the units are less self-contained. Upper levels of management often share responsibilities with operating units and help to guide the interdependencies between units. The distinction between "business" and "parent" is less clear-cut, and break-up or spin-off options are harder to conceive and implement. Focusing on the parent and questioning its added value is therefore less obviously relevant.

With the understanding that we have now gained of the workings of interdependent structures, we are in a position to provide a more thorough account of the role of the parent in such structures. We argue that these structures place some particular demands on parent managers, and tend to call for a more hands-on style of parenting. We also examine the different tasks carried out by the parent's functional support staff, and recognize that, in large companies, there is often more than one level of parenting. We conclude that the sharp distinction between the parent and the businesses does break down, and that parenting activities are more widely distributed in interdependent structures. Nevertheless, we continue to believe that a focus on the skills and added value of upper levels of management is a necessary discipline and a key ingredient of organization design. In particular, the parent is vital to the success of structured networks.

Parenting Roles

Upper levels of management have two essential roles to play. The first concerns the minimum or obligatory tasks needed to manage and maintain the existence of the corporate entity. The second concerns adding value to the operating units within the company.

Minimum Corporate Parenting Role

All corporate management teams have to carry out some unavoidable tasks, such as fulfillling obligatory legal and regulatory requirements and basic governance functions. Legal and regulatory tasks include, for example, preparing annual reports, submitting tax returns, and insuring that relevant health and safety or environmental legislation is observed. Any corporate entity must discharge these compliance responsibilities.

It is also necessary to undertake basic governance tasks and show due diligence in representing shareholder interests. The top management must establish a structure for the company, appoint the senior management, raise capital, and handle investor relations. It must also implement some form of basic control process, so that it can authorize major decisions, guard against inappropriately risky or fraudulent decisions, and check that delegated responsibilities are being satisfactorily exercised. The extent of these necessary governance and due diligence tasks is hard to determine precisely. The strict legal requirements are limited, so it is more a matter of what the chief executive feels obliged to do in order to satisfy fiduciary duties to the shareholders.

We call these unavoidable activities the minimum corporate parenting role. They are the bare minimum necessary to maintain any corporate entity in existence.

Value-added Parenting Role

We have argued that any valid corporate strategy needs to be based on a clear view of how value can be added by the corporate parent. The main ways in which the parent intends to add value, which we call parenting propositions, should shape both the responsibilities retained by the parent and the influence that it exercises.

Different companies concentrate on very different parenting propositions. Dow emphasizes manufacturing excellence, and has a strong corporate manufacturing function to influence its businesses and co-ordinate multi-business manufacturing sites. Rio Tinto adds significant value through using the expertise of its corporate technical staff to improve the planning of mining operations. BP has pushed hard to create a high performance culture throughout the company by agreeing stretching perform- ance contracts between business unit heads and the CEO. Virgin leverages its widely recognized corporate brand into a whole variety of businesses, from airlines through financial services to Internet access. The corporate parent's role needs to reflect the nature of its value-added parenting propositions.

In complex, interdependent structures, there are some particular parenting challenges associated with both the mini- mum and the value-added parenting roles. These will be dis- cussed next.

Parenting Challenges in Interdependent Structures

In interdependent structures, parent managers face some demanding challenges. Compared to parent managers in SBU- based structures, they

- retain, or share with other units, more responsibilities;
- are more involved in guiding co-ordination between units;
- are less able to exercise control through unit-specific, objective, output-based measures of performance; and
- need to pay more attention to the design and working of the organization.

More Responsibilities

In companies that place less emphasis on autonomous, self- contained business units, the parent may retain, or share, more responsibilities. For example, the parent may play an active role in creating an integrated strategy that will be accepted throughout the company, building on experience, skills, or resources at the center, and may establish the "rules of the road" in terms of policies and constraints that regulate the decisions of all the units.

In many professional service firms, for instance, the managing partner and executive committee are closely involved in proposals for service-line extensions, geographical expansion, partner promotions and transfers, and pricing policy changes. Individual offices or practice areas recognize that they must share responsibility with the firm-wide management on these issues, and that the managing partner will often take the lead in formulating proposals and pushing through decisions.

A typical example of the responsibilities of the parent in interdependent structures is provided by Infineum, a medium-sized speciality chemical company. The company, formed from a joint venture between Exxon and Shell, is a global leader in a range of additives sold to the oil and petrochemicals industry. It is organized into three product groups, which in turn are broken down into a total of about 15 separate profit centers. However, the product groups and profit centers are mainly concerned with marketing strategy and tactics, since research and development, manufacturing, and sales are all centralized functions – core resource units in our terminology. The company's structure is shown in Figure 6.1.

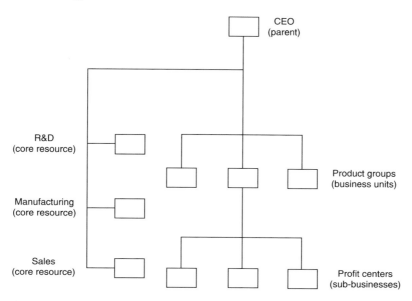

FIGURE 6.1 Infineum Company Structure

Clearly, the profit centers in Infineum are far from self-contained. Decisions about which research projects to pursue, how to rationalize production sites around the world, and how the sales force should approach common customers are all shared between the profit centers, the product groups, the central functions and the corporate management. Although there are processes in place for consultation between all interested parties, it is frequently necessary for the corporate CEO to take the lead. He is in the best position to see and make corporate-wide trade-offs; he has a greater depth of experience and contacts in the industry; and all the units look to him to provide a coherent direction for the group. Although he is insistent on pushing profit responsibility down to the product groups and profit centers, the CEO cannot avoid playing a key role in making major decisions. Even if the corporate parent managers are keen to decentralize, in structures of this sort they are compelled to share or retain some vital responsibilities.

If the organization design makes it essential for the corporate parent to exercise certain responsibilities in order for the company to function, the minimum parenting role is more extensive. Equally, if the parent is less committed to the autonomy of self-contained SBUs, it may perceive and be willing to pursue a wider range of value-added opportunities.

Guiding Co-ordination

With more interdependencies between operating units, the parent also needs to play a more active role in guiding co-ordination and networking between units. In our description of Citicorp's Global Corporate Banking Group in Chapter 4, we showed that co-ordination between product groups, customer-focused industry groups, local offices, and shared infrastructure depends on some active parenting from group level. Group management establishes the nature of the relationships between units, defines the key processes for collaboration, and is directly involved in promoting linkages and in arbitrating disputes when necessary. Decisions about customer priorities or about service discounts can easily get bogged down in the complex web of relationships between different Citicorp units, unless the parent is willing to establish clear ground rules for collaboration and to intervene as arbitrator when necessary.

The extent of the parent's role in guiding interdependencies between units depends on the importance and difficulty of the linkages between units. In Motorola, a Communications Group (referred to as the Communications Enterprise) was set up in 1998. This group included all Motorola's communications products and services, and was organized around major customer groups, such as Personal Communications (consumer), Network Solutions (carriers), and Government, Commercial, and Industrial. These customer-facing business units replaced product-based business units, and were set up to provide more integrated solutions to customers' communications needs. There was, however, a need for co-ordination between the businesses in several areas, such as standards and system architecture, co-ordinating subscriber needs and system infrastructure, and platform development. The Communications Enterprise management oversaw horizontal co-ordination processes in all these areas, although different business units played a lead role in each of them. The purpose of setting up the Communications Enterprise was to give more emphasis to integrated customer solutions and to create better links across Motorola's communication businesses. These co-ordination challenges were so important for Motorola that they justified setting up a new group level of management to address them.

In interdependent structures, the parent has an essential minimum role in establishing the conditions under which co-ordination through self-managed networking can flourish, and is likely to need to be more involved in adding value by facilitating difficult links between units.

Control Issues

In interdependent structures, tied relationships between sister units can reduce pressures for self-correction. Furthermore, sharing of responsibilities between the parent and the operating units, and among the operating units, makes strong accountability for unit-specific performance targets harder. Given Monsanto's highly interdependent structure, built to support its aspirations as a life sciences company, it would have been inappropriate for CEO Bob Shapiro to focus the accountability of unit managers exclusively and tightly on unit-specific performance. This could have undermined the desire for cross-unit collaboration and made it more difficult for them to work together to realise uncertain, long-term, "white space" opportunities in life sciences.

In interdependent structures, unit-specific measures of performance need to be complemented with performance measures for groups of units that work with each other. Judgments about the contribution of different units to group-wide results are also needed. Shapiro's task was not only to assess how well the Pharmaceuticals business was performing, but also to take a view on how well it was contributing to Monsanto's wider goals in life sciences, a target that was harder to measure. Monsanto needed a more sophisticated control process, in which the parent had a close knowledge of how the units were performing, including what they were contributing to each other (see Chapter 4 for more details about Monsanto).

Moreover, for overlay units, project units, core resource units, and shared service units, profitability is either irrelevant or less important as a performance measure, and other suitable bottom-line measures of performance can be hard to find. The number of new drug candidates taken into development per year, for example, is a simple, objectively measurable, and important target for a pharmaceutical research core resource unit, but it does not encapsulate all aspects of good performance for such a unit. This means that the parent must use a wider range of performance measures, and should be more concerned with the details of what the unit is doing. "Output" goals that can be readily measured may have to be combined with "input" measures that require more subjective assessment, in order to exercise adequate control. Performance contracts cannot rely on simple, objectively measurable output goals.

As a result, control is more complicated for corporate parents in interdependent structures. The parent must have sufficient knowledge and time to assess the contribution of each unit to other units, to deal with a more varied range of performance measures, and to make subjective judgments of performance based on a close understanding of what is going on in each unit. The due diligence control aspects of minimum parenting are more demanding, and the opportunities to add value through the control process call for a more sophisticated understanding of performance on the part of the parent.

Fine-tuning the Organization Design

All corporate parents need to monitor how well their chosen organization designs are working. But, in interdependent structures, there is more need for constant fine-tuning of the design to make sure that it is achieving the purposes for which it was established. Are responsibilities, relationships, and performance measures clear enough to facilitate self-managed decisions and networking? Are any critical links between units being under-managed, and should the parent play a more active part in setting up co-ordination mechanisms or influencing the units to collaborate? Are performance measures and control processes striking the right balance between simplicity and sophistication? Should the relative powers and responsibilities of overlapping units be adjusted in the light of changing circumstances? Should a simpler, less interdependent structure be considered?

At a minimum, corporate parents must insure that the organization design is not leading to unworkable conflicts and confusion. More positively, the parent can add substantial value by creating a design in which the interdependencies allow the whole to be worth more than the sum of the parts.

"Hands-on" Parenting

The upshot of these challenges is that the parent is integral to the working of the corporate structure. The parent must carry out a wider range of minimum responsibilities and is likely to be drawn into a more influential added-value role. Instead of a largely hands-off relationship with self-contained operating units, the parent needs to have a closer, more hands-on relationship with the units that report to it.[2] To play this role effectively, the parent needs more knowledge of the units, and a greater feel for their operations and critical success factors.

In smaller or more focused companies, such as Infineum, the corporate CEO can play a hands-on role. In larger or more diverse companies, a hands-on role is likely to overload corporate-level management, and it is intermediate parent levels, such as groups or divisions, that play the hands-on role. For example, in Philips the Lighting Division does much of the active parenting of the group's lighting businesses, and in Motorola the Communications Enterprise is the hands-on parent of the communications businesses. In survey-based research on the extent of parent influence, we have found that, in general, the higher the level of relatedness in a group's portfolio of businesses, the more influence the parent attempts to exercise.[3]

Given suitable parenting competences, hands-on parenting can add high value. But hands-on parents also face some value destruction pitfalls. If they have insufficient skills or poor staff support, they may hinder, rather than help the businesses. If they are too prone to interfere, they may inhibit the initiative of unit managers and take on tasks for which they are ill-suited. In one company we researched, the chief executive was renowned for sponsoring synergy initiatives that everyone knew would have limited pay-off, but which soaked up inordinate amounts of scarce management time. His hands-on attempts to push these initiatives became a major distraction from other more important priorities for managers down the line. And, in an *Economist* article on Coca-Cola's problems under Doug Ivester, CEO from 1997–99, the company was heavily criticized for becoming too centralized. Charlie Frenette, head of Coca-Cola in Europe, made a graphic comment: "If I wanted to launch a new product in Poland, I would have to put in a product approval request to Atlanta. People who had never even been to Poland would tell me whether I could do it or not".[4] Misguided hands-on parenting is even more damaging than misguided hands-off parenting.

But an unwillingness to play a hands-on role where it is needed is a major parenting pitfall in interdependent structures. We worked with a large, vertically integrated, multi-business chemical company which operated a number of shared production sites and whose customers often bought products from more than one of the businesses. The company was structured into business units, core resource units, and overlay units, with complicated transfer pricing mechanisms to take advantage of the interdependencies between the units. Not infrequently, there were disputes between the units about issues such as "unfair" transfer prices or the allocation of scarce production capacity. When this occurred, the parent would almost always refuse to get involved, claiming that the units ought to know best and should resolve things between themselves. The result was endless wrangling, a long history of compromise decisions that satisfied no one, and eventually a craving for more decisive leadership by the parent. Parents in interdependent structures must recognize that the demands on them will be greater than in SBU-based structures, and they must be able and willing to play the role required of them.

Parent Functions

The corporate parent consists of senior line managers such as the chief executive, the chief operating officer, and the division heads, supported by staff functions. Particularly in complex structures, the parent's support functions can play a variety of roles, some of which overlap with operating unit roles. Parent functions are also frequently involved in the provision of shared services and corporate resources. And in some companies, lead business units take on some of the responsibilities that would otherwise have been performed by parent functions.

Minimum Corporate Parenting Staff

One important role for the parent's functional support staff is to develop specialist expertise relevant to the minimum corporate parenting activities, and to assist senior line managers in performing them. Research carried out by the Ashridge Strategic Management Centre has allowed us to estimate the number of staff required for the minimum corporate parent role. These numbers can be strikingly low. For example, a company with 10 000 employees in total can handle minimum corporate parent activities with only about 15 staff, while a company with 50 000 employees needs only about 43 staff for these tasks (see box, Minimum Corporate Parent Staff). Table 6.1 shows 1998/1999 data for the total number of staff in the departments mainly concerned with minimum corporate parent activities (general management, legal, financial reporting and control, treasury, and tax) for four companies with lean headquarters: BAT, ITT, Ocean, and Nucor. Since the staff in these departments will be carrying out some activities that go beyond minimum corporate parent requirements, the numbers probably overstate the true size of the minimum corporate parent staff in each case.

What is more, significant economies of scale in minimum corporate parent activities are possible. The size of minimum corporate parent staff tends to increase by no more than about 50% with each doubling of company size. Large companies should have a lower proportion of minimum corporate parent staff than small ones.

Focusing on the minimum corporate parent staff achieves three purposes. First, it shows how small a truly lean corporate headquarters can be. The benchmarks derived from the Ashridge survey represent a challenge for most companies: how could we carry out the minimum necessary tasks of the corporate

TABLE 6.1 Lean Minimum Corporate Parent Staffs

	Company size (no. of employees)	No. of staff in minimum corporate parent departments
BAT	141 500	44
ITT	58 497	55
Ocean	11 400	17
Nucor	6 800	17

center in a professional manner with a staff of no more than, say, 20 people? This forces some tough-minded thinking about the size of the corporate headquarters.

Second, the discipline of reducing minimum corporate parent staff numbers reduces inadvertent value destruction. Due diligence is often a matter of checking what the businesses are planning or doing, a responsibility which even well-intentioned and competent corporate staffers with time on their hands can easily convert into unproductive interference and second-guessing. To avoid this sort of value destruction, planning and control activities that simply fulfill minimum corporate parent responsibilities should be strictly limited.

Third, minimum corporate parent staffing provides a good baseline for designing the corporate center. The obligatory tasks that any headquarters must carry out account for only a small proportion of most corporate center staff numbers. Any staff over and above those needed for minimum corporate parent tasks must then be justified with a clear value-added rationale.

Minimum Corporate Parent Staff

The Ashridge Strategic Management Centre's survey gathered detailed data on the size, cost, roles, and departmental composition of headquarters staff in over 600 companies located in the USA, the UK, France, Germany, the Netherlands, Japan, and Chile. It also collected information on overall company sizes, the nature of the businesses in each company (e.g. relatedness, geographical spread) and the policies of the corporate center (e.g. influence levels, linkages between businesses).

Through statistical analysis, we were able to identify the factors that are the most significant drivers of corporate headquarters staff. From the analysis, we produced "ready reckoners" for the total corporate center staff and for each department that calculate "par" (i.e. median) staff numbers for any company, adjusted for a variety of factors reflecting its size, the nature of its businesses, and the policies of its corporate center.*

Par staffing of minimum corporate parent activities can be assessed by focusing on general corporate management, together with the treasury, taxation, financial reporting and control, and legal departments. These are the main departments concerned with minimum corporate parent activities, and are present in over 90% of all companies. Staff numbers in these departments are similar in the USA, the UK, France, Germany, and the Netherlands. To benchmark staff numbers involved in minimum corporate parent activities, we used our ready reckoners to estimate par staffing for these departments, on the assumption that the departments are not trying to influence the businesses, responsibilities that have more to do with value-added parenting than with the minimum corporate parent role. Since these departments perform other tasks (e.g. service provision) that go beyond the minimum corporate parent role in many companies, we also used lower quartile numbers as our benchmarks.

The resulting benchmarks for European companies are shown below. US benchmarks are approximately 25% higher.

Company size (no. of employees)	Staff required for minimum corporate parent role	Minimum corporate parent staff per 1000 employees
2 000	5	2.5
5 000	9	1.8
10 000	15	1.5
20 000	23	1.1
50 000	43	0.9
100 000	65	0.6

Other common departments (present in over 80% of companies) are corporate planning, government and public relations, internal audit, and human resources. Using similar assumptions in the ready reckoners for these more discretionary departments adds around 5 staff to minimum corporate parent staff numbers for a company with 10 000 employees and around 15 for a company with 50 000 employees.

* For a full description of the ready reckoners, see *Corporate Headquarters: An International Analysis of their Roles and Staffing*, David Young *et al.*, Financial Times Prentice Hall, 2000, and *Benchmarking Corporate Headquarters Staff*, David Young and Kay Dirk Ullmann, Ashridge Strategic Management Centre, 1999.

Value-added Parenting Staff

Some parenting propositions depend heavily on functional staff support. For Dow, high-quality staff groups in the manufacturing function play an essential role in helping senior parent managers to create and deliver value. The same is true of Rio Tinto's mining technology functions. But other parenting propositions have less to do with corporate staff. In BP, the performance culture depends much more on line management than on finance or planning staff. And in Virgin, the value of the brand is enhanced more by Richard Branson personally than by the activities of the tiny corporate staff. Staff in parent functions can help to add value by developing specialist expertise relevant to the parenting propositions.

Given the diversity of parenting value propositions, it is not surprising that the Ashridge survey of corporate staff shows a wide variation in the size and composition of value-added parenting staff. Since the corporate strategy for adding value differs between companies, the required value-added parenting staffs are bound to differ.

What is clear from the Ashridge research, however, is that companies with a high level of linkages and interdependence have more than twice as many corporate staff as companies with little interdependence. Furthermore, the level and nature of corporate functional influence is a driving factor in shaping headquarters staff. For example, companies that guide most IT decisions from the center have IT departments over ten times larger than companies with a more decentralized approach.[5] Corporate parent functions in the US tend to be substantially larger than those in Europe, mainly because US companies generally have more influential, and hence bigger, functional departments in areas such as IT, purchasing, marketing, and R&D.[6]

Size of staff, however, is only one indicator of effectiveness in delivering the desired influence. Indeed, the survey shows that large headquarters staffs are not generally rated more effective in supporting corporate strategy than small ones. The skills of the staff and the value added from their activities matter more than their numbers or cost.

Large parent functions may be fully justified, provided they are genuinely needed to support value creating parenting propositions. It would clearly be wrong for a Dow or a Rio Tinto to cut back on the staff groups that are critical to their corporate strategies. But where the value-added rationale is vague or unconvincing, or where the evidence suggests that the actual impact on performance has been limited or even negative, parent functions are ripe for downsizing or elimination.[7]

The Role of Parent Functions

The purpose of parent functions is, therefore, to develop specialist expertise in activities relevant to minimum parenting tasks or parenting propositions. They should assist senior parent managers in discharging obligatory compliance and due diligence tasks, and in influencing and adding value to the operating units. Table 6.2 summarizes the role of parent functions.

Parent functions report to senior line managers in the parent, and should not act without their support and authority. Parent staffs that pursue their own agendas, independent of their senior line managers, are liable to provoke resentment and resistance in the operating units, even if they believe they are

TABLE 6.2 The Role of Parent Functions

Purpose	To achieve benefits by focusing on specialist expertise relevant to minimum parent activities and parenting propositions
Responsibilities	To assist parent management in discharging obligatory compliance and due diligence tasks, and in influencing and adding value to the operating units
Reporting relationships	Reports to senior parent managers who have ultimate authority over decisions
Lateral relationships	Works with other parent functions as part of the parent management team, and influences and adds value to operating units
Accountability	For contributing to the effectiveness and added value of the parent

adding value. Parent functions should work closely together as part of the parent management team, and need to cultivate good relationships with other units in order to be able to exercise productive, value-added influence. There is a delicate balance to be struck between acting as policy-maker and policeman, and providing helpful advice based on a depth of expertise.

Parent functions should be accountable for contributing to the effectiveness and added value of the parent. Surprisingly few companies, however, make an explicit attempt to measure how much net value parent functions are adding. We believe that this is an error, and that corporate function heads should be required to report on the value that their departments have added, at least annually. Shell has recently adopted this discipline for its corporate center, and it has sharpened its thinking about the real sources of parenting value-added, and about the staff resources needed to support them. The opinions of business managers should be given strong weight in making the assessments of value-added, and can provide a salutary balance to the views of overoptimistic corporate staffers.

Sometimes the role of parent functions overlaps with, or at least contributes to, overlay or project units. If the parent's value propositions are to do with issues that cut across business units, such as helping them to do a better job of serving shared customers or of combined new product developments, the parent's staff may take the lead in convening co-ordination committees, advising on overlap issues, and providing specific expertise. But an alternative option for the CEO is to set up an overlay or project unit to focus its attention on the relevant issues. Under this option, managers who would otherwise have been part of the parenting staff will now be likely to form part of the overlay or project units, or at least to work closely with them. The distinction between parent functions and overlay or project units can therefore become blurred.

In Chapter 5, we discussed core resource and shared service units (see Tables 5.5 and 5.6 and pages 167–174), treating them as operating units which take on responsibilities that the business units would otherwise have discharged themselves. An alternative is to view such units as part of the parent, helping to add a particular sort of value for the business units. Viewing core resource and shared service units as part of the parent should have little impact on their basic role, except perhaps that they should work more closely with other parts of the parent's management team.

Companies are more inclined to view core resource and shared service units as part of the parent in situations where a single functional department, such as IT, plays a variety of roles. If the IT staff, for example, help to implement basic corporate reporting processes (minimum parenting), provide expert advice on major IT investments in the businesses (value-added parenting), develop and run systems that are crucial for competitive advantage in the businesses (core resource provision), and offer some types of basic transaction processing (shared service provision), the department is clearly playing multiple roles. Indeed, individual members of the department may split their time between two or more of these roles. In these circumstances, it is natural to regard the staff playing the core resource and shared service roles as part of the parent.

Functions that play multiple roles are, however, dangerous, since the different roles and relationships can interfere with each other. In one company, a confused member of the corporate IT function complained to us that, in the morning, he was supposed to be telling businesses what to do (adding value through establishing a corporate policy) and, in the afternoon, selling them his services (shared services). It is difficult both for the staff and for the business units to avoid mixed messages and ambiguous relationships in these circumstances.

In our view, the different roles of staff members in the corporate departments need to be clearly distinguished to avoid loss of focus. At least, individuals need to be clear about the different roles they are playing, and hence about what behaviors are appropriate when. Preferably, the different roles should be separated out into different units, each with its own distinctive and cohesive role.[8]

In summary, parent functions contribute to minimum corporate parenting activities and to value-added parenting propositions. It is also possible to regard core resource units and shared service units as part of the parent, and we need to recognize that the roles of overlay units and project units can overlap with those of parent functions. Figure 6.2 shows the full range of types of staff and units that can be found in and around the parent.

Lead Business Units

It is possible for specific business units to take the lead on behalf of the parent on issues such as product development or customer liaison. A business unit with especially strong technology in a certain area may be given a responsibility and a budget to help other businesses develop products that use this technology, or the business unit with the highest sales level to a key account may act on behalf of other units in developing the overall relationship. Lead business units may therefore act as core resource or shared service providers, or may take on added-value parenting tasks that would otherwise have been performed by parent functions.

This sort of development has been widely discussed, and is advocated by writers such as Sumantra Ghoshal and Chris

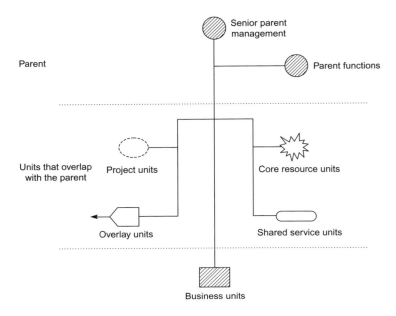

FIGURE 6.2 The Extended Parent

Bartlett, who believe that "transnationals" need to distribute power away from the corporate center and create less hierarchical relationships. Our own research suggests that lead business units can play a useful role, but can also become confused between their business unit and lead unit roles. In one company, the German subsidiary had been given a lead role in developing a particular technology. Although this subsidiary possessed excellent skills in the technology, it failed to act as an effective lead unit, because the German general manager almost always insisted that priority be given to the interests of his own unit rather than to globally desirable developments. This led to friction with other national units and with the corporate center. The reason for the German general manager's behavior was a conviction that his performance would be assessed more on the profitability of Germany than on the role played by Germany as global lead unit for the technology.

Organization designers need to make clear the nature of any lead unit responsibilities and accountabilities. Otherwise lead units face confused and conflicting priorities. As a result, they end up in turf wars with other units or with the parent, and fail to deliver either as business unit or as lead unit through the compromises involved.

We have also found that, despite the interest expressed in lead business units, only about a quarter of companies in the UK use them. In those that do, the practice is usually limited to a single functional area, and there does not appear to be a strong trend to increase the use of lead units.[9] Lead units are not yet as prevalent and influential as their proponents would like.

Parenting Levels and Reporting Relationships

In some companies, there is more than one level of parent: for example, corporate, group, and division may each be separate levels above the business units. In a few companies, the parenting role is divided between two different lines of reporting, resulting in a matrix structure at upper levels. It is quite common for the main parenting relationship to be complemented by a so-called "dotted line" or secondary parenting relationship. All these arrangements need to be understood to assess the nature of parenting in complex structures.

Corporate Parents and Intermediate Parents

In larger companies, the role of the parent is often shared between two (or more) levels of management. The operating units report to intermediate parenting levels, such as groups or divisions, and the intermediate parents report to the corporate headquarters. In large, complex multinationals with many business units, such as Philips, there can be several levels of parent management (see box: Parenting Levels in Philips).

Parenting Levels in Philips

With businesses ranging from consumer electronics through professional systems to lighting, Philips is one of the world's largest multinationals. Headquartered in the Netherlands, its sales were Dfl38 billion and its operating profits Dfl4.3 billion in 2000. It had 220000 employees operating in 60 countries. Figure 6.3 shows Philips's organization structure, focusing on the Lighting Division and, within it, on the Lamps business group.

The corporate level management consists of about 400 people. It concentrates on minimum corporate parent activities, portfolio changes (including M&A), and selected corporate parenting propositions such as corporate brand management and senior management development.

Lighting, which is one of the six product divisions, has a total of 47000 employees, of which 50 work at the divisional level. Division management is concerned with financial review and challenge, planning processes, human resources, IT/e-business platforms, purchasing, communications, and quality management: issues which are relevant throughout the division.

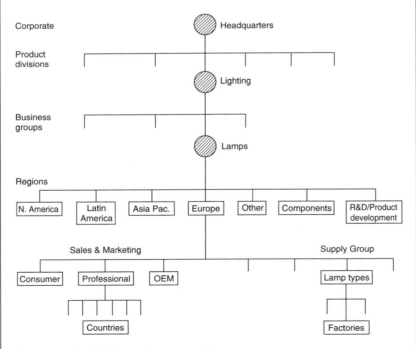

FIGURE 6.3 Philips's Parenting Structure

Within Lighting, there are four business groups, of which Lamps is the largest. Lamps has 28 000 employees, but only five work at the Business Group level. The main task of the Lamps level is to improve cross-regional co-ordination. In most cases, the Regions are supposed to sort things out themselves, but sometimes the Business Group management has to arbitrate or take decisions. Lamps is held accountable for the long-term value of the business.

The Regions (Europe, North America, Latin America, Asia Pacific, Other) are, in effect, the business units. There is also a Components business unit, whose sales are about 80% to in-house customers, and a core resource unit for R&D. The Regions are organized into Sales and Marketing Channels and Supply Groups (buying, manufacturing, and distribution). For purposes of cross-regional co-ordination, there are committees with representatives of the respective Regional Sales and Marketing and Supply Groups. The Regions are primarily accountable for profitability, measured by return on net assets.

Sales and Marketing consists of three Regional Channel-based organizations, serving Retail, Professional, and OEM (original equipment manufacturers) customers, with sub-units in each country. These sub-businesses keep track of local margins and costs. Within the supply chain, the organization is broken down by lamp types. The Supply Group is a cost center. The profitability and asset utilization, covering Sales & Marketing and the Supply Group, for different lamp types can, however, be tracked by the accounting system.

The Philips structure therefore has three levels of parent (Corporate, Product Division, Business Group), each with a distinctive role, above the Regional Lamps business units. There are also profit-responsible sub-units, for specific channels, countries, and lamp types. It is not unusual for large, multi-business, multinationals such as Philips to have four or more levels of profit-responsible management.

Every extra level of parent management brings with it the danger of duplication, redundancy, extra overheads, and contradictory parenting influences. A series of levels, each of which repeats the work of lower levels, but with progressively less detailed knowledge of the areas involved, is a sure recipe for parenting value destruction, and should be avoided. But a differentiation of roles, in which all levels have distinctive and complementary added-value tasks to perform, is much more defensible.

Ideally, the corporate headquarters concentrates on minimum corporate parenting and a few high-level parenting propositions, while intermediate parents are mainly concerned with more hands-on parenting propositions that relate specifically to their businesses. In GE, for example, Jack Welch has concentrated on a small number of corporate-wide parenting propositions such as "Workout", "Boundarylessness" and, more recently, "destroyyourbusiness.com", while the main groups such as GECS play a closer-in parenting role for their businesses, interpreting the corporate parenting propositions in terms that are specifically relevant for their industry sectors. Intermediate parent levels are needed when the corporate headquarters has insufficient detailed knowledge and competence to fulfill all the parenting needs and opportunities of the operating units.

A hands-on role for intermediate parents implies that the groups or divisions should be composed of units with similar parenting needs, often with a high level of interdependencies. The intermediate parent can then develop the skills to handle the specific parenting needs of the units and to guide the interdependencies. In Philips, arbitration on detailed co-ordination between the Regional Lamps business units is handled by management in the Lamps business group, two levels below the corporate headquarters, which would be much too distant to tackle these issues. Hands-on parenting is easier and more productive with a relatively focused portfolio of businesses.

But groups and divisions are often created for reasons that have little to do with the parenting needs of the units within them. Power politics, personal ambitions, management succession, location, or accidents of history are all factors that influence the formation of groups. In these circumstances, the intermediate parents often have no more cohesive and homogeneous portfolios of units than the corporate parent. It is then difficult for the intermediate parents to play distinctive, hands-on added-value roles which are complementary to the corporate parent.

Span Breakers

A further common reason for forming groups has to do with span breaking. The purpose of span breakers is to extend the parenting reach of the next level up in the corporate hierarchy.

Conventional wisdom suggests that no manager should have more than a certain number of direct reports. Some managers argue that this "span of control" should be no greater than 4 to 6; others, such as Jack Welch, favor much larger spans, with as many as 20 or more direct reports. In our research, we have found spans of control ranging from under 3 to 30 or more.[10] There is evidently a wide variation of views on appropriate spans of control.

We believe that the span of control should be driven by the nature of the parenting tasks being performed, rather than by any mechanistic formula. If the upper level limits itself to minimum corporate parent tasks only, it is possible to have wide spans of 10 or more reports. Indeed, narrow spans will, in these circumstances, encourage second-guessing and unnecessary interference, simply to keep the upper level manager occupied. If, however, the upper level is playing a more hands-on role, with substantial retained responsibilities and value-added influence, parent managers are likely to need a closer understanding of each unit reporting to them. They will therefore have to spend more time on each unit, and will be able to handle fewer direct reports. Hands-on parents with a reporting span of more than six to eight units may indeed be overstretched.

If the design criteria lead to groups of a size that are too large for a suitable span of control, it can make sense to break up the groups and install span-breaker managers. Instead of, say, 24 units all reporting to the CEO, three sub-groups could be created, each with their own span breaker, who in turn reports to the CEO. The span breaker is not playing a different parenting role from the CEO, but is acting on behalf of the CEO to extend his reach. In effect, the CEO and the span breakers represent a single layer of management. The span breakers should therefore avoid creating extra levels of review and separate staffs and overheads. In one company, the span breakers were referred to as "peripatetic chairmen", constantly travelling between business units, with very small offices of their own and "half a secretary". Span breakers should, as far as possible, work together with the CEO as a unified parenting team.

In practice, span breakers often do become more of a separate layer, and set up their own review and influence processes. "Empire-building" by span breakers is one common explanation, but often it is because the span breaker has not been told sufficiently clearly that the role is no more than an extension of the CEO. In any case, there is significant risk of value destruction if span breakers build a separate layer. At best, they become an extra level of review that slows decisions down and adds cost. More seriously still, they may start to act at cross-purposes with the CEO, leading to confusion and ambiguity for the units.

For span breakers to work effectively, it is necessary to design reporting and influence processes that closely integrate the roles of the CEO and the span breakers. It is also necessary for group and division managers to be clear about whether they are intermediate parents with a separate added-value role or simply span breakers working closely with the CEO.

Divided Reporting

In multi-dimensional structures, operating unit managers sometimes report to more than one boss. In ABB, for example, the heads of the national operating units used to report both to the national country manager and to the global business area manager. In such situations, the two bosses share the parenting tasks. For example, the country boss may be the primary line of reporting for budget approval and monthly monitoring, while the global product division boss may take the lead on strategy and investment allocation. The division of responsibilities should reflect the distinctive competencies and concerns of the different dimensions of upper level management.

Divided reporting of this sort, often referred to as matrix reporting, can reinforce the multi-dimensional focus of an organization. But by no means all multi-dimensional organizations have divided lines of reporting. Business units and cut-across units, such as overlays or project units, can all report to the same parent manager. Interdependent structures do not have to imply divided or matrix reporting.

Divided reporting is not easy. To work well, it requires clear agreement about who is primarily responsible for what, and a process for reaching a collective view on parenting responsibilities that are shared between the bosses. Such agreements may be possible in principle, but are liable to break down in the face of specific issues and crises. Are the operating company managers failing to meet their profit targets because the strategy is flawed (business area responsibility) or because the implementation is poor (country responsibility)? With divided reporting, it is often harder to decide what sort of parenting intervention to make, even if the two bosses have agreed in principle how to split the responsibilities. And the process of reaching agreement on how to intervene will almost always result in slower, less decisive interventions.

Divided reporting also causes potential conflict for operating unit managers. It is harder to respond to two bosses, each with separate agendas and sometimes pulling in different directions. Most managers much prefer clarity about their main reporting lines, and regard divided or matrix reporting as a nightmare. In consequence, divided reporting has become a relatively rare and unpopular form of parenting. Less than 10% of US and UK companies now have matrix reporting,[11] and even ABB, long the leading advocate of a balanced matrix, has abandoned it. Most companies now opt for clear primary reporting lines, even if there is also a secondary, or dotted-line, reporting relationship.

Dotted-line Reporting

A "dotted-line" reporting relationship is a typical example of the sort of vague term, which can mean different things in different situations, that is commonly used in organization design. We therefore need to make clear how the term "dotted-line reporting" is used in this book. With dotted-line reporting, there is a clear line of reporting to the main boss, who has ultimate authority, but there are some other secondary or dotted-line reporting relationships. For example, business function heads may report to the business unit general manager, but also have a dotted-line relationship to a corporate parent function head, or business managers in a specific country may report to the global business head, but also have dotted-line relationships to a local country head. The dotted-line boss is concerned with specific, identified issues, and has some influence on them, but the primary boss clearly remains the main authority. Dotted-line reporting may be designed into the formal structure, or may evolve more informally through networking and personal influence.

Dotted-line, or secondary, reporting is easier and much more common than divided reporting. It can be a good way to implement and legitimize certain types of functional influence. Finance staff in the business units, for example, are primarily part of the business units' management teams, but also have a secondary reporting relationship to the corporate finance director, who can use this relationship to check that common reporting standards are used throughout the company and that financial managers develop appropriate skills to do their jobs. A functional dotted-line can help to raise professionalism in the function, and does not usually cause conflicts for the functional managers concerned. It is not unusual for staff in functional departments such as human resources, IT, finance, and planning to feel an allegiance to their functional communities, with dotted-line reporting to a senior functional manager in the parent, as well as to the operating units in which they work.

Dotted-line reporting can also help business units to achieve their purposes. Business units will have a primary reporting relationship along the main dimension of business unit defin-ition (e.g. country to region to worldwide corporate HQ), but may also have a secondary reporting relationship along a different dimension (e.g. product group). The dotted-line relationship means that the local units must stay in touch with the product group, listen to its advice and persuasion, and even accept its authority in certain limited areas (e.g. product positioning for global brands). This provides additional parent-ing influence for the units, without fundamentally compromising the main reporting line.

So dotted-line reporting can be a useful complement to the primary reporting relationships. Nevertheless, dotted-line reporting brings with it some of the same dangers as divided reporting. The more powerful and demanding the dotted-line boss, the greater the risk of conflict with the main line of report-ing. But the weaker the dotted-line boss, the less impact the relationship will have. Dotted-line reporting is a tricky tight-rope to walk, and the extent of the responsibilities of the dotted-line boss need to be clearly laid out (see Country Managers box).

Country Managers

Many multinational companies, such as ABB, Cargill, Philips, and Shell, have reduced the power of country managers in recent years. As businesses have become increasingly regional or global in their competitive scopes, the global product dimension has taken over as the primary reporting line, and the role of national country heads has become less important. Nevertheless, most multinationals continue to have some sort of regional or national manage-ment structures. What role can regional or country managers play in global companies?

One possibility is for country managers to share the parenting tasks with global product heads, in some form of divided or matrix reporting. For example, the country man-ager may be concerned with operating issues and performance against budget, while the global product head may take the leading parenting role on strategic issues and major investments. Due to the potential for ambiguity and confusion in such arrangements, this is no longer a popular arrangement.

A second possibility is for the country heads to act in a secondary or dotted-line reporting capacity. While the main reporting line is clearly to global division heads, country managers can add some value by focusing on selected local issues. Typically, they have a role in helping operating units to maintain good relations with government institutions and with large local customers. They may also help to identify local business development opportunities, especially if these opportunities might otherwise fall between divisions or receive insufficient attention from global divisional management. Country managers also have some minimum parenting role in terms of compliance with local legislation, fiscal issues, and so forth.

Third, country managers can head up shared service units that provide services for the operating units in the country. Facilities management, payroll services, and fulfillment services are common examples of the services that can report to the local country manager. More rarely, country managers can also manage core resource units: in Shell Chemicals, for example, local operating company managers run shared manufacturing operations on behalf of all the Shell Chemicals global business units.

Last, country managers can provide hands-on parenting for local units that need more attention than they can get from the global product divisions. In one company, a country manager described his role as "getting involved in the nursery (small, new businesses), the orphanage (businesses with no other obvious home), and the infirmary (seriously sick businesses)."

Country managers can therefore play several different roles and the title "country manager" can consequently mean different things. So it is important for the organization designer to make clear what role is intended. The country manager role is never an easy one, but it is made much more difficult if the scope of the responsibilities involved is not properly spelled out.

The Relevance of Parenting Concepts

In complex structures, we have seen that the parent consists of a variety of levels of line management, supported by different types of staff. The parent, particularly at group and division levels, is often more hands-on, and shares more responsibilities with the operating units than in simple structures. There is therefore a spectrum of general management levels, from the corporate CEO through intermediate parent levels, down to business units and, eventually, sub-businesses. While the differences in role between a hands-off corporate level CEO and a deeply involved business unit general manager are clear, there are several shades of gray along this spectrum (see Table 6.3). The picture is further complicated by the existence of span breakers, and by divided and dotted-line reporting.

Corporate or divisional functions can also play a variety of roles. In addition to supporting minimum and value-added parenting, they can act as core resource and shared service units, and they can undertake tasks that overlap with overlay and project units. Moreover, lead business units can take on some of the roles that would otherwise be performed by core resource or shared service units, or by parent functions at corporate or divisional levels.

It follows that the distinction between "the parent" and "the operating units" is often blurred, and that parenting responsibilities are distributed more widely through the organization. Does this mean that the concepts of corporate parenting are no longer valid or useful?

Our conclusion is that a simplistic use of parenting concepts may be less relevant and helpful in complex structures. It may

TABLE 6.3 A Spectrum of General Management Roles

	Authority/Influence/Autonomy	Accountability
Hands-off corporate parent	Retains responsibilities or exerts value-added influence in a few areas and exercises due diligence control, but does not interfere in most issues	Profit-accountable for corporation as a whole
Hands-on intermediate parent	Retains substantial responsibilities, exerts extensive value-added influence, guides interdependencies between units, and exercises due diligence control, but accepts that he should not interfere in most day-to-day operating issues	Profit-accountable for group or division
Business unit general manager	Freedom to operate with limited interference from the parent, except on issues where parent retains responsibility or believes it can add value, and without consulting other units. Willing to collaborate with and help other units, provided it does not damage own business unit results	Strongly profit-accountable for business unit
Sub-business head	Some freedom to operate without consulting business unit general manager and other units; but must accept business unit general manager's authority on issues that matter to business unit strategy and performance, and must work with other sub-businesses as part of business unit management team	Profit-accountable for sub-business, but subject to contributing to overall business unit profitability

not always be possible – or useful – to identify precisely which management units are and are not part of the parent. Nor will an emphasis on questions about why we need a parent at all yield much insight, since the parent (broadly defined) is integral to the organization, whose separate parts could clearly not function on their own. Equally, to insist that the parent can only be justified if it is adding value to largely autonomous business units is bound to misrepresent the parent's role in interdependent structures, since the structure is not based on self-contained, autonomous units.

On the other hand, there is much in the parenting concepts that is relevant and powerful in complex, interdependent structures.

- Parenting advantage, that is to say the objective of creating more value out of a group's portfolio of businesses than any other owner could, is still an essential concept. The quest for parenting advantage should remain the fundamental driver of corporate strategy and structure, and the parenting advantage test is highly relevant. What are the sources of value creation on which the corporate strategy rests, and if an interdependent structure with several levels of parenting has been chosen, does this reflect the corporate strategy to achieve parenting advantage, or has it emerged for other reasons? Complex structures and reporting relationships only make sense if they are necessary to create as much value as possible.

- The redundant hierarchy test is critical in multi-level organizations. Does each level have distinctive, complementary, value-creating responsibilities, and does it have the knowledge and competence to discharge them effectively? Indeed, since the upper-level managers in the parent have more demanding responsibilities in complex structures, the issue of whether they have the necessary parenting skills is especially important. Value destruction by the parent in interdependent structures is a very real risk. It may not be possible to do without a parent, but the wrong sort of parenting can cause serious damage. A realistic assessment of value destruction by upper levels, and of how it can be minimized, continues to be a highly worthwhile discipline, with powerful practical implications for management.

- Although in practice there is a spectrum of general management levels, with less clear distinctions between parents, business units, and sub-businesses, it is still worthwhile to recognize the essential differences in role between them. In principle, the business unit has critically different responsibilities and accountabilities from the parent to which it reports and the sub-businesses which report to it. In particular, the business unit has more autonomous decision-making powers than its parent, which must usually work through influence on the business unit, or the sub-business, which must accept that the business unit general manager will have the final word on many important issues. Even a hands-on parent must recognize that primary responsibility for most decisions rests with business unit managers. Even independent-minded sub-business heads must recognize that their main task is to work as part of the business unit general manager's team. Otherwise the "business unit" shifts up or down a level, together with the primary profit accountability. Questions about which units have primary decision-making authority and profit accountability, and about how other management levels should work with them to optimize results, remain worth asking.

- Given distributed parenting, with a variety of units contributing to the overall parenting task, detailed thinking about the specific responsibilities of all the units that are involved in parenting is necessary. To achieve clarity about the roles and responsibilities of different management levels and units, it is useful to lay out explicitly their respective contributions to the overall parenting tasks. And, because some staff departments and lead business units play multiple roles, distinguishing between these roles is important to avoid confusion about how they should be discharged, and consequent value destruction.

- The role of the parent is vital in designing and managing interdependent structures as effective self-managing networks. As a result of knowledge and competence limitations, the parent should attempt to decentralize most decisions. But, to make the network work well, it will have to retain certain responsibilities and be willing to arbitrate on disputes between units. Its influence and authority is essential in establishing clear unit roles, protecting specialist cultures, facilitating difficult links, exercising control, and adjusting the organization to the changes it faces.

Although a sharp distinction between the parent and the operating units is often less feasible in interdependent structures, many of the questions prompted by the parenting concepts therefore remain relevant and powerful.

If the language of "parenting" is felt to be misleading, these questions can be rephrased in terms of corporate value-added, hierarchical relationships and the roles of different management levels and units. But our investigation of complex, interdependent structures has reinforced our belief that such questions are of vital importance, and that the parenting concepts, properly used, provide the best way of addressing them. Good parenting is a *sine qua non* of structured networking.

7

An Overview of the Design Process

We now want to turn to the question of how managers can go about making organization design decisions,[1] addressing what we see as two weaknesses in the approaches managers are currently using to solve their design issues.

The first weakness is that managers do not have a rigorous analytical approach to the topic. Most feel the need to create design criteria at the start of the project, but find this task difficult. Most fail to be sufficiently creative or generate a satis-factory range of options. Most do not have the tools to challenge and test the concepts that they come up with. Finally, most do not have a satisfactory way of communicating the solution they develop to the managers who must make it work. As a result, the decision process is often highly subjective and can be influenced more by the power and preferences of senior managers than by rigorous analysis.

For example, in one major power company, the CEO felt that insufficient attention was being paid to the jurisdictions in which the company operated. The company was organized into a generation business and a delivery business, but most of its sales were still regulated by four different jurisdictions. It was neces-sary not only to have an organizational face for each of the four regulators, but also to plan a strategy for each jurisdiction and co-ordinate the two businesses to insure the strategy was achieved. The jurisdictional dimension was both an operating challenge, in terms of community and regulator relationships, and a strategic challenge, in terms of optimizing performance in that territory.

The CEO assigned the task to one of his senior managers. It proved to be a tough task. Would it be necessary to create an additional dimension in the structure and, if so, what powers would the jurisdictional managers need? Who should these managers report to? How much of the work could be done by existing central functions such as Legal and Finance or delegated to the businesses? Her approach was thorough. She defined all the tasks that needed to be done, and asked a range of managers whether these tasks should be centralized or decentralized, creating in the process a massive responsibility grid that captured the opinions of those consulted. She was then faced with the task of pulling a solution out of this analysis. As the deadline loomed, she fell back on instinct and her assessment of what would be politically acceptable; but she was not confident that her proposed solution was the best available. "Surely there must be some way of testing whether this is a good solution," she asked, "other than presenting it to the senior management group and seeing if they like it?"

The second weakness in the approach managers normally take is that they have no method for creating "structured networks". They do not know when they have done enough design. Existing design tools – the process re-engineering tools of process maps, responsibility grids, approvals hierarchies, and job descriptions – draw managers, faced with enterprise-wide design issues, into more detail than they can handle. As a result, they either ignore the detail, assuming it "will be worked out as we go along", or develop too much process and detailed structure, killing initiative and individualism.

One manager leading a project to redesign a major retailer was trying to decide how much detail to go into. In particular, he was concerned about the relationship between the development division, in charge of format development and category management, and the operations division, in charge of stores, supply, and transport. It was not difficult to think of issues where the two divisions would need to work together – how much shelf space to devote to a category, how to tap into the knowledge that store managers have about customer reactions, and so on. The problem was in deciding how many of these processes would need to be laid out in the design rather than left to the managers concerned to develop for themselves. Moreover, the manager was not sure whether the processes needed to be defined before deciding whether the proposed solution would be workable.

His analytical mind caused him to believe that the processes did need to be defined before the design was chosen, but this was proving impractical. There was too much work to be done. He had therefore come to the opposite conclusion. "I may be a rebel, but I think we should let them work it out over time. We should go with this design, let them play with it for three months, and then push to have the processes written down." But he was not comfortable. "The trouble is, how will we know if we have forgotten something important, and how do we keep the business moving forward while everyone is focused on internal stuff?"

Our process addresses both these problems. The steps in the process – define criteria, develop options, test, and communicate – are not new (see Figure 7.1), but the rigor is. The fit drivers are used to develop design criteria; the taxonomy of units helps managers develop options; the tests insure that each proposed solution is thoroughly challenged; and the communication step makes sure that the design result provides enough guidance for the managers who must make it work. While managers leading design projects must ultimately get the commitment of senior managers to their proposals, they need a rigorous design process in order to convince themselves that they have an excellent solution before they try to sell it to others. Moreover, the process makes it possible to involve a broad range of managers in exploring options, avoiding the secrecy that often accompanies design efforts.

The second benefit of the process is that it helps managers find the right balance between structure and networking: it helps them design "structured networks". Here the taxonomy and the tests play a crucial role. The taxonomy helps managers to create

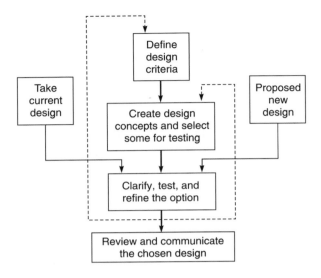

FIGURE 7.1 Making Design Decisions

design concepts that can work as networks: the units are defined and the relationships between units are articulated. The tests guide managers to design "just enough" additional structure and process to make the network of units function together as a purposeful organization. Rather than allowing staff to "play with it for three months", the manager from the retail company could have used the taxonomy to define more clearly the relationships between the development and operations divisions (Are they both business units? Is one an overlay? Should the development division act as a core resource unit?) and the tests to identify the few "difficult links" that need some additional design input.

The process we are describing is, therefore, not just a few commonsensical steps, but rather a systematic framework for addressing design problems.[2] In this chapter, we will focus on describing the process and addressing process issues that were frequently raised in our research. In Chapter 8, we will focus on the tests, because they are the most important part of the process and can be used on their own without the other steps. In Chapter 9, we will run through a detailed example.

The design process we are suggesting should be used by managers facing major structural issues: the redesign of the whole enterprise; the reorganization of a division that contains a number of business units; the introduction of a new organizational level. It is a process that is most appropriate when managers want to change reporting relationships, levels of centralization, or the definitions of units. The need for a redesign can stem from a merger or break-up, or from a major change in the environment or strategy. It can also occur because the current organization is not working as planned.

For example, David Roberts, the chief executive of Barclays Business Banking Group, wanted to move from an organization structured mainly by geography and by product to one that paid more attention to "financial solutions for customers" and to economies of scale in infrastructure areas, such as transaction processing. He wanted to create an interdependent organization with three axes – products, markets, and infrastructure.

Another example involved an enterprise-wide redesign at Cargill. Cargill operates a wide range of businesses, including agricultural commodities, food ingredients, and food products. The design team's brief was a complete organization redesign to achieve a better fit with a new corporate strategy. The aim was to become "the global leader in providing agrifood chain customers with solutions that enable them to succeed in their businesses." The project involved breaking the existing divisions into more than 100 operating units, assembling the units into clusters, designing the roles of the clusters or "platforms", reassessing the role of the corporate center, and developing coordination processes and performance measurement processes for the units.

A third example, which is referred to extensively in Chapter 9, involved a company we will call Global Foods. Its European Snack-foods Division was concerned about growth. Its core products were mature, and the division had diversified into other related sectors. These new product categories were not making as much progress as managers had hoped. The division wanted to give them more attention: to place them at the center of their growth strategy. Senior managers in the division had decided that some reorganization would be needed to achieve this.

Organization design challenges of this nature – enterprise or architecture challenges – can be contrasted with challenges such as the redesign of the relationship between marketing and manufacturing within a business unit, the design of the job of a product manager, or the design of the order to delivery process. For these "operating" challenges, the tools of process re-engineering are more appropriate than our tools. Our principles and tests may be able to contribute something to operational design issues, but they are not the focus of this book.

Where to Start the Design Process

There are three possible starting points to the process: start with the current design, start by defining the design criteria, or start with a proposed new design.

Logically, the process should start with a definition of the design criteria, which is how most consultants tackle the problem. It is hard to select a new design without first defining the objectives. In practice, however, managers often prefer to start from a different position, and in some situations this makes sense. For example, managers may be concerned about whether the current organization is a part of the problem or not. By assessing the current situation, they can decide whether or not a new design is needed.

Other managers start with a clear idea of what they think is the answer. Their vision may be based on instinct, experience, imitation of a competitor, or the latest organization concept. Their concern is not with theory, but with whether their new concept is likely to work.

Whatever the starting point, the step "Clarify, test, and refine the option" is at the heart of the design process. If the design is flawed, the problems will be exposed and the design team will need to make refinements, generate some new options, or go back to the start. While no process can guarantee that managers make good choices, by pointing out the strengths and weaknesses of the options, the tests can show up areas of prejudice and self-interest, thus reducing the influence of politics and power struggles.

Define Design Criteria

For managers starting at this point, the step involves using the four fit drivers – product-market strategies, corporate strategies, people, and constraints – to develop design criteria. For example, for "product-market strategy", the analysis would be:

- list the sources of competitive advantage and the operating initiatives planned for each product-market segment; and
- take each source of advantage and initiative, note the organizational implications and turn them into design criteria.

A *source of advantage* in some product-market segments might be close customer contact involving superior applications technology. In other words, the company is expecting to win in the marketplace by working with customers to solve their problems. This has the following organizational implications:

- the market-facing units probably need to be set up to focus on customer groups with different kinds of problems. This will allow different units to develop skills in different kinds of customer problems;
- the market-facing units probably need to be business units, because these units will have high motivation for making the difficult commercial trade-offs about how much free support to give each customer; and
- the market-facing units will need to have technical experts within their units rather than drawing them from a central technical function. This will further encourage focused skill development and insure high responsiveness.

The design criterion that emerges from this analysis would be: "insure that the market-facing units are business units, with control of their own applications technology, targeted on different customer types."

An *operating initiative* relevant to a number of segments might be to establish e-commerce systems to interact with both customers and suppliers. The design criterion would be: "Insure that the design allows for dedicated attention to be given to the e-commerce project."

For a situation that involves four or five product-market segments, the analysis needed is significant, but achievable. In the Cargill situation, involving more than 100 different product-market segments, a thorough analysis of all the design criteria from all the product-market strategies becomes an unwieldy task. The solution is to do the analysis either on an as-needed basis (i.e. do the analysis only when an issue is raised by one of the tests) or by sampling product-market segments until the additional analysis is not providing any additional design criteria. Because the four fit drivers are revisited in the fit tests, care needs to be taken to avoid "analysis paralysis" at this stage. Weaknesses in generating design criteria will be picked up in the testing step. Focusing on the few important sources of advantage and operating initiatives is one way of avoiding excessive analysis.

For "people", the analysis would be:

- list senior managers who will have prominent positions in the new organization, irrespective of the design chosen, and assess their strengths, weaknesses, and preferences;
- list other managers with particularly relevant strengths or skills;
- list any limits there may be to the type of people who can be recruited into the organization; and
- take this list of strengths, weaknesses, preferences, and recruiting limits, note the organizational implications, and turn them into design criteria.

If the chief executive prefers to work one-on-one rather than, leading a team, this needs to be converted into a design criterion: "Insure sufficient decentralization to avoid creating a decision process at the top of the organization that depends on a team or committee." If it is hard to recruit marketing managers in less developed countries, a design criterion might be: "Insure sufficient centralization of marketing or marketing recruitment to overcome local skill shortages."

Design criteria need to give specific guidance on some aspect of organization design. Criteria such as "minimize organizational boundaries", "maximize the capacity for organizational learning", or "cut the time it takes to make decisions" are too general to be useful. They have not been converted into sufficiently precise organizational implications. On the other hand, the criteria must not become a straitjacket: they must not be so constraining that they define the solution. We have found that developing criteria from the fit drivers is the best way of finding the middle ground between too much precision and too much generality.

The four fit drivers provide information about the specifics of the organization, its environment, and what it is trying to do. To develop criteria that reflect the unique situation of a particular organization, managers need to derive them from the four fit drivers.

The process of developing design criteria can result in a large number of considerations, some of which may conflict. Once the full list has been generated, priorities need to be set to resolve conflicts. A shorter list of the most important criteria that must be borne in mind throughout the design process is required. The full list of criteria will, however, be used to help select options in the next step.

Create and Select Design Concepts

There are two ways of creating options – intuitively in a group process, or analytically using the design criteria. The analytical process involves five steps:

1. Use the most important design criteria to define "responsibility groupings" – clusters of responsibilities that require focused management attention.

2. Choose one dimension of responsibility grouping as the primary reporting structure and, using the role labels, fit the other groupings around this structural backbone.

3. Create a few different "design concepts" with the same structural backbone.

4. Choose another dimension as the structural backbone and generate some more design concepts.

5. Scan the set of options generated by checking that it includes at least one simple and one more complex alternative.

A "design concept" is not a full organization design. It consists of the boxes (the units), the lines (who the units report to), and, most important, the unit roles (their broad responsibilities and accountabilities as well as guidance on their lateral and vertical relationships). It does not contain all the processes and co-ordination mechanisms that will be needed in the final design.

It is important to generate design concepts rather than fully worked blueprints. This is because it is extremely time-consuming to develop fully worked blueprints, and the time investment needed discourages managers from considering many options. Design concepts can be developed quickly, making it possible to lay out many alternatives without investing huge amounts of time in each. A fully worked blueprint should not be developed until after a choice has been made between design concepts. In our decision process (Figure 7.1), the last two steps "Clarify, test, and refine" and "Review and communicate the design" help convert a design concept into a fully worked blueprint.

It is also important to develop a range of design concepts. This insures creativity and overcomes blinkered thinking. In most design projects, managers do not consider enough options before making their choice. For example, in the power company, the manager considering the jurisdictional design issue was only articulating two alternatives – a centralized model and a decentralized model. We have noted that this is common because many managers do not have the language with which to articulate subtle differences between options. Fortunately, the roles taxonomy is a powerful tool for defining and articulating different options, and can be used to create subtle variations. For example, a secondary dimension of focus, such as the jurisdictional dimension, can be an overlay, a project unit, a business unit, a shared service, or part of the parent. As a result, the manager considering the jurisdictional project could have easily articulated six different models:

- a decentralized model, where most of the jurisdictional responsibilities are allocated to the generation and delivery businesses;

- a centralized model, where the responsibilities are allocated to an additional central function with "parenting" authority over the businesses;

- an overlay model, where the responsibilities are allocated to a unit that has a pressure group responsibility to maximize jurisdictional earnings, but little authority;

- a shared service model, where the responsibilities are allocated to a unit that provides a service to the businesses and the parent;

- a project unit model, where the responsibilities are distributed among the existing businesses in such a way that a project team needs to be formed in order to put together a jurisdictional plan; or

- a business unit model, where the jurisdictions are set up as business units that buy services from the generation and delivery businesses.

The taxonomy of unit types provides a set of building blocks which simplifies the task of creating an initial set of options. But the role labels should not be constraints. Within each generic option, it is possible to create further variations. For example, it would be possible to set up the responsibilities for relationship management within each jurisdiction as a shared service and the planning responsibilities as a parenting function. It would also be possible to set up an overlay unit that had some authority over certain decisions – for example, changes to service levels, or capital investment decisions.

A good way to use the taxonomy of roles is to deliberately give units different labels. For example, in a geographically organized company wanting to give more emphasis to the product dimension, the products could be "business units", "sub-businesses", "overlays", "core resource units", "project units" or "part of the parent unit". Each option has implications for the rest of the organization. By trying out each option, managers can be confident that they have considered a wide range of different solutions. Trying different role labels is not the only way of stimulating creativity, but in our experience it is powerful.

Our research revealed that managers have comparatively little patience for generating options. As soon as an option is created that looks like it might do the job, managers want to move on to the next stage of analysis – testing the option. We don't recommend this approach, but we don't want to be dogmatic. An option can be chosen, tested, found wanting, and then another option can be created. In other words, it is not essential to create all the options at one point in time and then test them in the next step. An iterative process is possible. The advantage of spending time on option creation is that it helps innovative thinking. In an attempt to develop a wide range of options, managers are forced to think of solutions they might not produce under different circumstances. Presuming the analysis has proceeded as we suggest, managers normally develop between three and seven generic options, each of which has between two and five variations. Given this large number of options, how should managers select which to evaluate? The answer is to use any method the group feels comfortable with. The selection process is not crucial, because the tests will help identify any inadequate options. Hence an intuitive process, which involves selecting the design with which top managers feel most comfortable, may be sufficient.

A more analytical process for choosing between design

concepts involves scoring the options against the list of design criteria. The options with the best overall score should be selected for testing. In practice, a combination of analysis, intuition, forced ranking, and the preferences of the most powerful managers is normally used to decide which options to test.

Allowing an intuitive process to dominate opens the door to politics and power. Managers are quite likely to choose an option that is acceptable to the most senior person in the group. Alternatively, they may be over-influenced to choose an option that clearly provides jobs for the most senior managers. While this should be discouraged, it is not a critical problem. Any weak points in the option will be flushed out during the testing stage.

Clarify, Test, and Refine the Design

Before a design concept can be tested, it needs to be clarified. What exactly does this mean? If the option has been generated from the "creating and selecting" step, it will already be clear enough. But if the current design or some other proposal is being tested, the option often needs clarification before testing can begin. Here the roles taxonomy is essential. The option needs to be converted into a design concept: boxes (how responsibilities are grouped), lines (reporting relationships), and roles (nature of lateral and vertical relationships).

We have frequently found ourselves reviewing a proposed design and having to ask basic questions, such as "Is such and such a unit a business unit?" In the case of the retailer, mentioned earlier, we met with the project leader just after he had successfully presented the proposal to a group of senior managers. The design had been approved and his presentation had been part of early communication to a wider audience. However, when we asked whether the development division was a business unit, an overlay, or parent function, he found the question difficult. "We have not decided yet. I expect each category will need to be measured on profitability, so I suppose they will be business units." He then continued, "But isn't the important thing that they need to work together with the formats and the operations units? We have been stressing the need for collaboration, not the different identity of the units."

We responded by saying that units in an organization always need to work together in some way. What is important in a design concept is to think about what sort of relationships need to exist for the organization to perform well. Hence our roles taxonomy. Stressing collaboration is not sufficient. Until the relationship between a category unit and a format unit has been specified as "team", "service provider/client" or "mutual self-interest", we believe that the design concept work has not been taken far enough.

Once managers have clarified the design concept, they can apply the nine tests. How to execute the nine tests is described in Chapter 8 and further illustrated in Chapter 9, so here we will not discuss the analyses involved. However, as part of the overview, it is worth understanding the purpose of the tests and how they can best be used.

A design concept is an organizational outline. It does not define the processes and mechanisms that will be needed to make it work. It includes a broad description of the responsibilities and relationships, but it needs to be fleshed out during the testing process. The tests, therefore, are not only about judging whether the option will work. They are about helping the designer make the additions, adjustments, and embellishments that will turn a design concept into a workable design. They are about turning a design concept into a "structured network". The tests can also be used to refine and improve an existing design.

In particular, the tests help managers achieve "just enough" design. As we have pointed out throughout this book, one of the big challenges of good design is to balance the objective of self-management with that of order: to promote self-organized networking, but with sufficient structure to have a well-functioning organization. The tests are critical to solving this tension. Structure and processes should be added to a design concept only so far as is needed to satisfy the tests – no more and no less. If the difficult links test points to a link that will not work effectively through self-managed networking, adjustments and additions need to be made to the design to resolve the problem. But, once sufficient additions have been made to pass the tests, no more is needed. The tests not only assess whether the design will work, they also guide managers to produce "just enough" design.

For example, the manager leading the project in the retail company could have taken his design work further by applying the following tests:

- the *difficult links test* would have helped him pinpoint those co-ordination issues that require special solutions, such as how the organization decides about the opening or closing of new retail space;
- the *specialist cultures test* would have helped him think about whether some units needed more separation, for example whether the design needed a new businesses unit in which wholly new concepts could be incubated outside the main structure; and
- the *accountability test* would have helped him think about the performance measures to use for "categories" and "formats", which would in turn suggest that these units need to be overlays or business units rather than functions.

Each test draws managers' attention to an aspect of the design that needs more clarification. The design team can then develop additions and refinements that address the issues raised by the test, knowing that, when they are finished, they will have done "just enough" design. For example, once "solutions" have been developed for all the difficult links, the design team will know that other relationships between units can be left for the managers concerned to work out for themselves. In the same way, the accountability test helps managers focus on those units that will be difficult to control. It encourages managers to search for innovative ways to measure performance or to find some other way of achieving accountability, such as insuring the unit reports to a parent manager with a particularly good feel for the issues in the unit.

There are a number of ways in which a design concept can be "fleshed out". Most managers think of *co-ordination mechanisms* as the glue that holds the different parts of the organization together and makes relationships between units effective. In practice, however, there is a much longer list of refinements and additions that can be used to address issues raised by the tests. Co-ordination mechanisms are not the only way of creating "structure" in the "network":

- Changes can be made to the allocation of responsibilities so that an awkward relationship becomes more self-correcting. For example, a mandated service relationship can be changed to one where both sides have a choice.

- Changes can be made to the role, skills, or resources of the parent level, so that parent managers have the time and ability to intervene when necessary. For example, to solve an issue about how to co-ordinate global pricing across a regional structure, the company could appoint a corporate marketing vice-president capable of intervening wisely when the regional units are sub-optimizing pricing.

- Performance measures and incentives can be used to insure that managers do not have conflicting motivations. For example, bonuses can be given on combined group performance rather than separate performance by unit.

- Different people can be appointed to important jobs. For example, managers who have previously worked successfully together can be appointed to insure a potentially awkward relationship has the best chance of working.

- Cultural levers such as behavior norms and leadership style can be used to set the right ground rules for interactions between units.

We devote much of the next chapter to the different kinds of refinements and additions that can be made. The important message to take from this chapter is that there is a range of solutions to issues raised by the tests. Co-ordination mechanisms are only one of a number of embellishments that can be introduced to make a design concept, or an existing design, better able to pass the tests.

We recommend that managers apply the fit tests first, since these tests often identify knock-out factors that cause an option to be rejected. The fit tests narrow down the range of options that need to be considered. The good design tests should follow the fit tests. Their value is more about helping managers refine and embellish the design concept. The good design tests can result in knock-out factors; but, more normally, they encourage designers to develop processes, mechanisms, and other adjustments that will make the option workable.

When the tests throw up knock-out factors, the design should be abandoned and another one selected for testing. If the tests reject an option, the answer is to go back to the "creating and selecting" step and select another option. If the process started with the current design or a popular proposal, the next step may be to begin by defining design criteria as a preliminary to option development.

There is some duplication between different tests. Also, it is often necessary to repeat tests to check adjustments or additions to the design. This duplication and repetition is healthy: it is part of doing a thorough job, and involves revisiting analyses from different angles. We have never found that time spent on the tests has been wasted.

The chosen design should be the one that performs best in the testing process. In our experience, managers rarely test more than one or two options in any detail. Usually the preferred design emerges quite quickly, and the tests are used to refine and improve the design. Sometimes a dilemma emerges between two designs, each of which has different strengths and weaknesses. In this situation, leaders need to decide, but only after they have involved as many managers as possible in discussing the tests and assessing the trade-offs. If "due process" has been seen to be done, those with opposing views are much more likely to support the final decision.

Review and Communicate the Design

Once an option has been tested, refined, and chosen, the design process is almost complete. However, there is still some work to do. People need to be allocated to the main jobs, the design needs to be reviewed for clarity, and it needs to be communicated.

This step involves examining each unit, deciding how the top team of the unit will be chosen if it has not already been appointed, and assessing whether the team has enough guidance to start operating. The key question is about communication. Are the role definitions, policies, processes, and mechanisms described in a way that will allow the managers to start work without further guidance? The temptation in this step is to provide additional detail rather than more powerful communication. The previous step will have resulted in "just enough" design. This step is about finding a way to help the managers involved understand what is intended.

So long as a design has been thoroughly tested and managers have thought long and hard about the refinements and additions that are needed to address the issues raised by the tests, the design will include enough but not too much detail: it will be a "structured network". We have found, however, that managers find our advice difficult to take on faith: "Don't I need to develop job descriptions for every position?" "Surely I need to define the details of the target setting process?" "In my last company we produced a corporate policy manual; isn't that part of what I need to do?"

In most cases, the answer is no. If sufficient process and design has been done to address the issues raised by the tests, the design job is complete. For example, if there is an HR function at the center tasked with managing a pool of senior managers across the company, it is not the job of the organization designer to define the policies that the HR function will need to put in place to do its job. This is something that the HR managers need to work out together with the heads of the businesses.

"But what if I have missed something in the testing process?" persisted one manager. This is a valid concern. Our solution is to have a final review of the design. We look at the new design from the position of the management teams running each of the important units. Ideally, the design should be examined through the eyes of every management team, but the time involved often makes it more practical to focus on the important units.

Having chosen a unit to focus on, the analysis involves reviewing all the important relationships that the management team has outside the unit. The list should include relationships with external groups such as customers, trade unions, suppliers, and other stakeholders. It should also include all internal relationships, both lateral and vertical. The objective is to double-check that the design, in its final form, provides enough information for managers to start working. The question for each relationship is: "Are there any constraints on how the unit's managers should approach this relationship?"

If there are no constraints, if the unit can operate at arm's length, there is no problem. If there are constraints, either in the form of a relationship definition provided by the design or in the form of co-ordination policies or processes that are defined as part of the design, there is a follow-up question: "Are the responsibilities, role definitions, policies, or processes clear enough to allow the managers concerned to start working without further guidance?"

If the answer is no, something has been left incomplete from the testing process. Either an issue has been overlooked and should now be addressed, or the solution to an issue has not been defined in sufficient detail. Either way, the designer should go back to the test concerned and redo the analysis.

The communication itself involves judgments that are best taken together with some of the managers concerned. What is clear on paper is often not clear in the heads of managers. In fact, managers frequently read between the lines, looking for more constraints and policies than have been specified. This is particularly true in situations where the design is more decentralized or more "self-managed" than before. Managers read into the design some of the old rules, even though these have now been dropped. The opposite can also be true. In situations where the design is becoming more centralized and more interdependent, managers frequently underestimate or overlook some of the new constraints that have been added.

The tools of communication are similar to the tools of design – structure charts, role definitions, process maps, decision grids, job descriptions, and policy manuals. The skill is to avoid misusing these tools by letting them lead managers into adding more detail than was intended in the design. For example, it is common to produce job descriptions as part of a new design. Once this activity is initiated, it can take on a bureaucratic life of its own. The people producing the job descriptions try to include all the responsibilities of each manager rather than defining just enough to enable the manager to work effectively in the new design. "Role descriptions" is a more useful term in this context. The same can happen with decision grids. Instead of focusing on those decisions that are confusing or "difficult", a decision grid often covers all the decisions affecting a particular issue or relationship. This results in too much definition rather than "just enough" detail. The taxonomy of roles and relation-ships is also very useful in the communication process, so long as managers are familiar with the terms used.

It is also important to explain the rationale for the new design. Managers gain a fuller understanding from knowing why something has been chosen or changed. As we will point out in the last section of this chapter, involving managers in the design process is the best way to insure that they understand the thinking that lies behind the judgments that have been made. One useful measure is to lay out the weaknesses in the design. Every design is a compromise that makes some objectives easier to achieve and others harder. It can be helpful to define those objectives that will now be more difficult, those relationships that will be harder to operate, and those accountabilities that will be harder to measure.

Managers can be myopic about organization, throwing their hands up in disgust at the things that are difficult without balancing these negatives against the positives. If this analysis is provided as part of the communication process, it not only makes managers feel that the pros and cons have been properly analyzed, it also helps them see the trade-offs. As one consultant pointed out to us, "Managers only ever understand the strengths of an organization once they have changed to a different one. Their focus is frequently on the negative, on what is not working well today. The art is to help them see the trade-offs that lie behind these negatives." A list of the negatives that are being lost and the positives that have been created can help to silence any cynics ready to undermine any change.

Questions and Answers About Designing an Organization

During organization design projects, certain questions frequently come up. In this last section, we will give our answers to some of these questions. This will also serve as a summary of some of the key aspects of our proposed design process.

1. Where should a design project start?

We have attempted to answer this question with our Figure 7.1. The analytical approach starts by defining design criteria. However, in practice it is sometimes better to start either by testing the current design or by examining a proposed solution.

An advantage of starting with the existing organization is that managers often feel strongly about those features of the existing organization that are awkward, without fully appreciating the good parts of the current design or why this design was created in the first place. By starting with a review of the current organization, managers can get a more balanced view of the issues they will face when testing a new design. For managers who are uncertain about where to start, our rule of thumb is: "Start with the existing design. Clarify it and test it."

2. Who should we involve?

The ideal answer to this question is to involve those who will be affected, but this is usually not practical. A project team becomes unworkable above a certain size, and the majority of managers need to focus on keeping the current organization working smoothly, not planning for a change in organization. As a result, most design projects are driven by relatively small project teams. This seems unsatisfactory. Not only do the majority of managers feel less committed to the change than is ideal, but the design team frequently fails to understand important issues. We therefore believe in involving as many managers as is possible and practical.

One of the benefits of our design process is that the framework of the analysis makes it possible to expose the thinking and accommodate inputs from many parts of the organization. Recognizing the danger of distracting the whole organization, we have found it useful to widen involvement at three points – option generation, testing, and review.

It is possible to run a series of workshops, covering large numbers of managers, on both option generation and testing. Not only do these workshops have the benefit of educating managers about organization issues, they also insure that knowledge in the field is brought to the design team. In addition, they demonstrate due process and help generate commitment.

When it comes to "review and communication", all managers need to be involved in judging whether the design blueprint provides them with sufficient information to start working. Sessions with the managers of all important units are essential both to communicate the design and listen to their concerns and misunderstandings. If the work has been done thoroughly, these sessions will be mainly about communication. However, in most cases new issues emerge from these sessions which require some small design adjustments. They should be viewed as part of the checks and balances in a good design process.

The design team itself should usually be limited to fewer than seven managers (including consultants), but should not be smaller than three. This is the minimum size of design team that is needed to prevent blinkered thinking. Moreover, the design team should continue to operate for the first month or two of the new design, acting as a point of first inquiry for issues that come up.

There are also advantages in creating a steering group of three or more senior managers who will pay special attention to the design project. Often this steering group is, by default, the company's executive committee, although this group is frequently too large and too burdened with other agenda items. A separate steering group insures some separate attention for the project. The steering group should also continue to meet for some months after the new design has been put in place, to act as the keeper of the design's integrity.

For managers who are uncertain about who to involve in a design project, our rule of thumb is: "Involve as many as practically possible." There are dangers in this. New designs disrupt the status quo and existing power structures. Managers often have hidden agendas and pursue self-interest before organization logic. Nevertheless, with a robust design process, it is possible to involve large numbers of managers. There is no excuse for the secretive processes that some companies still use.

3. How far down the organization should we design?

This is a problem for managers involved in a top-down design effort. Should we just design the layer below and let the managers in that layer design the layers below them? Or should we design two or three layers down?

Some senior executives believe that they should only design the layer that reports directly to them, in order to promote decentralized decision-making about the design of lower levels. However, most companies' organization designs cover a number of layers.

In our view, the organization design should go down far enough to make clear the intentions of the designer. For top-down enterprise-wide designs, this is likely to involve specifying the roles of all the main building block units, at least down to the level of the business unit, and often including the sub-businesses. For managers uncertain about how far down to design, our rule of thumb is: "Design as far as is necessary to convey your intentions, and in any case at least as far as the business unit level."

4. How much should we specify?

We have addressed this question fully in the main text of this chapter. The answer is "just enough to resolve issues raised by the tests". However, since this is such an important point, it is worth emphasizing once more.

Some organization designers seem intent on laying out every responsibility in an organization. Ideally, they would like to specify every action for every individual in the organization – and in some command-and-control organizations this is often what it feels as if managers are trying to do! Moreover, there is a logic to this level of detail in situations where tasks are repetitive. Time and motion studies, process re-engineering, and skills training are largely aimed at creating this mechanistic outcome.

However, in turbulent environments this objective is not only unrealistic, it is unhealthy. The time it would take to design all the responsibilities in an organization would be prohibitive. The world would have changed before the design was finished! Moreover, creative, idiosyncratic people, who are the driving force behind today's organizations, are not prepared to be allocated machine-like tasks. They want broadly defined responsibilities that allow them to use their skills and ingenuity. Finding the right level of specification has become an essential part of good design.

Therefore, for managers uncertain whether they have done too much or too little design, our rule of thumb is: "Do enough to satisfy the tests, but no more."

5. What should we do about the "soft" issues – culture, values, and attitudes?

Effective organizations include much more than structure, roles, people, and processes. They include aspirations, attitudes, beliefs, behavior norms, loyalties, ambitions, rivalries, commitments, and relationships. As a result, design teams often ask what they should be doing about these "softer" issues.

Our response comes in three parts. First, the design process we are suggesting does address some of these softer issues. Most importantly, it addresses the issue of relationships between the units in the organization and the performance measures that will be used to assess progress. It also addresses the skills, attitudes, and style that managers will need to have to be effective in particular "pivotal" jobs, and the behavior norms that will be needed to make difficult relationships work. In other words, although the design process appears to be focused on structural issues, it does address soft issues so far as these are needed to resolve problems raised by the tests.

Second, we see many of the soft issues of organization, such as culture and commitment, as outcomes rather than inputs. A good design will help create a healthy culture and high levels of commitment, not vice versa. In other words, for a company keen to develop a "collaborative culture", we would suggest attention to organization design as the first step. If the relationships between units have been well constructed, a collaborative culture, to the degree that it is needed, will emerge.

Third, we believe that much of the soft side of organization is best managed during implementation. It is not easy to design in advance. It is best managed by "walking the talk" and "leading by example". If the company wants a high performance culture, then the leaders must be intolerant of mediocre results and walk their own talk with their own staff functions.

For those managers uncertain over how much attention to give to the soft issues, our rule of thumb is: "Get the design right first and worry about the additional soft issues during implementation."

8

Nine Tests of Organization Design

Our analysis of the principles of organization design in Chapters 2 and 3 led us to propose nine tests – four "fit" tests and five "good design" tests (see Figure 8.1). These tests are at the heart of our approach to organization design.[1] They not only provide a rigor that has been lacking in most of the design projects we researched, but they also help managers achieve the difficult balance of creating a design with "just enough" structure and process: a structured network.

The tests can be used in two ways. They can be applied to a proposed new design concept with the intention of testing whether the concept is viable, and, if it is, refining and adding to it so that it becomes a fully worked blueprint. This chapter focuses on this use of the tests. We assume that a project team has worked through the design criteria and option generation stages, has selected one or more design concepts, and is now facing the challenge of testing them.

However, there is also another way in which the tests can be used. They can be applied to an existing organization to identify its strengths and weaknesses and to help managers decide whether it should be changed. The analyses that need to be done are the same for both ways of using the tests. The difference is in the conclusions. If managers are testing an existing organization, the objective is to create a list of strengths and weaknesses. We illustrate the use of the tests on an existing organization in Chapter 9.

FIGURE 8.1 Nine Tests of Organization Design

When applied to design concepts, the tests have three purposes:

- to identify whether the design has some major flaw or "knock-out" factor;
- to help managers understand the strengths and weaknesses of a design so that they can be weighed against other designs; and
- to help managers refine and improve a design concept, so that it has just enough structure, process, and definition.

The third of these three purposes is probably the most important. The tests help pinpoint issues that need to be addressed. Managers then need to find solutions to the issues to improve the design. Finding solutions requires creativity and knowledge of what is likely to work in the organization concerned. We therefore begin by looking at what to do when an issue is raised by one of the tests.

What to do When an Issue is Raised

The purpose of the tests is to identify the weak points in a design concept and insure that managers pay enough attention to issues they often overlook. The ideal outcome is that the design passes all the tests. However, in situations that require multi-dimensional structures, this is unlikely, since every design concept is, by definition, a compromise. It will give more attention to one dimension at the expense of other dimensions. It may insure that a specific co-ordination is successful, but at the risk of insufficient specialization. It may have units with clear accountabilities but less flexibility. We can expect almost all designs to raise some issues.

When a test points to an issue, the first reaction should be to consider which additions or changes to the proposed design would reduce the negative impact of the issue. For example, in a simple structure of business units based on products, the market advantage test would signal an issue if the strategy included an ambition to provide "one face" to large common customers. Only a structure with a unit focused on "large common customers" would pass this test without question.

There are, however, ways of adding to the simple product structure to achieve something close to the "one face" objective. For example, the company could co-ordinate customer relationships by creating "account managers", either as part of the parent or as lead individuals within the product units, or by forming "account teams", involving the sales managers from each product. In fact, it is usually possible to develop several ways of achieving some, if not most, of the original objective without compromising the design concept. We will refer to these ways of addressing issues as "refinements", "additions", "embellishments", "changes", or "solutions". The reason for having so many words to describe the same thing is evident in Figure 8.2. None of these words, on their own, quite captures the full range of ways of addressing issues. The process of testing is, therefore, primarily a process for refining the design. As the proposed design is tested, it is embellished with solutions to the issues that are raised. This often involves going back and forward between different tests looking for solutions that give the best balance of outcomes. None of the solutions will be perfect: each will have some unavoidable negatives. But, as the impact of the issue is somewhat, if not totally, reduced, it is less important in the final evaluation. The tests, therefore, not only help managers refine their designs, they also alert managers to the strengths and weaknesses of each design, making it possible to choose between competing alternatives.

By the end of the testing process, a design concept (lines, boxes, and roles) is likely to have been significantly refined. Refinements may include adding co-ordination mechanisms, providing guidance on people selection, allocating responsibilities in more detail, and changing parenting propositions. Figure 8.2 lists the types of addition and change that are commonly used to address issues. The goal is to refine all issues, without changing the basic design concept. For certain issues, it

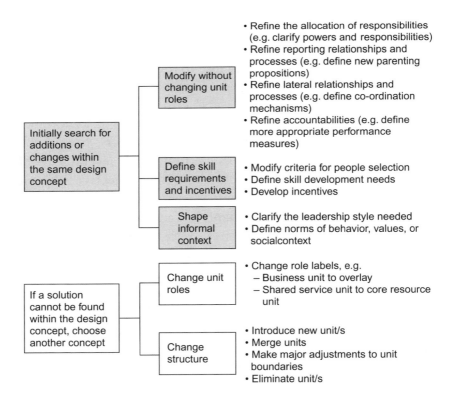

FIGURE 8.2 Additions and Changes to Address Issues

Based on a figure first produced by Risto Pentinnen of McKinsey & Co.

proves impossible to find a "good enough" solution. When this happens, the issue becomes a knock-out factor, in which case the design concept should be discarded and another option chosen for testing. This is much more likely to occur for the "fit" tests than for the "good design" tests. If the design does not give the right balance of attention to the strategic priorities (market advantage test), it is usually necessary to choose another design concept. If the design requires people with skills that are scarce or unavailable (people test), this is usually also a knock-out factor. On the other hand, if the design gives too little autonomy to one unit (specialist cultures test) or centralizes pricing decisions too high up the structure (redundant hierarchy test), there are normally solutions that can be grafted on to the structure without altering the overall concept.

The fit tests should be applied first, because they are more likely to identify knock-out factors. The good design tests can then be used to refine and select between different options, all of which are basically fit for purpose. But both sets of tests should be repeated to insure that additions and refinements do not raise new issues. The testing process, therefore, consists of the following steps: first, clarify the design concept using the taxonomy of unit types; second, use the fit tests to confirm that the design concept is viable; third, use the good design tests to refine the design so as to minimize the impact of issues raised; fourth, scan the tests again to make sure that changes or additions to the design have not raised issues with other tests; finally, weigh up the advantages and disadvantages of the refined design and decide whether it is the best option (see Figure 8.3).

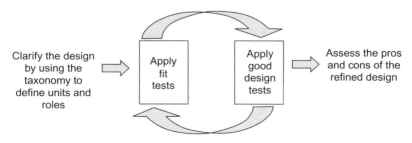

FIGURE 8.3 Testing a Design

Fit Tests

The fit tests are derived from the four drivers of fit described in Chapter 2 (see Figure 2.4 on page 45).

The fit tests are particularly useful in choosing between design concepts. Proposals that do not meet one or more of the fit tests are unlikely to be viable: the best course is usually to abandon the design and try another option. As we discuss the fit tests, we will give particular emphasis to this pass or fail dimension. But the fit tests can also be used to refine and improve a design. We will discuss this aspect of the tests more fully once we have introduced all four tests.

Market Advantage Test

"Does the design allocate sufficient management attention to the operating priorities and intended sources of advantage in each product-market area?"

The purpose of this test is to check that the structure gives sufficient attention to:

- the needs of the customers in each product-market segment; and
- the sources of advantage and major operating initiatives that management believe will help them succeed in each product-market segment.

The market advantage test makes sure that the design is customer-focused. It addresses the degree to which the design will help the organization succeed in its chosen marketplaces.

The test involves the following steps:

1. Insure the design pays sufficient attention to the chosen product-market segments:

   - list the product-market segments the company is targeting;
   - check that there is a market-facing unit dedicated to each important target segment;

- where a dedicated market-facing unit does not exist, decide whether the structure gives sufficient attention to the segment.

A product-market segment is a loose term. It can be used to describe the segment "mass-market cars" or the segment "high-performance hatchbacks". The listing of segments should therefore take account of the business diversity of the part of the company being designed. If the company has a broad spread of businesses, like General Electric (GE), the segment listing might be as broad as "aero-engines", "white goods", "asset-based financial services", etc. If, on the other hand, the design candidate is the financial services division, then the segments would be different financial products, probably further divided by geographic market, such as "aircraft leasing in Europe" or "receivables financing in Mexico".

The target segments will have been defined by the strategy. Hence the listing of segments may involve no more than pulling them off the strategy document. In situations where the target segments are unclear, some prior strategy work will be necessary. If a new design is required, despite an unclear strategy, then the target segments should be defined in a workshop of senior managers.

Having listed the target segments, use the test to decide whether the design pays each segment sufficient attention. If the segment has a market-facing unit dedicated to it, it has sufficient attention. Market-facing units are business units, sub-businesses and overlays. Shared service units can also be market-facing if they have external customers.

If an important target segment does not have a market-facing unit dedicated to it, it may be a knock-out factor causing the design to be rejected. This is, however, a matter of judgment. Different managers may disagree. A target segment that is not addressed by any unit is clearly a knock-out factor. A target segment (e.g. a currently small but growing e-commerce channel) that is addressed by a unit with broader responsibilities is a cause for concern: the segment may not get sufficient attention because managers are distracted by broader responsibilities. A target segment that is addressed by an overlay is also a cause for concern: the managers in the overlay may not have sufficient influence to insure the segment is properly served. Ultimately, however, "sufficient attention" is not a scientific term. The purpose of this part of the test is to insure that managers consider whether the design is sufficiently market-facing. If it is not, some adjustment needs to be made to the design, or it should be abandoned and another chosen.

2. Insure the design pays sufficient attention to the planned sources of competitive advantage and operating initiatives:

- list the sources of advantage and operating initiatives planned for each target segment;
- identify any sources of advantage or operating initiatives that require co-ordination across unit boundaries;
- decide whether the design includes solutions for insuring these sources of advantage and operating initiatives will get sufficient attention.

Sources of advantage are the ingredients of product/ market strategy. A source of advantage may be new product development, closeness to customers, low-cost manufacturing, superior government relationships, etc. If these are not clear, some additional strategy work will be required to clarify the issue. In the meantime, the design team can convene a group of relevant managers and make a stab at defining the necessary information, signaling that the judgments may need confirming before the design is finalized.

Major operating initiatives include things like the launch of a new product, the implementation of a new IT system, the building of new capacity, etc. Every target segment will have some operating initiatives associated with it. Clearly there is an overlap between "sources of competitive advantage" and "operating initiatives": most sources of advantage are achieved through operating initiatives. The value of the two concepts is completeness. With both concepts, all the most important factors relating to the target segment will be recorded.

Once the sources of advantage and operating initiatives have been identified, this part of the test involves looking for situations where co-ordination across unit boundaries will be necessary. For example, a source of advantage in one segment may be superior new product development. If the unit focused on this segment needs to co-ordinate with a central research function in order to develop new products, then the source of advantage requires co-ordination across unit boundaries. Alternatively, if the source of advantage comes from economies of scale in production, it may be necessary to co-ordinate manufacturing across numerous units if they are each focused on small or local segments.

As we have already pointed out (see co-ordination principle, page 52), co-ordination within a unit is easier than across unit boundaries. Hence any source of advantage or operating initiative that requires cross-boundary links should be a cause for concern. The judgment is about whether managers in the new design will pay sufficient attention to the link.

3. Where there are concerns about the effectiveness of links, they should be referred to the difficult links test.

In a complex organization there will be many sources of advantage and many operating initiatives that depend on cross-boundary links. This is what makes the organization complex. The market advantage test is not intended as a detailed audit of each of these links. This is the role of the difficult links test. The purpose of the market advantage test is to make sure that "sufficient attention" has been given to the sources of advantage and operating initiatives: in essence it is about making sure that the units and reporting relationships are broadly in line with the strategy. Inevitably there is an overlap between the market advantage and difficult links tests, but it is a healthy overlap that encourages managers to look at the issues of unit design and links between units with care.

As we pointed out in Chapter 2, organization designs are often not sufficiently based on what is needed for successful strategy implementation. The market advantage test therefore challenges the choice of operational units from the perspective of the marketplace strategies. Its purpose is to make sure that the choice of units reflects the product-market strategies the company has chosen. It can be argued that the definition of the market-facing units is as much a strategy task as an organization-design one; but the purpose of the test is to make sure the marketplace strategies have not been overlooked in the organization design.

As with all the fit tests, there is a high level of overlap between the analyses needed for this test and the work needed to develop design criteria (see Chapter 7, page 229). A design that has been carefully crafted to meet the design criteria will normally "pass" the fit tests without raising awkward issues.

Parenting Advantage Test

"Does the design allocate sufficient attention to the intended sources of added-value and strategic initiatives of the corporate parent?"

The purpose of this test is to insure that the structure gives sufficient attention to the creation of value from:

- the chosen parenting propositions; and
- the planned strategic initiatives.

The parenting advantage test is focused on the corporate and intermediate parent levels in the organization and aims to insure that the design makes it easy for these levels to add value to the operating units.

The analysis involves:

- listing the main parenting propositions and strategic initiatives, and
- judging whether the design gives them sufficient attention.

A parenting proposition is a way in which a parent level adds value to the operating units that report in to that level. It might be "to help with government relations", "to encourage the development of certain kinds of e-commerce", "to provide functional support in areas of corporate core competence, such as research", etc.

Parenting propositions are the ingredients of corporate-level strategy. Often companies do not have clearly articulated propositions, and analysis is needed to identify the parenting propositions. (See box: Defining Parenting Propositions, later in this chapter.)

Strategic initiatives are the major actions planned by corporate management: for example, plans to sell the operations in Portugal; implement a corporate-wide ERP (enterprise resource planning) system; make acquisitions to expand in technology X; and decide whether to outsource IT.

Once the parenting propositions and strategic initiatives have been defined, the design is scanned to see if it gives them "sufficient attention". If there is a parent unit dedicated to the parenting proposition or strategic initiative, sufficient attention is probably not an issue. If, however, the proposition or initiative has been allocated to a parent unit that is also responsible for five or six other major propositions or initiatives, the designer would have cause for concern. If the implementation of a parenting proposition or initiative is shared between a number of parent units, the designer would also have cause for concern. However, as with the market advantage test, sufficient attention is a matter of judgment.

Often managers need to understand the actions that are required to implement a parenting proposition or initiative before they can judge whether the attention is sufficient. If this level of detailed understanding is not available, comparison can be used. Will it be easier to foster knowledge sharing between business units that are part of the same division than if they are spread across different divisions? Will it be easier to create a performance culture if research is decentralized to the business units or located in a core resource unit? Will it be easier to sell the Portuguese operations if they are set up separately or as part of the Spanish unit? Will technology acquisitions be easier if the acquisition team is located in the technology division or at the center?

Another way of making judgments is to involve the managers concerned. Do the managers who are going to lead the implementation of a new ERP system believe that the design will hinder or help them? What do the lower-level managers think? Managers who will have to carry out the operational tasks to insure the new system works in the field are often best placed to make such judgments.

This leads us to a broad point that is relevant for all the tests. Involving middle level and lower-level managers in the judgments is important. In the first place, by giving them a stake in the design process, it helps gain more of their support for the final decisions. In the second place, it is a good way of obtaining valuable information that is expensive, if not impossible, to collect in any other way.

Even where middle managers are involved, judgments are rarely black or white: there are usually different ways of achieving the same initiative. However, the test raises issues that need to be taken into account in the final judgment about the option.

People Test

"Does the design adequately reflect the motivations, strengths, and weaknesses of the available people?"

The purpose of this test is to make sure that the people needed in the organization are both able and willing to make the design work. Since the vast majority of responsibilities will be carried out by managers operating in a self-managed network, co-operation and enthusiasm are critical. Not only do the managers need to have the right skills, they also need to be enthusiastic about the design.

The amount of analysis required by this test will depend on the complexity of the design. In a simple structure, it may be necessary to test only the skills and motivations of a few top managers and the heads of the main units. In a complex organization, on the other hand, it may be necessary to extend the scope: to include managers in corporate functions and managers lower down involved in relationships between units. In general, however, the test involves the following analyses:

- list the members of the top team and judge whether the design fits their skills and preferences, and will gain their commitment;
- identify other individuals with particularly valuable skills, and judge whether the design uses these to advantage;
- list the "pivotal jobs" in the new structure and judge whether the company has or is likely to be able to recruit or develop the skills needed;
- identify any influential managers who are likely to lose status or cherished roles and judge whether they have been appropriately compensated or neutralized; and
- assess the current or likely level of enthusiasm for organization change in general and the new design in particular.

We will now explain each area of judgment in more detail and discuss the assessments that need to be made.

The *top team* can be 2 people or 20. The criterion for inclusion in the top team is membership of the highest level executive committee or equivalent body. These are the individuals who are most important to the design.

Judgments about skills and preferences do not need to be fine-grained. If the CEO is a marketing type and the design has limited her role to performance management, problems are likely to emerge. If the head of finance would prefer to have the finance functions in the new business units reporting directly to him, there will be awkward relationships in this area. If the IT core resource reports to the chief executive officer (CEO) and the chief operating officer (COO) believes this undermines his effectiveness, the design is questionable.

Problems with the top team normally require a design that fits their skills and preferences more closely. We have often encountered organizations where one half of the executive committee is pulling one way and the other half is resisting. The result is nearly always unsatisfactory. The only alternative to choosing a different design is to change the membership of the top team – which is not usually a practical proposition.

All organizations contain some *particularly valuable individuals*. Sometimes they are members of the top team, but not always. The judgment is to identify whether these individuals have jobs that capitalize on and extend their skills. If a few individuals seem to be under-exploited, managers can probably make small adjustments to improve the design. If large numbers are involved, then a new design is probably needed.

Pivotal jobs are those outside the top team that are particularly important to the success of the design. They normally include the heads of all the important units, and managers in functions that are involved in critical cross-unit relationships. The judgment is not only about whether the required skills exist today; it is also about whether the skills can be developed and sustained in the future. It involves assessing how far existing skills need to be changed, the availability of skills in the outside market, and the type of career paths needed to sustain and develop the skills in the longer term. A design that cannot be staffed with competent managers should be abandoned.

All new designs create *losers*. The purpose of this part of the test is to make sure that sufficient attention has been given to the down-side of creating losers: they can become cynics and undermine the new design. The analysis requires two difficult judgments. First, losers with influence need to be distinguished from those whose support is less important. Second, the degree to which these influential losers have been compensated or neutralized must be estimated. Neither decision is easy. So long as thought has been given to the problem of losers, however, managers can reduce the danger of resistance to the new design.

The final part of the people test concerns the *mood for change*. Unless the majority of managers are in favor of some change, the new design is less likely to be successful. This part of the test is only rarely a knock-out factor because, with appropriate propaganda and argument – and providing the design is a good one – views can be changed. By considering managers' views, it is possible to avoid launching a new design on an unwilling organization. Knowing that the test will be faced also encourages managers to prepare those not involved in the project for what is coming.

Feasibility Test

"Does the design take account of the constraints that may make the proposal unworkable?"

The purpose of the feasibility test is to make sure that the proposed structure can be implemented. Like the people test, the feasibility test can involve a great deal of analysis or very little, depending on the number of constraining factors.

The analysis involves:

- scanning the environment to identify constraints;
  - legal and government issues;
  - institutional and stakeholder issues;
  - other external issues, such as local culture;
  - internal issues, such as internal culture or systems;
- testing the robustness of the design against each constraint.

It is not appropriate here to describe all the analyses that can be done in support of this test. We will, however, explain each category of constraint and comment on some of the judgments involved.

Legal and government issues include a range of constraints imposed by governments, regulators, and the law. In some countries, it is not possible to do business without setting up a separate joint venture with a local partner. This clearly imposes constraints on the choice of design. In the utilities industry, regulators often insist on keeping regulated and non-regulated business activities in separate organizational units, limiting the ability to solve co-ordination issues by creating one unit. Although legal and governmental issues are important, they are not usually a dominant influence on the design.

On the other hand, *institutional and stakeholder* issues may have a big impact on organization design. Companies with dominant shareholders will have to pay due regard to their preferences. Companies in industries with powerful unions, like the British printing industry in the 1980s, will need to pay particular attention to this relationship. The stock exchange imposes some rules on its members, such as those concerning minority shareholders. These rules discourage companies from choosing to invite minority stakes in parts of the company. In situations where a minority shareholder might provide additional insulation for a unit requiring a specialist culture, the rules act as a constraint.

Internal issues include corporate culture and broad capabilities. IT systems often constrain organization design. Managers may want to move from a country-based structure to a product structure, but the current systems may not be able to report performance by product. The constraint of legacy systems has been particularly severe in financial services. Another common internal constraint is culture. Some organizations find it easy to do things that others find difficult. While there is no commonly accepted way of understanding a culture, we have found it useful to identify the "root causes" of an organization's strengths and weaknesses. For example, in an organization with a strong performance culture but poor co-ordination between units, the root cause may be an incentive system that gives large bonuses for unit performance but not for co-operative behavior. Any new design that relies on cross-unit processes will need to change the incentive system and recognise that managers may find it hard to play by the new rules.

The feasibility test typically raises a number of implementation issues. Some will be serious strikes against the design, such as a legal problem or a systems limitation. Others will be more minor, such as the need to fine-tune the company's incentive system, or set up a separate unit in Nigeria to comply with government rules. The test is useful in flushing out these implementation issues.

At what point do feasibility problems become knock-out factors? If in doubt, it is best to record the problems and make sure they are taken into account in the final assessment. However, comparative analysis is also useful. If it is possible to design a structure that has the same advantages minus the feasibility problems, then these problems are knock-out factors.

Summary of Fit Tests

In order to keep the explanation of the fit tests to a minimum, we have focused on whether the test is passed or failed. We have shown that it is possible to knock out a design based on the results of only one test. However, usually managers will want to run through all of the fit tests at least briefly before deciding to reject a design concept.

For example, a major utility company was considering a new organization that would move the company from a functional structure to a business unit structure. The top management team wanted to drive commercial thinking down into the organization on the presumption that this would cause managers in charge of generation plants or transmission wires to be more commercial about their maintenance and capital spending plans. Their preferred structure was one that divided the organization into five business units – trading, generation, transmission, delivery, and supply.

After putting the proposed design through the tests, they decided to delay their decision until they had resolved issues that emerged in three of the fit tests. The feasibility test raised issues about management information. The current accounting systems could produce profitability data by jurisdiction but not by business unit. Moreover, as they discussed possible solutions to the problem, they realized that it would be difficult to devise a transfer pricing system that did not bias the commercial judgments. They felt that it would be better to wait until the systems and transfer pricing arrangements had been developed before they changed the structure. This concern was reinforced by the people test. Not only were the chief finance and chief legal officers resisting the move because of concerns about accountability, the managers who would be in charge of the new businesses were not wholly enthusiastic. Moreover, the CEO had doubts about the ability of these managers to cope with the ambiguities that the new structure would create. More work was needed to prepare the individuals and the skills before a change would make sense.

The third concern came from the parenting advantage test. The initial plan was to set up the new businesses and gradually give them more power and authority as they developed. But the parenting advantage test demonstrated that no parenting propositions had been defined. "Based on the current logic, we will gradually give authority to the businesses until we spin them off," explained the head of strategic planning.

After debating the tests, the company's executive committee concluded that the proposed new structure should be reconsidered or delayed, and they defined an agenda of issues that needed to be addressed over the following six months. In fact, the issues took longer than anticipated to resolve and the company chose in the end to move towards a business unit structure in phases. A division with responsibility for buying fuel and wholesaling power was set up after seven months and, after another six months, the rest of the organization was split between generation and distribution. The fit tests had helped to significantly improve the organization plans.

The fit tests are not only about deciding whether or not to use a new design. They can also be used to help refine the design. In Chapter 2, for example, we described how Cargill used the parenting advantage test to refine the role of the corporate center in its new organization. Clearly, if refinements can be found that will address problems raised by the tests, they should be added to the design. Often, however, issues raised by the fit tests are hard to resolve, and so act as knock-out factors.

The fit tests are the first line of attack on a proposed design. They question whether the design is broadly fit for purpose, given the resources available and the opportunities that are at the center of the strategy. Once a design has passed the fit tests, there is a reasonable chance that it can be made to work. However, the fit tests will need to be revisited after the good design tests have been completed. The structure may have been adjusted in ways that alter some of the earlier judgments. So the fit tests are often applied twice, first to assess whether the design concept makes sense, then to insure that the embellished design still fits the strategy, people, and constraints (see Figure 8.3).

Good Design Tests

The good design tests are drawn from the good design principles in Chapter 3 (see Figure 3.3 on page 93). As we have already explained, these tests are most helpful in refining a design concept and clarifying its strengths and weaknesses. Where a test raises an issue, the result will normally be to add to or refine the design in order to reduce or eliminate the negative impact. The tests are as much an aid to the design process as a stress challenge to a completed design.

Difficult Links Test

"Does the organization design call for any "difficult links", co-ordination benefits that will be hard to achieve on a networking basis, and does it include "solutions" that will ease the difficulty?"

The purpose of the difficult links test is to make sure that all the important links in the design work effectively. It involves:

- listing all the important links between units;
- assessing whether the links are likely to be "difficult";
- developing "co-ordination solutions" where possible; and
- deciding whether any of the links are "unworkable" and, if so, whether they constitute a knock-out factor.

The analysis carried out for the market advantage test is a useful starting point for identifying difficult links. The test will have listed the sources of competitive advantage and the operating initiatives that need to be managed across unit boundaries. In addition to these lists, it is useful to consider the analysis from the parenting advantage test. The parenting propositions and the strategic initiatives can both point to important areas of value creation that may involve cross-unit links. Finally, it is useful to examine each of the major units in the structure, and list the important links each has with others.

Developing a list of important links is a demanding task. In a complex situation there may be many hundreds of links. There is little alternative to a diligent scanning of the relationships between all important units in the structure, but the checklist shown below can be helpful.

1. **Shared know-how**: The benefits associated with the sharing of knowledge and competence across units. This may involve sharing of best practice in business processes, leveraging expertise in functional areas, pooling knowledge about how to succeed in separate geographic regions, sharing product or market know-how, and so on. The emphasis that many companies give to leveraging core competencies and sharing best practices reflects the importance of this type of link.

2. **Shared tangible resources**: The benefits from economies of scale and elimination of duplicated effort when physical assets and resources are shared – for example, when businesses use a common manufacturing facility or research laboratory, or share personnel.

3. **Pooled negotiating power**: The cost or quality benefits that can be gained from purchasing scale. It also covers the

benefits from joint negotiation with other stakeholders such as customers, governments, universities, etc.

4. **Co-ordinated strategies**: The benefits that arise from aligning the strategies of two or more units – for example, by reducing competition between units (allocating export markets) or co-ordinating reactions to competitors (multipoint competition).

5. **Vertical integration**: Co-ordinating the flow of products or services from one unit to another. Benefits come from lower inventory costs, shared product development, better capacity utilization and improved market access.

6. **Combined new business creation**: The creation of new businesses by combining know-how from different units, by extracting activities from different units to put into a new unit, and by internal joint ventures or alliances between units.

Deciding which links are "difficult" is also hard. The key question for each link is: "Given the roles allocated to the units involved, will self-managed networking between the units produce a good outcome?" In other words, are the role definitions sufficient guidance for the managers involved or will they find the link difficult without more guidance? In Chapter 3 (see page 63), we described at some length the type of reason that can make a link difficult. Below, we have converted these ideas into a checklist for use in the analysis.[2]

There are four reasons why a link between two or more units may not proceed smoothly on a networking basis:

- **Perception blockages**: The managers concerned may not spot the benefits available due to:
  - parochialism or inertia;
  - lack of appropriate contacts or information;
  - lack of experience, skill, or perspective.

- **Evaluation biases**: The managers concerned may misjudge the costs or benefits due to:

- previous experiences that bias assessment;
- inappropriate evaluation methods or processes;
- misperception of corporate priorities.

- **Misaligned motivations**: The managers concerned may not be motivated to give attention to the link due to:
  - local or personal incentives and interests;
  - frictions, rivalries, and mistrust;
  - hard-to-compensate win/lose issues.

- **Capability limitations**: The managers concerned may not have the capability to implement the link appropriately due to:
  - lack of experience, skills, or resources;
  - need for clearer collaboration processes;
  - organizational constraints.

Once a difficult link has been identified, the question is whether some change or addition to the existing design concept might ease the problem. For example, Citibank's structure, discussed in Chapter 4, involves customer-based units working closely with product and geographic units. Recognizing that some of these links would be difficult, Citibank has designed some process solutions, such as a process for global customer account planning. To help these processes work, Citibank also supports a "customer-comes-first" behavior norm for all the units and has made sure that parent managers are able and willing to get involved and arbitrate over disputes. As a result, a structure that looks at first sight as if it might fall foul of the difficult links test is able to pass satisfactorily. Equally, BP's peer group process, also described in Chapter 4, provides a means of overcoming co-ordination difficulties.

To illustrate the analysis needed to identify solutions to difficult links, we can take a typical example: one between a shared service unit and the business units it is serving. If the design constrains the relationship, insisting, for example, that the business units have no alternative but to get their service from the shared service unit, a difficult link may be created. If the service does not meet the requirements of the business units or if the demands of the business units are unreasonable, the units will have a hard time resolving their differences. In terms of the above checklist, there are misaligned motivations and capability limitations due to the constraints on the relationship between the units, which lead to divergent motivations and reduce the ability of the units to resolve their differences.

When the test brings to light a situation like this, some of the types of change or addition in Figure 8.2 can be used to consider ways of solving the problem. These will be discussed more fully in Table 8.1 overleaf.

The list of ideas in Table 8.1 is no more than a list of possible solutions; the sort of list that might emerge from a brainstorming session. Some of the ideas have more potential for smoothing the link than others. But the table illustrates the range of solutions that should be considered when deciding which additions or refinements to make to the design. Managers often presume that the solution to a difficult link must be a co-ordination mechanism. In reality, there are many different ways of solving the problem. Our checklist helps insure that managers consider the full range.

As part of this research, we wanted to produce a framework for matching co-ordination solutions to types of difficult link. However, solutions seemed to be situation-specific. For most difficult links, it is possible to think of five to ten different ways of resolving the difficulty. Choosing the way that will work best in a particular organization depends on the specifics of the people involved, their skill levels and motivations, the history of previous experiences with similar kinds of links, and so on. Rather than trying to benchmark best practice or deduce the answer from some co-ordination framework, we advise managers to focus on the reason why the link is difficult and, using our checklist, generate a range of possible solutions.

Having developed a list of ideas, managers must choose one (or more likely a combination) and graft it on to the design. For example, in Table 8.1, let us suppose that the chosen solution

TABLE 8.1 Ideas for Easing the Shared Service Link

Types of addition or change	Ideas
Modify without changing unit roles	
Refine the allocation of responsibilities	The business unit could have the responsibility for setting the price for the service (the price the unit is prepared to pay) and the shared service unit could have responsibility for deciding whether to do the work. This would make it possible for the service unit to retain the business, though potentially at the expense of making losses (*probably not workable*).
Refine reporting relationships and processes	With other units, the business unit could sit on a board that governs the shared service, or the shared service could be an official joint venture between the business units. This would place the onus on the business units to change the management of the shared service if it was not delivering the goods (*promising*).
	The management of the relationship between the shared service and the business units could be defined as a parenting proposition and a parent appointed with the skills and time to make it work (*needed for a solution that requires arbitration or parent involvement*).
Refine lateral relationships and processes	Design a process for negotiating service-level agreements between the businesses and the shared service, with provision for arbitration by senior managers (*might be expensive in management time*).
Refine accountabilities	Devise a performance measure for the shared service based on the expressed satisfaction of the business units (*probably necessary anyway*).

Define skill requirements and incentives

Modify criteria for people selection	Make sure that the person running the shared service has the best interests of the businesses at heart or is an individual whose crusade is improving shared services (*makes sense if we can find someone with these attitudes*).
Define skill development needs	Design a skill development program for the shared service manager, to insure that she understands the main ways in which the shared service can be improved and the priorities of the business units (*necessary for most of the solutions suggested*).
Develop incentives	Make sure that a significant part of the compensation of the shared service head is based on the level of business satisfaction. Also include a reward for the business heads based on how good, in quality and cost terms, the shared service is. This latter reward will encourage the business heads to work with the shared service to improve it, rather than rely only on tough negotiations (*seems sensible*).

Shape informal context

Define norms for behavior, values, or social context	Define a norm of behavior that is based on what is best for the company as a whole. Resolve all issues using this criterion (*desirable provided it is compatible with unit accountability*).
Clarify leadership style/skills needed	Make sure that the leaders to whom the service unit and business units report are knowledgable about the economics of the service unit and the needs of the business units, and/or make sure that the leaders are wise arbitrators, with no biases on this issue (*makes sense if leaders have these skills, but probably not worth changing them if they don't*).

was to set the service up as an informal joint venture, governed by the business units. The units' performance would be measured against satisfaction levels as well as unit costs. This solution would then be added to the design concept.

Choosing the best solution involves a combination of intuition about what will work in the organization and a quick review of the other tests. For example, the unofficial joint venture solution might create a problem with some of the other tests. It might reduce the ability of the shared service to develop a specialist culture because of domination by the business units. It might reduce the parent's ability to create a performance culture because of the shared responsibilities. It might reduce flexibility, because the joint venture partners would need to agree to any major change. The final choice is not a scientific one. It is a matter of balancing the pros and cons to arrive at the best available solution.

The final part of the analysis sequence is to judge whether the chosen solution is "good enough". Managers might conclude that none of the ideas will significantly ease the relationship between the service unit and the businesses. For example, there may be a long-running dispute between the service and the businesses, and previous attempts to solve it have not worked. When this happens, the link becomes a knock-out factor.

Some types of links are very hard to find solutions for. As we explained in Chapter 3 (see page 65), when the link requires frequent judgment calls from the next level up or involves a win/lose trade-off that is difficult to compensate, it will be hard to find a refinement to the design that solves the problem. The only solution is to change the structure so that the link is incorporated within a single unit. This amounts to rejecting the design concept and choosing another option.

But, when is a link important enough to become a knock-out factor? Again, there is no definitive answer. It is a knock-out factor if management believes that there is another structure available which will solve the problem and is not significantly worse on some other dimension. As a result, it is often wise to scan the options and the other tests before declaring a link to be a knock-out factor. With experience, we have found that it is relatively easy to judge when a problem is a knock-out factor or simply a weakness that can be acknowledged in the final assessment of the design. If in doubt, those with less experience should treat the problem as a weakness rather than a knock-out factor.

Specialist Cultures Test

"Do any 'specialist cultures', units with cultures that need to be different from sister units and the layer above, have sufficient protection from the influence of the dominant culture?"

The purpose of the specialist cultures test is to identify parts of the organization that need more independence than the design currently allows.

The test involves:

- listing all units with cultures that need to be different from the dominant culture of the company or the division to which they belong;
- assessing whether the specialist culture is in danger of being dominated;
- adding to or changing the design so as to provide more protection where needed; and
- deciding whether any of the "exposed" specialist cultures are knock-out factors.

Specialist cultures exist when the critical success factors of a unit are different from those of its sister and parent units. Hence, the first step in the analysis is to note units that are different from those to which they are closely connected. The next step is to examine the critical success factors of the units to understand the nature of the differences. For example, a speciality chemicals unit that is part of a bulk chemicals division would be a candidate. An analysis of the differences in critical success factors would quickly confirm that the speciality unit needs a specialist culture (see Table 8.2)

Specialist cultures are common. For example, a shared service unit normally has critical success factors different from the business units it is serving. An overlay often has critical success factors different from the business units it is interacting with. A quick scan is usually enough to identify where issues of specialist culture exist.

Specialist units are in danger of being dominated, if the level they report to and the units they most frequently interact with have critical success factors that are both different from theirs and similar to each other. In these circumstances, the dominant culture can overwhelm the culture of the specialist unit. If the specialist unit is in a division of other units, each of which has its own unique culture and operating priorities, then there is less chance of domination, because there is no dominant culture. If, however, the unit is a speciality chemicals unit in a division of bulk chemicals units reporting to an intermediate parent staffed by managers from the bulk units, then there is high potential for domination.

Once a specialist culture is considered to be at risk, the next step is to think of ways of providing the unit with more protection without changing the basic design. For example, a senior manager might be put in charge of the unit, making it easier for the unit to resist inappropriate external influence. Alternatively, the unit might be given greater autonomy, such as freedom from the human resource policies that are imposed on the other units.

The checklist on page 252 can be used to help generate a range of ideas.

TABLE 8.2 Critical Success Factors Analysis

Bulk chemicals	Speciality chemicals
Feedstock costs	Customer relationships
Operating costs	Technical service skills
Asset utilization	Applications selling skills
Scale	Product development
Location near a port	Location near feedstocks or customers
Regional	Global

- More responsibilities can be allocated to the unit, helping to insulate it from its parent and sister units. Ultimately the unit can become an independent company with the parent holding only an investment stake in it, and having little more influence than a shareholder.
- The unit can report to a different layer in the hierarchy.
- Accountabilities can be focused on bottom-line measures so that the unit has more freedom to act in whatever way it chooses, so long as the bottom-line targets are met.
- Parenting propositions can be carefully screened for their effect on the unit. Those that could have negative side-effects can be dropped as far as this unit is concerned.
- The managers in the unit can be appointed for their independent attitudes, insuring that they resist inappropriate impositions.
- Managers in the unit can be given particularly powerful unit-dependent incentives, encouraging them to focus on what is good for the unit rather than seeking to fit in with the dominant culture.
- Parent managers and managers in sister units can be educated on the business model of the unit so that they are more sensitive to the unit's special needs.
- Parent managers can be selected for their knowledge of the nature of the specialist unit, or for their hands-off style.
- The norms of behavior and values relating to this unit can be made explicit, and the differences with the dominant culture exposed.

As this list shows, it is possible to generate a number of different ways of providing protection for a specialist unit. The final step in the analysis, therefore, is to choose some of the ideas to add to the design, or conclude that none of the solutions will work. In the latter case, the risk of domination becomes a knock-out factor, and another design concept should be developed.

In Chapter 9, we discuss in some detail the ways in which a company we call ESD handled specialist culture issues in designing some new overlay units.

Redundant Hierarchy Test

"Are all levels in the hierarchy and all responsibilities retained by higher levels based on a knowledge and competence advantage?"

The purpose of the redundant hierarchy test is to insure that the parent levels in the hierarchy above that of the operating units (business units, shared service units, core resource units, overlays, and project units), in other words the parent and intermediate parents, have clear value-adding roles and the skills and resources needed to execute them:

- identify each level in the hierarchy above the operating units and list the functions that are part of the level;
- for each level, identify the parenting propositions ;
- where the parenting propositions are weak, or there are concerns about the knowledge or resources in the "layer", try making changes and additions that solve the problem; and
- finally, decide if any of the hierarchy issues are knock-out factors.

Identifying the levels in the hierarchy involves tracking the reporting relationships from the operating units to the corporate center. Sometimes there is only one level of parenting. Sometimes there are several levels, although usually not more than three. In a large international company there may be as many as 20 intermediate parent units. In a small geographically-focused company there may be no intermediate parent units at all.

Once the parenting levels and units have been identified, the functions or major areas of responsibility within each unit need to be listed. In some cases, the unit is little more than a line manager and a finance executive. In others, it may include a number of functions, each staffed with many employees.

With the benefit of this data, the remainder of the analysis is designed to expose parenting layers that do not have convincing parenting propositions, or have too much or too little functional support. First, articulate the parenting propositions for each parenting level. The list of parenting propositions developed for the parenting advantage test is the ideal starting point. Each level can be assessed against the list. It often proves hard to identify parenting propositions for some levels. Sometimes this will be because the level is a span-breaker and is helping to execute the propositions of the level above. At other times it will be because of a design flaw: an additional level has been added without sufficient thought (see box: Defining Parenting Propositions).

Defining Parenting Propositions

A parenting proposition is a statement about why actions by the parent are needed to create some value and what, in broad terms, the actions will be.

For example:

"The technologies of the new economy have created new opportunities and threats that are disrupting many markets. Our units are so focused on driving operating performance improvements that they are likely to underinvest in analyzing and exploring e-business issues. By engaging them in an e-business planning process and providing support through our corporate alliance with Oracle, we expect to be able to improve their response to these new opportunities and threats."

There are five broad categories of parenting proposition:

Select propositions involve creating value by acquiring units or people for less than they are worth or disposing of activities for more than they are worth.

Build propositions involve helping units significantly expand their size and scope of activity, for example by helping with globalization and product range extension, or by raising growth ambitions.

Stretch propositions involve helping units significantly improve costs, quality, or profitability, for example by setting stretching targets, providing benchmarks, or intervening to raise performance levels.

Link propositions involve helping units to work together in ways that they would find difficult if left to themselves, for example by facilitating co-ordination, centralizing activities or providing knowledge management support.

Leverage propositions involve finding ways to exploit a central resource, such as a brand, a relationship, a skill, or a patent, in new markets or businesses.

These five categories are useful areas to consider when defining parenting propositions. The key, however, is to think through in detail the factors that cause an opportunity to exist in the first place and the parenting skills and actions needed to help the organization address the opportunity. It is important to keep in mind the requirement that the parent has a knowledge and competence advantage. Parenting propositions must be built around a logic that explains why the parent is better placed than the units to contribute.

In our experience, managers are much too easily satisfied with parenting propositions that do not add significant value. For example, a frequently cited parenting proposition is "the provision of wise, objective council on strategy and major decisions." Undoubtedly this does add value, but not usually enough to cover the inevitable costs and down-sides of having an extra layer. To cover these costs, a parenting proposition needs to be able to increase the performance of the reporting units by at least 10%. Using this crude definition of when a convincing parenting proposition exists, redundant hierarchy judgments become easier. It is worth noting that the 10% criterion is a powerful logic against having many layers. With three layers above the business unit, the total parenting added value needs to be at least 30%!

Another problem is that a level may have too much or too little resource to execute its propositions. The knowledge and competence of the level may also be inappropriate. For example, a span breaker is unlikely to need any supporting functions, normally drawing on those of the level above. In contrast, an intermediate parent responsible for Europe, trying to create added value by co-ordinating manufacturing, managing pan-European customers, and integrating back office functions, will need a lot of resource, knowledge, and competence. To be effective, the parent responsible for Europe needs to have skills and resources in manufacturing, major account management, and back office integration, as well as functional support in areas such as finance and HR.

This step in the analysis – identifying problems – requires a good deal of experience using the parenting proposition concept. It also requires experience in judging what level of competence and resource is needed to execute a given proposition. Fortunately, the analysis does not call for fine-grained judgments. The objective is to spot major problems, not fine-tune minor issues. We are looking for redundant parenting or badly designed parenting levels where either there is no parenting proposition or the proposition is not matched by the resources allocated.

If the test identifies a problem with one or more parenting layers, the next step is to try to improve the design in a way that solves the problem. The problem is normally a knock-out factor if there are no convincing parenting propositions. However, before jumping to conclusions, it is worth considering some alternative parenting propositions. A workshop with the units reporting into the layer, including managers from the layer, is a powerful way of confronting the issue.

If the problem is a concern about skills or resources, the checklist from page 252 can be used to stimulate creative solutions. For example, extra functions can be added, or redundant functions removed. Working groups of managers drawn from the businesses can be set up to provide additional skills or resources. Processes of interaction between the parent and the units can be designed around the skills available.

When these remedies are not enough, the methods for implementing the parenting proposition can be changed. For example, a proposition to create value from developing a core competence in marketing can be implemented by setting up a central marketing function at one extreme or by fostering a network of relationships between marketing professionals at the other extreme. One of these alternatives may fit the skills of parent managers best.

In one company we worked with, the design involved appointing two senior vice-presidents (SVPs) to oversee each of the company's two main business groupings. This would free the CEO to spend more time on new business development. The design, however, failed the redundant hierarchy test: no parenting propositions had been defined for the SVP layer.

One solution was to decentralize one or more of the CEO's parenting propositions to the SVP layer. For example, the CEO had been effective at driving a performance culture through the company's planning and budget processes. This parenting proposition could be delegated to the SVPs, a solution which was favored by the SVPs, one of whom wanted to move his offices away from the corporate headquarters. The CEO, however, was reluctant, believing that his involvement in budgeting and planning was essential. An alternative solution was to define the SVPs as span breakers, whose role was to help the CEO execute the corporate-level parenting propositions rather than create an additional layer in the structure. The company chose the second solution, which meant preventing the SVPs from building their own staffs or moving out of the corporate headquarters.

By using the redundant hierarchy test, many companies have been able to cut out layers of management, downsize corporate and divisional functions, and refocus the remaining parent-level managers on responsibilities that add more value.

Accountability Test

"Does the design facilitate the creation of a control process for each unit that is appropriate to the unit's responsibilities, economical to implement, and motivating for the managers in the unit?"

The purpose of the accountability test is to make sure that all units have effective accountabilities that are low in cost and highly motivating.

The test involves the following analyses:

- For each unit, which factors exist that may hinder the creation of an effective control process?
    - Does the unit have any lateral relationships that are not self-correcting?
    - Are there any important dimensions of performance that cannot be assessed with "appropriate" measures?
    - Does the parent have sufficient feel and status to rely on more subjective, informal controls?
- For each factor, look for refinements and adjustments to the design, such as changes to unit responsibilities, design of lateral relationships, improvements to the skills of the parent, or the choice of performance measures, that will make it easier to create an effective control process.
- If refinements and adjustments cannot be found, the test may be a knock-out, and an alternative design concept may need to be chosen.

A common cause of accountability issues comes from lateral relationships that are not self-correcting. The lateral relationships surrounding each unit need to be examined to identify those which involve shared responsibilities imposed by the structure. The key signal of these "imposed-shared responsibilities" is that the units cannot agree to disagree: they are obliged by the structure to work together. Imposed-shared responsibilities prevent units from putting pressure on each other to change their behavior or improve their performance, since neither side can walk away.

Imposed-shared responsibilities occur when senior managers make it mandatory for units to collaborate. For example, overlay units are required to influence business units, acting as a pressure group to advance their interests. In a company with global business units and country overlays, country managers cannot act independently of the global businesses. Equally the global businesses cannot ignore the pressures from country managers. Imposed-shared responsibilities like these are also characteristic of core resource units, project units, and sub-businesses. All these types of units are typically required to collaborate with sister units. Shared service units' relationships with other units are also sometimes set up on a mandatory use basis. Where shared responsibilities are imposed, it is easy for each unit to argue that performance problems are caused by the other units: neither party can be held fully accountable for the outcome.

There are a number of ways to reduce the impact of imposed-shared relationships. For example, overlay units may be given power over certain decisions. A product overlay may have power over development spending or use of the brand. A country overlay may have power over the local marketing budget. Core resource and shared service units can be set up on a voluntary use basis or they can operate as a joint venture owned by the units they serve. The result of reducing imposed-shared relationships is to increase the degree of self-correction and improve accountability.

However, self-correcting relationships are not always possible or optimum. Sometimes, as argued in Chapters 4 and 5, the best way to create value is to design a relationship that requires units to work together. In this situation, accountability is achieved by developing performance measures that enable the parent to track how well the relationship is working. For example, in a relationship between a category unit set up as an overlay and retail business units, measures such as customer satisfaction, stock-outs, wastage, and gross margin can be used to judge whether or not the relationship is improving performance. Furthermore, business units can be asked to assess the contribution of the category overlay units, and vice versa. Such assessments are not always objectively measurable, but provide some basis for judging how well the different units are working together.

The second major accountability issue therefore concerns the extent to which there are important dimensions of performance for any units that cannot be assessed with "appropriate" performance measures, using our Chapter 3 definition of appropriate (i.e. relevant, objectively-measurable, outcome-oriented, benchmarkable, few in number, clear, and economical to collect). If such measures are not readily available, the test challenges parent managers to use their ingenuity in searching for new, creative, and insightful performance measures that will be more appropriate. Companies such as Citibank and ABB have invested large amounts of time and money in identifying suitable balanced scorecard measures of performance for their units and in creating the information systems to make them operational. But for some units, such as an R&D core resource unit, it will always be hard to find appropriate performance measures (see Chapter 5), and disentangling the respective contributions of different units that are required to work together is not easy.

In situations where there are imposed-shared responsibilities and/or where it is difficult to find appropriate performance measures, parent managers have to rely on a more subjective and informal judgment of how well units are performing. This means that the parent-level managers must know enough about the units and have a good enough feel for their operations to make these judgments soundly, and in a way which will be trusted by the unit managers. This level of knowledge is comparatively rare. Also, informal control processes can be costly, with excessive demands on management time to acquire the necessary familiarity with the units. Only parent managers with a depth of relevant personal experience are likely to be able to exercise control cost-effectively in this way. The last component of the accountability test, therefore, concerns the availability of parent managers with these skills.

The design refinements that the accountability test can suggest correspond to the three areas in which issues can arise:

1. Clarification of responsibilities to reduce imposed-shared relationships and improve self-correction.

2. Fresh thinking about more appropriate performance measures.

3. Review of reporting relationships and parent management appointments, so that the parent managers of units with difficult accountability issues have a better feel for the operations reporting to them.

Conversely, accountability issues can become knock-out factors when the unit concerned is important, self-correction is weak, appropriate measures of performance cannot be devised, and the parent manager does not have the experience to judge when the unit is underperforming. When these conditions exist, the design is sufficiently flawed that it should probably be abandoned and another chosen.

Flexibility Test

"Will the design help the development of new strategies and be flexible enough to adapt to future changes?"

The purpose of the flexibility test is to insure that the design is "fit for the future". There are two key questions to ask:

- Does the design provide mechanisms for exploring new opportunities (or new resources) that might be overlooked by the existing structure?
- Will the organization be able to adapt to changes that may occur?

Innovating new ways to create value and adapting to change are two of the most frequently mentioned concerns of managers in charge of large organizations. Unfortunately there is no best practice answer to either concern. The flexibility test can, therefore, only be about whether some allowance has been made for innovation and change, not about whether the design incorporates the latest best practice ideas.

1. Insure the design has mechanisms for exploring new opportunities:
   - List some examples of new opportunities that the company might want to explore.
   - Consider whether the current structure would make for "fair exploration" of each opportunity.
   - If problems exist, consider ways of adding to the design that will provide solutions.

- If solutions cannot be found, decide whether this is a knock-out factor.

Deciding which new opportunities to consider is an imprecise task. Almost by definition, the analyst is unlikely to predict correctly which new opportunities the company should pursue. In these circumstances, choosing the list of new opportunities for testing is more about creating a demanding list than an accurate one.

The best way forward is to use a small workshop including a diagonal slice of managers drawn from parts of the organization that are knowledgable about products, markets, or resources. This group can be asked to create a list of 10 or so new opportunities that are not in the strategy but are typical of the new opportunities that the organization might face in the future.

It is not important at this stage that the list of new opportunities is particularly realistic. It will be a stronger list if it contains some items that managers immediately acknowledge with, "Yes; that is something we might consider in the future." But the list also needs to contain some "off the wall" ideas that may seem improbable.

With a list of new opportunities, managers need to decide whether the current design is likely to ignore them or whether mechanisms exist that will insure the opportunities are considered. This analysis is particularly hard. It depends on second-guessing what people would be most likely to do at some hypothetical point in the future. Nevertheless, it is normally possible to make rough and ready judgments. Will the current structure be highly supportive, neutral, or highly negative? For example, let us take the case of a car company. We will assume that the company is organized geographically with product development teams and other functions like human resources at the center and in each of three decentralized regions – Europe, Asia, and the Americas. One item on the new opportunity list is a new product idea – "a motorized office". It would not be difficult for us to conclude that the design would be "highly supportive" to this new opportunity. Any of the four product development teams could champion the idea, and the geographic structure would not hinder it.

On the other hand, an idea to change the way managers are compensated, moving, for example, from 100% salary to 50% bonus might fall in the "highly negative" category. Central human resource policies combined with regional differences would make this idea difficult to address. It would be necessary to get the agreement of all four human resource functions to be able to change the contract or even to experiment with variations.

For those new opportunities in the highly negative category, it is worth considering whether additions or changes could be made to the design. Because the new opportunities are speculative, the changes to the design would need to reduce the organization's natural resistance to the new opportunity without reducing its effectiveness on any of the other tests.

3M's multiple sources of seed capital for new products is one example of a mechanism that reduces an organization's natural resistance. A strategic planning system that allocates time to explore new opportunities is another. A policy of setting up multi-functional teams to assess and propose new ideas is a third possible solution. Some of the latest research in this area[3] recommends the appointment of opportunity "magnets". These are individuals with a roaming brief to spot new opportunities and act as magnets to pull together the organizational support required to move the projects forward.

2. Insure the design will be able to adapt to changes that may occur:

- List five or ten important changes that the organization may face in the next three to five years.

- Identify those parts of the organization that are likely to be most difficult to change.

- Blend the analysis from the previous two points and decide whether significant problems exist.

- Try to find additions or adjustments to the design that solve the problems.

- Where adjustments cannot be found, decide whether this is a knock-out factor.

We need say little about the first part of this analysis. Scenario analysis is an excellent generator of possible futures. One other source of ideas about what may change is the design itself. Any part of the design that has involved a "hard-to-make" trade-off is one where subsequent learning may cause managers to want to change their minds.

Identifying those parts of the design that will be hard to change is more tricky. The board, the executive committee, and any dominant units are normally hard to change. This is due in part to personal loyalties, in part to visibility, and in part to the power bases that senior managers defend. The result is that the topmost structure and the largest units are often the hardest part of an organization to change at short notice. An organization with many small units and no "barons" on the board is usually easier to change than one with a few dominant units, all of whom have board representation.

Rigidity also occurs where units have been woven into a tight web with many processes, policies, and co-ordination mechanisms. Because the units are no longer "plug-and-play" modules, any change can mean redesigning the whole web, something managers take on with reluctance. It is useful, therefore, to identify those parts of the design that are more web-like and less modular.

The third step in the analysis is to blend the work from the first two steps. Would any of the ten "important changes" require adjustments to the top structure or to those parts of the organization that are less modular? Does the rigidity in the current design make the company vulnerable to any likely area of future change? Positive answers to either of these questions point to potential problems.

With a problem defined, managers can use the checklist from page 252 to search for solutions that resolve or mitigate the problem. If no reasonable solution can be generated and the risk is viewed as high, the problem becomes a knock-out factor.

Readiness to change is not primarily a structural issue. More important are the attitudes of the managers concerned. If they are comfortable redrawing responsibilities or power structures and recognize the need for this, change is easy. If they do not, change is difficult. We should therefore take account of the type of people who will populate the organization. Where change is likely to be needed, the people in key appointments need to be change-friendly.

At companies like HP, reorganizations have been so frequent and job changes so much part of the culture that managers have become particularly flexible: they do not expect to hold a given set of responsibilities for more than a year or two. Frequency of organization change is, therefore, one way of increasing a company's capacity to adapt. While this makes the organization more flexible, it has costs in other areas: management attention may never focus on one dimension for long enough to build the needed advantages; accountabilities can become blurred because results are more dependent on the actions taken under the previous arrangements; and so on. Frequent reorganizations should only be planned if the need for flexibility is greater than the need for consistency.

Summary

The tests are a vital part of organization design. They not only provide an appropriate challenge process for an existing or new design, they also help managers decide how much structure and process to create and how much to leave to self-managed networking. Giving time to the tests is, therefore, essential both to insure that a thorough job has been done and to help managers find a happy medium between structure and self-managed networking: between an organizational straitjacket and an informed free-for-all.

Even if a design has been chosen using criteria developed from the fit principles, the tests will still identify many issues to resolve. This is because a design concept (lines, boxes, and roles) is an outline structure, not the finished article. Additional detail about areas of overlap, lateral relationships, accountabilities, and hierarchical processes are inevitably needed to flesh out the concept.

One of the important issues we have been addressing with the tests is the question of how much additional process and detail to add to a design concept. How many of the processes and detailed responsibilities should be defined and how many left to be designed by lower-level managers or worked out during the run of play? The answer is, just enough to satisfy the tests. For example, on the issue of cross-unit links, the designer only needs to create processes and mechanisms for those links that are expected to be "difficult". The vast majority of links can be left up to the managers involved. They should be encouraged to design their own processes in discussion with colleagues, and they will change them when circumstances demand. But these self-managed processes are not part of the formal design and should not be the concern of the organization designer.

In Chapter 4, we pointed out that interdependent organizations face difficult management challenges. Simpler structures have advantages, and we argued that complex designs should only be selected if they are strategically necessary. We therefore considered a tenth test – a complexity test.[4]

In the event, we decided not to include a separate complexity test. Instead, we treat the issue of complexity as a background to all the tests: we want to encourage managers to think about the cost/benefit trade-off every time they design an overlay, add a co-ordination process, introduce complicated performance measures, or create mandated relationships. The tests should lead to an organization that is as complex as it needs to be, but no more.

The trend toward more and more complex designs is not, we believe, inevitable. There is often a simpler solution that will give a better net result. We are, therefore, keen to emphasize the value of simple solutions. Throughout the design process, managers should be thinking simplicity. When designing a co-ordination mechanism, they should be looking for the simplest solution. When providing protection for a specialist culture, they should avoid complex governance processes or multiple parents unless there is no alternative. When making changes to the layers and functions in the hierarchy, they should search for solutions that reduce the number of layers and simplify functional connections. While we do not position complexity as a test, we do recommend that managers scan their designs with an eye for areas of unnecessary complexity.

The nine tests are our way of making sure that the principles have been properly considered and the compromises and trade-offs of a design fully exposed and analyzed. The design principles are sound concepts, but they can be hard to apply in a given situation. It is often more practical and rewarding to use intuition to make initial judgments about a new structure, and then test the quality of the judgments using the nine tests. By applying the tests and adjusting the design where necessary, managers can build a blueprint that achieves the qualities of a structured network.

9

The Design Process: The Example of Global Foods

In this chapter, we will go through the steps in our design process in detail using an example, Global Foods, to illustrate the analyses and judgments that need to be made.

It is based on a real situation we have been involved in. But, to insure that it remains anonymous, the situation is well disguised, allowing us to share the human frailties and politics involved. Some of the example will be in boxes, allowing readers to get the main messages without following all the detail.

In design terms, the problem is relatively simple. It has been chosen because it is a typical problem faced by many management teams and because its simplicity makes it easier to comprehend. However, as will become clear, no organization design is without its awkward issues.

The example concerns the European Division of a global foods company. We will call it the European Snack-foods Division (ESD) of Global Foods. The company's core products are savory snacks: potato chips, corn chips, other potato and corn products, and nuts. These products have been growth markets in Europe for many years, although more recently growth has slowed in the developed countries. In pursuit of growth over the last 10 years, the company has extended its product range into similar areas, such as cake snacks, savory biscuits, and dried mashed potato. The logic for these product extensions varies. All have higher market growth rates than savory snacks. Some share brand positioning. Some share ingredients and manufacturing technologies. Some are snack-type products and hence compete for similar eating occasions. All are distributed through similar outlets. All have similar product development and technical challenges.

There are, however, important differences. Cake snacks are sweet tasting. Mashed potato is a main meal product. Savory biscuits also have a link to the cheese course at a meal. Savory biscuits and cakes involve some different ingredients – flour – and a different manufacturing process – baking. ESD has had some successes with these new product categories, although none is as profitable as the core savory snack products. The mashed potato product still has not broken even.

Management in Europe decided to make these products a growth priority because sufficient growth was unlikely to come from savory snacks. Hence, they decided to pay more attention to the "new product categories". They also decided that additional attention could not be achieved just by emphasizing these products in the next planning round. Some change in organization design was necessary. ESD was currently organized into four business units designed around the four major countries in Europe – Germany, France, the UK, and Italy. Other countries in Europe were all attached to one of these four businesses. At the European level, there were functions for manufacturing, product development, and brand marketing. The majority of the personnel in each function reported to local functional bosses in each country, but the European functional heads had significant influence over the careers of senior managers in each function, as a result of which the country functional heads feel as though they had two bosses.

The problem at ESD was that the new product categories were not growing fast enough. Cake snacks had proved successful in Italy, but none of the other countries had invested much in developing their markets. Savory biscuits had small market positions in three countries, but there was concern about the quality of the product, and there had been a lack of brand development in all markets. The mashed potato product was achieving significant volumes, but, because it was manufactured by a third party, margins were low, leaving little money for investment in the brand.

Across all three products, management felt that the problem was too little attention and investment. Perhaps one of the products should be dropped and the effort invested in the others? But, because the products were minor factors in each market, the four countries were not paying significant attention to any of them.

Starting the Design Process

The managers at ESD chose to start by reviewing the current design. They wanted to know whether their current organization was a problem. They presumed that it was, but felt that they needed to confirm this before developing ideas about alternative ways of organizing. In terms of our design process figure (Figure 9.1), the managers at ESD started with the step "Take current design".

This led to the next step – "Clarify, test, and refine the option". The first part of this step involved laying out the

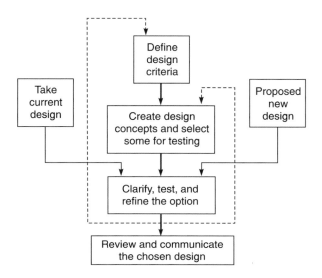

FIGURE 9.1 Making the Design Decision

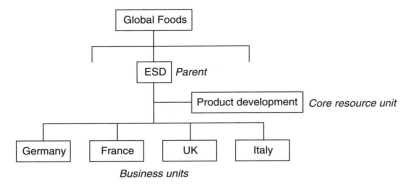

FIGURE 9.2 ESD Organizational Chart

existing organization, using the taxonomy of roles. Figure 9.2 was the result: the existing organization of ESD consisted of business units, a parent, and a core resource unit. When this was laid out, the managers felt uncomfortable. "It doesn't feel that simple," said one. "Surely we should have a lot of dotted functional lines on the chart. There are not many things that we do in the countries without some involvement from the corporate functions." After discussion, however, they agreed that the functional influences from manufacturing and marketing were part of ESD's parenting propositions: the dotted lines were the result of active parenting by ESD.

We will not repeat here all the analysis that went into testing the existing design. However, we can give a summary outcome (see box: Testing ESD's Current Organization). The judgments made about the current organization require deep knowledge of the strategies ESD was pursuing, the critical success factors of the new products and the way the organization was working. The net conclusion was that the organization seemed to be well designed for savory snacks products, but less well designed for the new products. ESD, therefore, launched a redesign project.

The rest of this chapter discusses the steps taken by ESD in the design process in detail.

Testing ESD's Current Organization

Tests	Comments
Fit tests	
Market advantage test	The sources of competitive advantage in savory snacks require the organization to be tightly integrated so as to get the benefits of scale and functional skill. The current country structure could be considered inappropriate because it fragments the organization. However, it appears to be working. The fragmentation does not seem to be a problem because of the influence of the central functions.
	However, the country structure and central functions do create a problem for the new product categories, especially where the sources of competitive advantage are different. For example, the branding strategies used for savory snacks do not seem to be working as well in cake snacks. In addition, the new product categories are not getting the attention from country managers that is needed.
Parenting advantage test	The structure is well designed for ESD's parenting propositions (see page 302). First, the strong central functions insure that manufacturing and product development skills are leveraged. Second, the country structure provides a level of decentralization and accountability that helps to create a performance culture.

People test	The design fits the current top team well. However, it does not fully utilize the skills of the number two within the product development function, nor does it capitalize on the skills of one of the marketing managers who has savory biscuit experience and has run a small business unit.
Feasibility test	Less relevant when testing a current design.

Good design tests

Difficult links test	Co-ordination works well in savory snacks, mainly because of the authority of the central functions. It works less well in the other product categories, because neither the functions nor the countries give them sufficient attention. The main "difficult links" seem to be between the countries and the new product managers within the central functions, and among the central functional managers themselves. There is no process for them to resolve differences.
Specialist cultures test	Because the new products have different critical success factors, they may need some autonomy from the savory snack business.
Accountability test	Currently the countries are easy to hold to account: most of their stakeholder relationships are self-correcting and their performance can be measured in terms of profit and market

share. Moreover, the CEO understands the business well and is able to "sense" when one of the countries is underperforming.

The central functions are more difficult to hold to account. Their relationships with the countries are not self-correcting and there are few objective, benchmarkable, outcome-based ways of measuring their performance. However, the top team works closely together, so that areas of underperformance are quickly pointed out by the countries or spotted by the CEO.

Accountability for the new products is a problem mainly because they are not set up as separate units. Because the responsibility for the success of these products is spread across functions and countries, it is hard to hold any unit responsible without developing performance measures at a level that would be considered intrusive.

| Redundant hierarchy test | The ESD layer has important parenting propositions – skills in product development and low cost manufacturing, and the ability to create a performance culture. |

Global Foods contributes to the functional skills through its functional knowledge in these areas. Its reputation Global Foods also influences retailers and suppliers.

| Flexibility test | The integrated nature of the existing structure and the fact that the countries and functions are on the executive committee make it somewhat inflexible: it will be hard to change the roles of the functions or the status of the countries. A more decentralized structure with more countries would be more flexible.

However, this is a fairly slow-moving industry, so flexibility is not the top concern. More integration with Global Foods may also be necessary in the future. The current structure is well designed for this change. |

Defining Design Criteria

Design criteria describe the objectives of the new organization and the constraints of the situation the company is in. They can be developed from analyzing the fit drivers – product-market strategies, corporate strategies, people, and constraints. This results in a set of design criteria that will guide the designer in developing an organization that fits the company's unique circumstances.

Here, we cannot go through all the analysis carried out by the managers at ESD, so we will just give some examples.

Product-market Strategies

To convert product-market strategies into design criteria:

- list the sources of competitive advantage and major initiatives planned for each product/market segment; and
- take each source of advantage, note the organizational implications, and turn them into design criteria.

Let us take the core business - savory snacks. The sources of advantage in this business are:

- *market share:* like most consumer products, costs such as distribution, product development, and marketing are volume-sensitive;
- *product quality:* product brands are built around innovative and high quality products;
- *transport costs:* the product bags contain a lot of air, making them expensive to transport more than one or two hundred miles; and
- *low costs:* the products sell mainly to the children's market where prices are low, forcing companies to minimize all overhead and non-essential costs.

The major initiatives planned in savory snacks were:

- expansion into Eastern Europe;
- launch of private label brands in Holland; and
- acquisitions in Germany and northern Italy.

The organizational implications of the sources of advantage and major initiatives are:

- the benefits of volume suggest that markets should be defined broadly rather than narrowly (i.e. the whole of Europe rather than separate countries);
- the importance of product quality suggests that units should be defined around products rather than market segments or geographies; certainly product development and quality control should be strong rather than fragmented functions;
- high transport costs imply that there should be a number of local factories: one issue will be whether these factories report to a manufacturing function, a country head, or a product head;
- the need for low costs suggests centralization and standardization where possible; and
- the major initiatives will each require some focused attention.

These implications were turned into design criteria, such as:

- define markets broadly, unless there are clear differentiating factors;
- centralize product development and quality control, except for products with clearly different needs;
- centralize manufacturing, except for products that need frequent market contact (i.e. where the links with marketing and product development are more important than the link with manufacturing); and
- insure sufficient attention is paid to Eastern Europe, acquisitions, and private label.

A similar analysis of the sources of advantage in the other product categories produced some different organizational implications and some additional criteria. For example, product differentiation and tailoring is much more important in cake snacks, implying the need for more segmentation by country. Mashed potato has high fixed costs in manufacturing and low transport costs, implying the need for more centralization.

Corporate Strategies

To convert corporate-level strategies into design criteria:

- list the main parenting propositions and planned strategic initiatives; and
- take each parenting proposition or strategic initiative, note the organizational implications, and turn them into design criteria.

The parenting propositions at ESD were:

- product development skills;
- low-cost manufacturing expertise;
- the reputation of Global Foods among retailers and suppliers; and
- management's ability to create a performance culture.

Strategic initiatives that relate to the design issue were:

- develop significant growth in new product areas; and
- expand into Eastern Europe.

These were turned into design criteria, such as:

- insure strong leadership is given to the product development and manufacturing functions;
- insure unit responsibilities are clear, separable, and measurable, implying that any move away from a business unit and sub-business unit structure would need to be done with care; and
- give added attention to new products and Eastern Europe.

The intermediate step of defining organizational implications is not necessary in this simple example. Moreover, it creates tedious reading. However, in a complex situation, we recommend that managers include the intermediate step, and define organizational implications before trying to articulate design criteria.

One of the difficulties of doing analysis of corporate strategies is deciding what constitutes a source of corporate value creation as opposed to a source of product-market advantage. For example, in ESD, product innovation is a source of advantage in each product-market segment, and it is also a source of value creation that is organization-wide. Eastern Europe is a major initiative for savory snacks and a strategic initiative for ESD as a whole. At this stage in the analysis, the overlap is not a problem: the overlapping strategies point to the same design criteria. Product development needs to be a core function that is strongly influenced by the center or tightly co-ordinated. Eastern Europe needs to be given sufficient attention within savory snacks and by ESD as a whole.

People

To convert the people driver into design criteria:

- list senior managers who will have prominent positions in the new organization irrespective of the design chosen, and assess their strengths, weaknesses, and preferences;

- list other managers with particularly relevant strengths or skills;
- list any limits there may be in the type of people who can be recruited into the organization (based on past experience); and
- take this list of strengths, weaknesses, preferences, and recruiting limits, note the organizational implications and turn them into design criteria.

The people issue provided some important design criteria at ESD:

- the company had a long history of promoting from within, and was not considering any changes in its top managers as part of this organization issue (although some reshuffling of responsibilities would be possible);
- most managers had grown up in the savory snacks business and their ways of thinking were strongly influenced by the "rules of the game" in savory snacks;
- the CEO of ESD liked to manage the division as a team, which created limits on the number of people he could have reporting to him;
- one manager, in marketing, had previously worked in the biscuit business, had strongly championed the savory biscuit product category, and appeared to have the qualities to run a savory biscuit business unit, if this design solution made sense; and
- the current technical function had a strong second-in-command, making it possible to release him or his boss for other tasks.

These implications were turned into design criteria, such as:

- build the design around the current management skills, such as the marketing manager with biscuit experience;
- isolate products that will not thrive in a culture dominated by savory snacks, but probably without setting them up as sub-business units (see next section, Constraints, for a further development of this criterion); and
- avoid creating a big "team" at the top.

As this example demonstrates, managers have idiosyncratic strengths and weaknesses. Not all of them can be identified as part of the design criteria: some may only emerge when a particular solution is being considered (for example, the fact that manager A does not get on with manager B). The objective at this stage of the analysis is, therefore, to set out the major issues that have an obvious impact on the choice of design.

Constraints

To convert the constraints driver into design criteria:

- list the legal and governmental issues that may impinge on organization design choice and convert them into design criteria;
- consider the requirements of each institutional or stake-holder group and convert any constraining requirements into design criteria;
- consider the broader external environment, such as the culture in specific locations, and decide whether this imposes any design criteria; and
- list the organization's strengths and weaknesses, especially those that relate to organization change, identify the root causes that lie behind these strengths and weaknesses, and use them to define additional design criteria.

Since the process of defining design criteria has been well

illustrated in the previous three sections, we will focus only on the last of the above points – root causes analysis.

The strengths of ESD included discipline, high standards, meeting performance objectives, and comfort with doing things the standard way. These all contributed to the performance culture and to low-cost manufacturing. The company's culture of product innovation was based on a deep understanding of value for money in this segment. Products were rarely the most innovative. Usually, they were the best value for money: classic rather than fashion products. As a result the company would frequently launch and relaunch products as ideas were developed for improving value for the consumer or the retailer.

ESD's weaknesses were a lack of strategic capability and difficulties in innovating outside its savory snacks approach to the business. This was at the root of the difficulty the company was having in developing the new product areas. Also, the company was arrogant towards the retail trade: marketing and sales managers felt that the trade did not understand the snacks category as well as it should. This did not harm ESD's core category because its products were strong. However, it made the trade less willing to "help" ESD get into new product areas.

Another issue concerned the relationship between the sales units in each country and the other functions. The sales units frequently wanted special treatment that the other functions were not prepared to provide. The other functions recognized that this increased costs. Yet the sales function felt that "special deals" were a way to get more support from the retail trade.

Defining root causes is always difficult and can be contentious. However, precision does not appear to be critical. What is valuable is to be aware of some of the powerful cultural and historic forces at work in the organization. At ESD, the root causes could be summarized as:

- a belief in value for money and hence little patience with innovation for innovation's sake, with "specials", with marketing frills, or with wasteful duplication or bureaucracy;
- an arrogance about the company and its way of doing things;

and

- strong central and functionally oriented leadership, resulting in discipline and little questioning or dialogue about the overall business strategy.

These implications were turned into design criteria, such as

- isolate from the main functional organization products or activities that require a:
  - positioning that is not "value for money";
  - close collaboration with the trade; or
  - creative strategizing.

For ESD, the root causes analysis underlines the value of giving the new product categories sufficient isolation. The implication is that the design challenge is particularly tough. The new products will need to have the scale and skill advantages that ESD has to offer, but at the same time remain separate from ESD's normal approach to business.

A full analysis of the four elements of the fit principle can generate a large number of design criteria. In the ESD example, we have only done enough analysis to illustrate the points we are making. Nevertheless, we have generated 10 design criteria. The full analysis generated many more. While this might seem like an unreasonable number, it is manageable. Many of the criteria reinforce each other or can be grouped into aggregate thoughts. Moreover, in a complex design there are many parts to the organization and most criteria only affect one part. The number of criteria that need to be kept in mind for any individual part of the design is, therefore, reduced.

Creating and Selecting Design Concepts

Once the design criteria are defined, it is possible to start creating design concepts. These can be created intuitively. For example each member of a group can be asked to write down her "preferred" option.

Design concepts can also be generated analytically. There are five steps:

1. Use the design criteria to define "responsibility groupings" – clusters of responsibilities that require focused management attention.
2. Choose one dimension of responsibility grouping as the primary reporting structure and, using the role labels, fit the other groupings around this structural backbone.
3. Create a few different options with the same structural backbone.
4. Choose another dimension as the structural backbone and generate some more options.
5. Scan the set of options generated by checking that it includes at least one simple and one more complex alternative.

A design concept is not a complete organization design, but it is more than lines and boxes. A design concept defines the boxes (units) and the broad accountabilities and relationships (roles). It defines the organizational units, provides broad job descriptions, and gives guidance on how the units are expected to interact. It does not lay out the detail of important processes; define which people should be in which jobs; or define performance targets or incentives.

Defining Responsibility Groupings

A responsibility grouping is a collection of responsibilities. Responsibility groupings should have some significance in terms of the design criteria. A grouping might be based round a function (product development), a market segment (Eastern Europe), a process (budgeting), a product (dried potato), a channel (large grocers), a parenting proposition (help with government relations), or some other dimension. Grouping responsibilities is a way of dividing up the total task of the organization into sub-tasks. In fact, designing an organization is basically about how the responsibilities are grouped.

At ESD, the definition of responsibility groupings started with those parts of the organization that are natural groupings. These are collections of operating responsibilities that are unlikely to need to be broken down further, given the design issue being analyzed. Often these natural building blocks are geographically distinct – a factory, a sales force in a country, or a research laboratory. Natural building blocks are not "natural" in the sense of existing independent of the problem being studied. They are "natural" in the context of the design that is being done and the current organization. They describe the maximum disaggregation that it is useful to consider, given the problem that is being addressed.

The natural groupings at ESD were deemed to be the factories (six in total), the country-based sales forces (one in each of the four main countries and eight others), the research laboratories (one in each of the four countries), the product/brand marketing teams (about twenty in the four countries and a further six at ESD level looking after the European brands) and the CEO's office. The factories could be further broken down into operating lines, but since there is no prospect of different operating lines in a factory reporting to anyone other than the factory head, further disaggregation was not felt to be useful. In a similar way, the sales forces could be broken down by region in a country, but little benefit would be gained from this.

On the other hand, the sales forces might be broken down by product. This might have been a useful further disaggregation because the design issue is about how to give extra attention to the new products. ESD's managers chose not to disaggregate the sales forces in the initial definition of groupings because they believed that the economies of scale from combining sales forces far outweighed the benefits of focused sales attention by product. They recognized that the design process could result in a subsequent decision to separate out a special sales force for one or more of the products. But, in their initial cut at the responsibility groupings, they decided to maintain a single sales force in each country. If there had been disagreement between the managers involved, we would have advised creating sales force groupings for each product in each country and an additional grouping to co-ordinate the sales activities in that country.

Issues like this occur every time an initial set of building blocks is produced. We have found that it does not matter greatly if some building blocks are a little more aggregated (or disaggregated) than turns out to be appropriate in the final design. On balance we encourage managers to disaggregate when in doubt. But a practical approach is needed. The designer does not want to disaggregate into so many small groupings that she cannot keep them in mind during the process of creating design concepts.

We have found that analytically-oriented managers devote too much effort to the issue of what is or is not a natural grouping. In our experience, this stage of the analysis is not critical. The decision about whether to divide the sales forces by product is not an issue worth spending much time on. During the option generation stage, it is possible to further divide the sales force to create, for example, an option with the products as complete business units. Moreover, the issue is also likely to be raised by the tests, either as a difficult link (between product units and country units over the allocation of sales force time) or as a specialist culture (do the products needs sales staff with a specialist culture?). Getting an initial set of responsibility groupings is an important first step in the analysis, but it does not preclude subsequent further divisions.

To the natural building blocks, additional groupings were added based on the design criteria. There need to be some manufacturing functional activities above the level of the factories (to maintain the low-cost manufacturing skill). There also need to be some equivalent groupings for the other functions, and a grouping for each of the new products, given their importance to the strategy. There should be a grouping for acquisitions, as well as one for private label and one for Eastern Europe. In other words, groupings are needed for all "activity areas" that are important to strategic success. The box below, Using Design Criteria to Define Responsibility Groupings, sets out the connection between the groupings and the design criteria.

Using Design Criteria to Define Responsibility Groupings

Design criteria	Implications for responsibility groupings
Operating strategies	
Define market broadly	Avoid grouping by market segment
Centralize product development	Have an ESD-level product development grouping
Centralize manufacturing	Have an ESD-level manufacturing grouping
Pay attention to:	
• new products	Have a grouping for each new product
• Eastern Europe	Have an Eastern European grouping
• acquisitions	Have an acquisitions grouping
• private label	Have a private label grouping
Corporate strategies	
Clear accountability	No implications for groupings
Strong leadership in:	
• product development	Have an ESD-level product development grouping
• manufacturing	Have an ESD-level manufacturing grouping
Pay attention to:	
• Eastern Europe	Have an Eastern European grouping
• new products	Have a grouping for each new product
People	
Build round current skills	Include groupings for all current units

Avoid creating a big team at the top	No implications
Constraints	
Isolate products that need different mental maps	Have a grouping for each new product
Isolate products that need different market positions	Have a grouping for each new product

The groupings developed from the design criteria may sometimes conflict with or reinforce the natural groupings. Where conflicts exist, the groupings should be broken down further or specified more clearly until the conflict is eliminated. For example, there might appear to be a conflict between having the factories as groupings and the need for an ESD-level manufacturing function. At this stage, it makes sense to have both. In different designs the factories may end up reporting to the manufacturing function or to the countries or, even, to the products. The ESD-level manufacturing function may also have different roles in different designs. It may be one of the dominant power bases in the organization with all the factories reporting in directly, or it may be designed as little more than a committee meeting of the country manufacturing heads.

To complete the list of responsibility groupings, ESD managers added groupings for other parts of the organization not highlighted by the design criteria or the natural building blocks. Central functional groupings such as finance, human resources, logistics, and IT were identified. Since they exist in the current organization and they probably need to exist in some form in the new organization, they were included in the overall list. Groupings were also added for each of the four countries. The final list of responsibility groupings is shown in the box below.

Responsibility Groupings

CEO's office

Operating areas (natural groupings)
  Factories, by country
  Sales forces, by country
  Research laboratories, by country
  Product brand teams (e.g. Scrunchy Chips), by country and at ESD level

Functional leadership and co-ordination (at a level above the country)
  Product development
  Manufacturing
  Other functions that currently exist (finance, brand marketing, HR, IT, etc.)

Country co-ordination
  Germany
  France
  UK
  Italy

Other areas needing attention
  New products (savory biscuits, cakes, mashed potato)
  Eastern Europe
  Private label
  Acquisitions

At this stage of the analysis, the responsibility groupings are not precisely defined: ESD had not defined precisely what was in "product development" versus "marketing", or which countries were included in Eastern Europe. Also, the responsibility groupings do not necessarily become units in the final design. For example, in different design concepts "Germany" could be a business unit, an overlay, a co-ordination mechanism, an intermediate parent, or an activity within the CEO's office (i.e. within the parent).

Choosing a Primary Reporting Line

The second step in creating a design concept is to choose a primary reporting line. In ESD the choice is between function, country, and product. Currently the organization is structured by country with strong functional parenting. It may make sense to consider options with function or product as the primary dimension, but initially the country is the obvious choice for the primary dimension.

The ESD managers chose to stick with the status quo, making country the primary reporting line. The bulk of the people in each operating area would continue with the country as their primary reporting line. Functional leadership would continue to be provided by strong parenting functions. The challenge was to decide how to give attention to the new products and other dimensions such as private label and Eastern Europe.

The role labels described in Chapter 5 provide a language for generating ideas about what to do with these additional dimensions. The initial design concept was to make product categories and private label into "overlays" and Eastern Europe into a "sub-business" within the German unit.

Creating Different Options With the Same Primary Reporting Line

While sticking with the same primary reporting line, it is possible to use the role labels to generate additional options. ESD managers generated a design concept with new products and private label as "project units" rather than "overlays". The project units would be time-limited units whose purpose was to develop and win organizational support for a strategy in the chosen product area. The units would be multi-functional, consisting of managers from each of the core functions involved.

Another design concept made the new product categories into parenting activities within product development. This would give them a power base from which to influence the country business units, although there was concern that they might be dominated by the savory snacks way of thinking.

A more extreme possibility was to set up the new products as additional business units. This would begin to undermine the countries as the primary reporting line. The countries would be responsible for savory snacks and operating activities such as sales. The new product business units would have responsibility for product development, branding, and manufacturing.

Trying a Different Primary Reporting Line

The alternative primary reporting lines are product or function. Since the main concern is about how to pay more attention to the new products, the first alternative that was considered was the product dimension. With products as the primary reporting line, the products become the business units. The factories, laboratories, and product brand teams would all report into one of the product business units. The responsibility groupings that then need to be considered are the countries, functions, Eastern Europe, and private label (assuming private label is not one of the product units).

One design concept had functions as part of the "parent"; Eastern Europe as a "shared service" sales force; private label in Holland as a "project unit"; and the country dimension was dropped altogether (see Figure 9.3).

An alternative design was for manufacturing to be a "core resource unit". All the factories could report to a central manufacturing function to form a "core resource unit". In this design Eastern Europe could be a "project unit", an "overlay", or part of the "parent". Private label would be a separate business unit (see Figure 9.4).

Additional options were generated with the functions as the primary reporting line. This made ESD into a single business unit rather than a parent. The primary reporting lines – manufacturing, product development, etc. – would be "business functions".

Using the roles taxonomy, many different options can be generated. For example, the responsibilities that are grouped

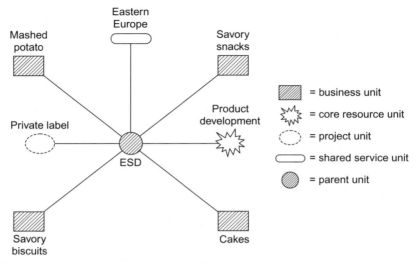

FIGURE 9.3 Products as Business Units

under the label "Eastern Europe" could be a "sub-business", an "overlay", a "project unit", or part of the "parent"; or the responsibilities could be handled through a co-ordination mechanism such as the planning process. This creates five options. The taxonomy of roles provides a means of quickly articulating these differences and, hence, generating many

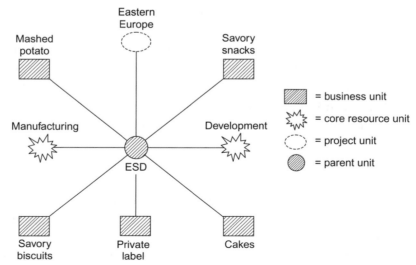

FIGURE 9.4 Products as Business Units – an Alternative Design

options. This proves to be invaluable in the design process. One of the problems we have often encountered is the difficulty managers have in articulating options. Often the discussion of options is limited to considering different primary reporting lines or choosing "a matrix" (i.e. multiple reporting lines). The taxonomy of roles helps managers to think through some subtle differences and articulate them for discussion and evaluation.

Scanning the Options

The final analytical step is to make sure that the set of options is broad enough. First, the list can be scanned to see if it includes any simple options. This insures that the managers involved have not overlooked a structure where the ease of operation would compensate for the loss of focus on secondary dimensions. The simplest option is to have one primary reporting line and self-contained units: a business unit with business functions as the primary reporting line or a portfolio of business units. Managers should examine the simplest option and consider whether a simpler solution can be added to the list.

Second, scan the list to see if it includes some complex options. This insures that the managers involved have been ambitious enough in looking for an option that achieves as many of the focus benefits as possible. If the sources of competitive advantage and parenting advantage only require attention to be given to one dimension, the search for complex solutions is time wasted. But, in most cases, attention is needed in multiple dimensions, suggesting that some complexity should be considered. So long as there is at least one option that includes sub-business units, overlays, and core resource units, managers can be confident that they have thought through some complex solutions. If none of the options is complex, managers should consider whether a more complex option should be added to the list.

ESD's managers had considered a wide range of options including both simple and complex ones. The scan did not suggest any new ones.

Selecting a Preferred Option

ESD's managers used an intuitive process to select an option for testing. First, they reviewed all the design concepts they had created and chose the three they felt were the strongest. The managers involved in this forced ranking were all familiar with the design criteria, but did not use the criteria explicitly to make the ranking. The box below explains this ranking process.

ESD's Design Concepts

ESD's managers defined three design concepts. The first was little different from the status quo. The brand marketing function would appoint senior brand managers to take the lead on each of the new products. These individuals would be asked to form teams including managers from product development, manufacturing, and the four countries. The teams would be charged with "parenting" these new product categories more heavily.

The second concept was to create "overlays" for each new product. Small teams of dedicated marketing and product development managers would be created for each new product category. They would be made volume- and profit-responsible for the category throughout Europe, but they would have no direct powers over the countries. They would have to work by argument and persuasion. They would report to a manager responsible for new products, the number two from the product development function, who would be appointed to ESD's executive committee.

The third concept was to make the three new products into separate business units, fully responsible for marketing, product development, and manufacturing, but dependent on the countries to provide sales. One proposal was that these three new business units should each have a seat on the executive committee and report to the CEO of ESD, but it was felt this would not suit the style of the CEO. Another proposal was that the new businesses should report to a

---

Director of New Businesses, but none of the existing managers appeared to have the skills needed. The final and preferred solution was that the three new businesses should report to the country most likely to promote the business: cakes to Italy, mashed potato to the UK, and savory biscuits to Germany. (see Figure 9.5 illustrating the three options)

The managers then chose one of the three design concepts as their preferred option. In fact, this option was evidently the preferred one early in the option generation process. The preferred option was to retain the countries as the primary reporting line and pay additional attention to the new products by creating overlays. The design involved appointing an additional member to the top management team to head up a "new products group" (see Figure 9.5). Within the new products group, each new product would have its own dedicated team consisting of marketing and product development managers. The manager who would run this new group was the second in command from the product development function. The job was viewed as an excellent development opportunity for this manager, who had some entrepreneurial skills and plenty of energy for tackling the issues. The main change was that the new products would now have a separate voice at the highest level.

The other issues – Eastern Europe, private label, and acquisitions – will not be the focus of our analysis. However, for completeness it is worth describing what they chose. Eastern Europe was to be set up as a "sub-business" reporting to Germany, and the private label opportunity in Holland was to be handled by setting up a "project unit" that included managers from marketing, manufacturing, and sales. Acquisitions would become a central service unit reporting to the central finance function.

Applying the Tests

The nine design tests are critical to any decision process about structure. Whether the analysis has proceeded in a logical order

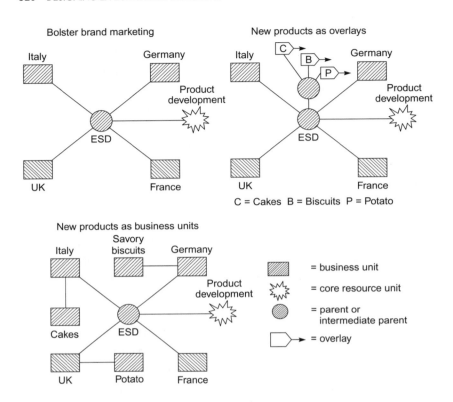

FIGURE 9.5 The Three ESD Options

from design criteria to option selection, or whether a domineering leader has plucked some proposed structure from his personal biases, the tests are the opportunity to apply rigor and objectivity to the decision.

It is inappropriate to go through all of the tests here. They have been well covered in the previous chapter. Instead, we will provide a summary of the test analysis ESD managers did on the option they chose. We will then discuss some of the issues raised in more detail. Before applying the tests, the managers had first to clarify the design they had chosen. Was the new product group a "parenting function" or an "overlay"? After some discussion, they decided it was an "overlay". The managers in charge of the new products would be held responsible for profit, volumes, and market shares and would be expected to significantly improve on the current performance. This meant double-counting the profits and volumes, which would also be the responsibility of the countries.

The box below provides a summary analysis of the tests with regard to this design. In general the option "meets" the tests, but there are some particular issues that we will focus on more closely.

Testing the Preferred Option at ESD

Tests	Comments
Fit tests	
Market advantage test	The solution is clearly a compromise. The new products are given some extra attention, but not the power to implement the conclusions they might come to.
Parenting advantage test	The new structure has not disturbed the ability of the organization to implement its parenting propositions.
People test	There was broad support for this solution because it did not disturb any of the existing power bases. However, there was an issue about the skills and resources needed by the head of the new products group. The manager from product development did not have some of the needed skills such as business strategy development. Also he had a savory snacks way of thinking, which might be a disadvantage for the new products. (Discussed in the text)
	There was some concern about whether ESD would be able to find managers for each new product with

	the skills to develop strategies and influence the countries to support them.
Feasibility test	There was some concern about whether the IT systems could cope with double-counting.

Good design tests

Difficult links test	Much discussion focused on the link between the new product "overlays" and the countries, since part of the current problem was the failure of some countries to give the new products sufficient attention. It was not obvious that the change in structure would solve the problem. Time was also spent discussing the link with the factories. (Discussed in the text)
Specialist cultures test	Concerns were raised about the lack of protection for the new products as specialist cultures. Wouldn't the savory snacks way of thinking, normal in the central functions and countries, over-influence them? (Discussed in the text)
Redundant hierarchy test	The parenting propositions for the head of "new products" and for the relationship between new products and the CEO were questioned. (Discussed in the text)
Accountability test	Although the relationships between the new overlay and the countries were tied, the structure did not have serious accountability issues. The overlay's performance could be measured by looking at the success of the new products, and the ability to compare performance across the new products

	was seen as a benefit. Moreover the relationships with the countries had some self-correcting features: the overlays would be motivated to win the good opinion of the countries in order to successfully influence them.
Flexibility test	The main flexibility concern was with appointing another manager to the executive committee (i.e. creating an additional power base that might be difficult to change at the top of the organization). However, because the head of product development was retiring in two years' time, and this would be the perfect next job for the head of new products, the constraint on flexibility was thought to be minimal.

We will now pick up on three of the issues raised by the tests – the difficult links issue, the redundant hierarchy issue, and the specialist cultures issue. These were major concerns of the managers, and they developed some interesting refinements and solutions. At the top of the list was the difficult link with the countries. How would the product units succeed in getting the countries to give the new products more attention than in the past? Three solutions were generated. The first involved an addition to the planning process. Prior to the normal planning process, managers inserted a "new product planning conference". This would be an annual event at which the new product teams and the countries would present their plans. The objective was to create a device to insure that the countries and the new product managers aligned their strategies. If the strategies were not aligned, this would be exposed at the highest level. The new products conference was run before the normal planning round to make it possible to insert any conclusions from it into the business plans.

The second solution was to give the overlays some marketing budget. This meant that if the manager in charge of cakes wanted to increase marketing spend in the UK, he did not need to persuade the UK marketing manager to free up some marketing budget from his other priorities. He could offer to provide the budget from his own funds. This gave the overlays something to trade.

The third solution was to create strategy teams for each new product. These teams consisted of managers from the new product unit, representatives from sales or marketing in each country, and the manager in charge of the most important factory for that product.

The concerns about the links with the factories were solved by locating the new product teams in the country with the lead factory, and on the same site as the factory relating to their product. This meant that the new product team and the factory manager would develop a close working relationship. This would help the new product team to learn the economics of manufacturing, and make it easier for them to consider the whole business model when they were developing strategy.

The redundant hierarchy issues were more complex. Was the head of new products an "intermediate parent" or a "span breaker"? Were the right skills and resources available? After some debate, it was decided that the head of new products was a span breaker: he was helping to execute ESD's parenting propositions. In terms of "functional skill reinforcement" and "enhancing the performance culture", there was no problem: the head of new products could act as a representative of ESD. But, with regard to the new units, there were some additional parenting propositions. To develop good strategies, the new units needed some protection from the dominant way of thinking (i.e. the specialist cultures issue). They also needed some support from a parent with strong strategy thinking skills. Finally, they needed help in influencing the countries.

In normal circumstances, the success of the design would depend largely on finding a manager with these skills to take the job. Unfortunately, ESD did not have the ideal candidate. Some compromise was necessary.

The solutions were as follows. The head of new products was sent on a general management program at INSEAD, Europe's leading management school, to give him additional skills and objectivity. He was also given a budget for using consultants to help develop strategies for the new products. It was felt that consultants would help bring some objectivity with regard to how far the new product strategies needed to be different from the strategies of savory snacks. Senior managers were appointed to run the overlay units, and they were told that they should be as pushy as they liked in promoting their products to the rest of the organization.

Despite all these additions and refinements, there was still concern that, in practice, the new products would not get the freedom they needed to develop radical solutions. However, managers agreed that, if they thought this was happening, they could give the overlay units more marketing budget or more influence over strategy, until they had sufficient independence and impact.

Reviewing and Communicating the Design

Once an option has been chosen, the design is almost complete. But there is still some work to do. The objective has been to create "just enough" design: so that it is a "structured network". What is now needed is to turn attention to communication rather than design. The final stage is to make sure that the design is ready for implementation.

When the chosen design was given a final review, issues of clarity and potential confusion were raised in two areas – the new product strategy teams and the relationship between the lead factory and the new product unit. We will focus on the issues raised by the new strategy teams.

The strategy teams were a co-ordination mechanism designed to bring together the managers from the relevant functions and the main countries. The intention was that this process would be led by the head of the new product unit, who would involve the other managers in a dialog about strategy until a common view and understanding was reached. The budget for consultants was expected to help the process.

One concern was about the status of these meetings relative to other meetings the managers might need to attend in their functions or countries: when there were conflicts, which meeting should take precedence? Another concern was the role that the country managers were supposed to be playing. Were they expected to act as representatives of their country, explaining the policies of the country to the team, or were they members of the team trying to develop the best strategy for their product?

The initial reaction of the ESD senior managers was to ignore the issues. "Where conflicts exist, the managers will need to judge the relative importance of the different priorities," said the CEO. "And the managers from countries need to act as middlemen between the new product unit, their country and their function." It was this thinking that had caused the managers to overlook these difficult link issues when they were doing the difficult links test. In the review, it became clear that the problem was likely to be more significant. The heads of the new product units would need to be able to rely on the participation of the functional and country managers. A quick scan of planned meeting schedules was sufficient to make the design team realize that conflicts could easily occur. Moreover, in talking to managers, it was clear that some would loyally represent their country or function. "My job will be to make sure that the new product strategy does not conflict with our country strategy," commented one. If this occurred, it would be hard to develop new solutions.

The first attempt to solve the problem did not work. The managers tried to solve the problem by laying out the meetings and responsibilities in more detail, to define what managers should do when faced with a conflict. The solution was rejected by the head of the new products unit. He said it would be impractical: "Strategy work does not fit into structured timetables." After further discussion, managers decided that, if the new products were at the center of the division's growth strategy, the strategy teams would have to take priority over other meetings. They also decided that members of the team should take their functional or country hats off while they were part of the strategy meetings, and that during the meetings they should think of themselves as working for the new product.

In most new designs, as in ESD, there are a few areas that need further clarification. Some are picked up during the review and communication step, while others are not identified until after the new organization has been announced. Once management has tested a design and concluded that it is the best option available, there are benefits in making the announcement quickly. Moreover, it is often easier to resolve issues together with the managers involved, once they know what jobs they have been allocated. Hence reviewing the design and early implementation often happen simultaneously. In fact, adjustments can continue for the first few months of the new design, as issues emerge. What is important is to recognize that further work is normally needed and, hence, a process needs to be set up for raising and resolving design issues and insuring that changes do not undermine the intent of the new design.

As part of the communication process, ESD managers emphasized both the strengths and weaknesses in the new design. They explained that the chosen solution was not perfect, but it was the best compromise. The competing demands of giving specialist attention to the new products and insuring integration with the rest of the organization could not be accommodated without some weaknesses. Moreover, the benefits of a geographic focus were too great to put at risk. They pointed to the following weaknesses:

- the relationships between the new products and the countries, which left the countries in control of decisions about how much attention to give to the new products;
- the role of the head of the group of new products, who did not have all the skills needed for the role;
- the abilities and seniority of the heads of each new product, who again lacked some of the skills that would ideally be needed; and

- the potential for the new products to be dominated by the savory snacks way of thinking.

While it is unusual for managers to declare skill weaknesses, the openness of the process ESD had been through made this seem appropriate. Moreover, by pointing out these weaknesses, managers were much more forgiving of each other as the new design bedded down. The management team was therefore able to approach the new design with their eyes open.

All new designs have some teething problems, and ESD's was no exception. After only five months, the manager in charge of the mashed potato product was replaced. It was felt that he did not have a strategic perspective or sufficient respect from members of the mashed potato strategy team. However, after 18 months' experience, the ESD CEO commented:

"It has worked. We made the right trade-offs. If we had taken control from the country managers, we would have lost the power we had in the marketplace and it would have been much harder to make the key decisions. We have also developed some additional management skills. We now have much more strategic capability."

The head of the new products group explained, "Without the open debate and structured analysis, we would have ended up with the new products being split between the countries [the third option they considered]. The discipline of the project pushed managers into discussing the trade-offs, and this of itself made a major contribution."

The main successes were a decision after one year to exit the mashed potato product and significant volume gains in the other two product categories. Most notably, there was now an aggressive campaign for savory biscuit products in France with major market successes. The campaign in France had been developed by the strategy team for savory biscuits led by the marketing manager from France. Previously, the French management team had resisted pushing this product because they were unconvinced by its potential. But, as a result of being part of the product strategy team, the French marketing manager had become converted to the potential for the product and was now implementing a creative new campaign.

In summary, faced with a tricky organization design challenge, the management team at ESD found a solution that worked for them. It was not radical nor spectacularly innovative, but it worked. The process of defining design criteria, laying out options, testing, and refining the options and, finally, reviewing and communicating the choice achieved their objective. ESD's managers felt that they had focused on the right issues and made well-informed judgments. They had anticipated most of the problems that subsequently came up, and felt confident going forward because they had discussed the alternatives. "We were rigorous", explained the head of the new products group. "We were able to focus attention on the issues rather than the politics, and that was a first for me."

10

Twenty-first Century Organizations

As we enter the twenty-first century, a number of trends in organizational design are emerging. Attractive ideas such as knowledge-sharing, freedom from hierarchy, and renewal are being explored. Leading companies are endeavoring to transform their organizations, leaving behind the baggage of the old economy and adopting a new paradigm more suited to the new century. In this final chapter, we review these trends and show why the concept of the network organization has become a popular response to them. But we also argue that network organizations risk failing some of our design tests. They will only pass the tests if they are designed as "structured networks" in accordance with the approach we have put forward in this book.

Trends in Organization Design

During our research, we encountered several major themes that drive current thinking about organizations. These include:

- multi-dimensionality;
- knowledge sharing;
- disaggregation;
- freedom from hierarchy;
- stretch for high performance; and
- renewal.

Respected academics and consultants have advocated these twenty-first century characteristics, and leading companies such as Dow, Shell, Cargill, and GE have embarked on major corporate transformation programs to introduce them into their organizations.

Multi-dimensionality

Multi-dimensionality is about moving away from SBU-based organizations (that are structured around one dimension) towards structures that make it possible to give management attention to two or more dimensions. Organizations based around a single dimension of focus are likely to be narrow, and unable to cope with the complex realities of today's competitive world. This concern, discussed extensively in Chapter 4, is leading to the adoption of multi-dimensional, interdependent organization designs.

In *Managing Across Borders*,[1] Christopher Bartlett and Sumantra Ghoshal argue that multinational companies need to combine both local responsiveness and global integration. They should become "transnationals", able to achieve focus on local geographic markets as well as on global opportunities for advantage. Bartlett and Ghoshal accept that few companies have as yet become fully transnational, but believe that organizations such as NEC, Ericsson, and Unilever are moving in the right direction.

Jay Galbraith, who has written widely about corporate structures, notes the emergence of what he calls the "front-back" organization,[2] in which front-end units focused on customers or channels of distribution work together with back-end units focused on products or technologies. This enhances competitiveness by achieving focus on both dimensions. Galbraith cites Acer, Citicorp, and Tetrapak as examples of companies that have adopted this structure. In Chapter 5, we pointed out that there are many possible variants on front-back structures, and that lack of clarity about how the front-end is supposed to work with the back-end is a danger. But we acknowledge that the underlying purpose behind such structures is often valid.

Transnationals and front-back organizations can be seen as modern versions of the familiar matrix structure. Matrix structures have for many years been canvassed as a means of achieving multi-dimensionality.[3] Indeed, Bartlett and Ghoshal assert that the essence of the transnational is to achieve a "matrix in the mind" of managers. But matrices, as we have noted, often get bogged down in conflict and ambiguity, and have failed to deliver for most companies. Galbraith has argued that the problems associated with matrix structures have more to do with the skills and experience of managers than with the desirability of the structure *per se*. Nevertheless, we need to recognize that multi-dimensional structures are bound to involve units with responsibilities that cut across each other, and which must therefore collaborate. Finding ways to achieve this without introducing the heavy hand of hierarchy or the laborious process of consensus-building is the challenge.

Knowledge Sharing

Current thinking about the sources of competitive advantage in the new economy stresses the importance of building and leveraging knowledge and competences.[4] Getting ahead, and staying ahead, increasingly depends on possessing distinctive skills and using them to find innovative ways of competing across all the businesses in a company.

A major theme for GE under Jack Welch has been "boundarylessness", in which all units within the company maximize learning from each other. In the boundaryless organization, every unit has an obligation both to seek out knowledge that is relevant to it from other units and to share its own knowledge with them. The organization's structure and processes should be designed to facilitate this by creating forums for sharing, establishing relationships between units that encourage sharing, and rewarding boundaryless behavior.

In terms of organization design, the task is to create the so-called "learning organization", popularized by Peter Senge and defined by David Garvin as an organization "skilled at creating, acquiring, and transferring knowledge, and at modifying behavior to reflect new knowledge and insights."[5] An environment conducive to learning, in which self-managed innovation and collaboration take place, is the key requirement. Raymond Miles, Charles Snow, and Grant Miles have reached similar conclusions with reference to new-economy companies such as Intel and TCG, a privately held Australian IT company, in an article with the arresting title of "TheFuture.org".[6]

But, however much a chief executive would like to create a learning organization, he or she cannot impose it. Managers cannot be ordered or compelled to learn from each other. Rather, it is a matter of designing conditions within a company in which a learning organization will flourish.

Disaggregation

The disaggregation theme brings together three trends: sharpened competition, increased outsourcing, and a much more active market for spin-offs and buy-outs. As competition intensifies, firms must concentrate increasingly on the activities they do best, and find ways of de-emphasizing or offsetting areas of relative weakness. Outsourcing provides a means of exiting from activities that are no longer regarded as sources of competitive advantage, and the range of services offered by outsource suppliers is becoming ever wider. Spin-offs or buy-outs give an alternative exit route. Disaggregation implies that progressive companies should establish a series of focused units, in which the performance of each unit can be assessed separately. The units can have trading and other links with upstream or downstream units, but there is no need for all the units to be under common ownership. Those capable of being highly competitive will be retained within the company. The rest will be outsourced or spun off.

The Boston Consulting Group (BCG) has made much of this trend, with its concept of "deconstructed" organizations. BCG attacks companies with traditional vertically integrated value chains, believing that successful companies need to embrace radical reconfiguration of the value chain. The Internet has given extra impetus to these developments.[7] Industries ranging from automotive retailing through financial services to newspapers are now facing deconstruction pressures. McKinsey has also argued for "unbundling" the corporation into more disaggregated units.[8]

Taken to extremes, deconstruction and disaggregation lead to the so-called "virtual" organization, which outsources all the main components of its value chain, retaining a role only as system integrator and overall strategist. This concept became popular in the 1990s, but there are few companies today that have become fully virtual. Even dot.com companies seem to be moving towards "clicks and mortar" rather than purely virtual structures.

A major issue for disaggregated companies is how to establish appropriate links and relationships, both within the company and externally, between the separate units that need to work together. Charles Handy[9] has suggested that the right model for this is a "federal" structure. The individual units have a high degree of autonomy, but co-operate together on a largely voluntary basis on those issues where there is a need to do so. Handy believes that companies like ABB and BP have shown the way. He expects more companies to follow them, and to take the federalist approach further. The federal metaphor is attractive, since it combines unit freedom (sovereignty) and voluntary collaboration within an overarching common framework.

Freedom from Hierarchy

In recent years, a strong ground-swell of opinion has built up that blames many of the ills of large companies on oppressive corporate hierarchies. To rectify the problem, it is argued, modern companies should empower their front-line managers to take the initiative, and reduce the burden of corporate overheads by moving to flatter, more decentralized organizations. As far as possible, the front-line units should be self-managing, able to set their own strategies and self-correct if needed, without the imposition of corporate policies, controls, and instructions.

Many writers have joined in the attack on hierarchy.[10] Among the most eloquent are Ghoshal and Bartlett, whose most recent book, *The Individualized Corporation*,[11] is a clarion call to invert the traditional corporate pyramid and de-emphasize formal structures, systems, and even strategies. In "individualized corporations", front-line managers are encouraged to make their own decisions, and senior managers' role is to provide a context that supports them. Ghoshal and Bartlett cite companies such as Intel, IKEA, and Komatsu, as well as GE, as ground-breakers. BP's reliance on peer groups rather than upper levels of management (see Chapter 4) is in the same spirit.

A related concept, put forward by Bruce Pasternak and Albert Viscio of Booz Allen and Hamilton, is the "centerless" corporation.[12] In centerless corporations, the traditional roles of the corporate center, to do with asset management, hierarchy, and control, are reduced to a minimum. Instead, a "global core" emerges, which concentrates on resource and capability building, interdependencies, and empowerment. These are laudable objectives. But it is important that the elimination of redundant hierarchy does not go too far. The corporate parent does have some necessary and value-added roles. We need to avoid throwing the (parental) baby out with the bathwater.

Stretch for High Performance

The trends discussed so far emphasize freedom and autonomy for individual units within the corporation. But the *quid pro quo* is that the units should strive for high performance. The desirability of building "high-performance" organizations is strongly advocated by consultants, such as McKinsey, and by corporations, including BP, Emerson, Granada, and Tyco. It has also been behind much of the value created by private equity investors in recent years. Moreover, it fits well with our control and commitment principle, with its emphasis on motivation and performance contracts. Twenty-first century companies may be more empowered and less hierarchical, but they seem likely to incorporate some tough performance disciplines.

There is, however, some tension between pressure for performance and the encouragement of innovation and interdependencies. The danger is that so much attention is given to next month's performance targets for each unit that creativity, mutual learning, and long-term corporate renewal suffer.

Renewal

Faced with rapid change and a stockmarket that demands sustained growth, today's companies need to be able constantly to reinvent and renew themselves. In addition to innovation and learning, this implies a need for flexible organization designs that can adapt to new and changing requirements. The renewal theme has led Jay Galbraith to put forward the idea of the "reconfigurable" organization.[13] Reconfigurable organizations are able to shift the balance of power flexibly between different dimensions of the organization, and so can refocus on new opportunities as they arise.[14] Project units that form and reform play a major part in reconfigurable organizations. To facilitate reconfigurability, companies must have information systems that are flexible enough to provide performance data on any product-market segments or activity groupings that could form part of the new structure.

A rather different approach to renewal and reconfigurability is taken by Shona Browne and Kathleen Eisenhardt.[15] They favor an approach to organizational adaptability which they call "patching", which is discussed more fully in Chapter 4. Patching, as practiced by companies like Hewlett-Packard and 3M, involves setting up small, loosely coupled units, but being prepared to make frequent, often small, changes in business unit designs and divisional charters. Drawing on complexity theory, Browne and Eisenhardt argue that this is the best way for large corporations to adapt in an uncertain environment.

Network Organizations

Putting together the trends we have discussed – transnationals, front-back organizations, boundarylessness, learning organizations, deconstruction, virtual companies, federalism, individualized corporations, centerless companies, high-performance organizations, reconfigurable structures, patching – the twenty-first century organization begins to take shape. It is best summarized as a network organization. The network is multi-dimensional and disaggregated, consisting of many different units, each with its own focus. It is populated by entrepreneurial managers, who interact spontaneously and flexibly to share knowledge, achieve competitive advantage, and implement the corporate strategy. It supports learning and collaboration through open personal contacts between the units. It has minimal hierarchy and strong empowerment of the units, which are largely self-managing and self-motivated to drive for high performance. And renewal is possible through flexibility in network relationships and redefinition of unit boundaries. Networks find favor with nearly all modern experts in organization design.[16]

We, too, are attracted by the network concept. Networks score well in terms of our good design principles, since they can:

- create units that specialize on different market segments and sources of competitive advantage;
- encourage co-operation between units by promoting interpersonal networking across unit boundaries;
- take account of knowledge and competence by decentralizing most responsibilities to disaggregated, focused units;
- reduce the cost of control and foster strong commitment through self-management to achieve high unit performance; and
- allow flexibility and adaptability by reducing hierarchy and power structures and promoting entrepreneurial responses to new opportunities.

Nevertheless, networks face several challenges, which our design tests highlight. These challenges concern network feasibility, the blurring of unit boundaries, the management of difficult links between units, the role of the parent, shared accountabilities, and the avoidance of confusion.

The Feasibility of Networks

To be feasible, networks depend upon the attitudes of the managers working in them, and the information available to them.

In a network, much depends on the motivation, flexibility, and co-operativeness of individual managers. Traditional organization man, who follows instructions, sticks to rules, and is suspicious about collaboration with sister units, guarantees that networks will fail. Fortunately, a new generation of managers seems to be emerging who relish empowerment, expect to adapt to changing circumstances, and find it natural to collaborate with others to realize corporate objectives. Often in our research we heard about the difficulties faced by older managers in adapting to the demands of network structures and about the comparative ease with which younger managers handle these requirements. Twenty-first century organizational cultures, and the attitudes of the "new managers" who work in them, seem to be in tune with network organizations.

A second precondition for successful network operation is a free flow of information to managers working within the network, and an ability to analyze performance in several dimensions. Unit managers need ways to find out if other units are outperforming them, so that they can take steps to learn from their colleagues; managers in overlay units and sub-businesses need to be able to track the results of their units, rather than have them submerged in aggregated business unit reports; and senior managers responsible for network design need to be able to cut information in a variety of ways to help them to decide which unit structure will work best, and to support decisions to change the structure.

Until recently, many companies' information systems were unable to cope with the sophisticated demands of a network structure. Driven by public reporting needs and by the finance function, they could not provide the richness, the wide access, and the flexibility that network managers need. But rapid developments in IT have now made it much easier to satisfy these information requirements. Powerful systems, such as SAP, can generate rich, tailored information with relative ease, and corporate intranets can make it freely available. Whereas it took ABB years and many millions of dollars to develop its renowned ABACUS (Asea Brown Boveri Accounting and Communication System) information system in the late 1980s, companies can now instal powerful modern information systems much more quickly and cheaply.

Two of the key constraints, individual attitudes and information availability, that have up to now held back the successful development of network organizations are therefore being overcome. No doubt there are still several companies that have work to do in this area, but it is becoming easier for network structures to meet the feasibility test as we enter the new millennium.

Networks and Unit Boundaries

In networks, there is some risk that specialist cultures will be contaminated by too much interaction with other units. Extensive personal contacts with other units are expected, in order to spread learning and shape attitudes. Even units that need to be different can experience pressure to pick up "best practices" from elsewhere and to conform to success formulae that have proved themselves in other units. But "boundarylessness", so desirable to encourage networking, is dangerous if it leads to unintentional domination of small, specialist units by ideas that are not suitable for them.

To pass the specialist cultures test, networks must maintain the boundaries around units that might otherwise be inappropriately dominated. To thrive, these units need to preserve a degree of separation and autonomy, and so must be allowed to participate in the network only to the extent that they can genuinely benefit from it. It is notable that GE, the pioneer of boundarylessness, nevertheless allows a great deal of autonomy to its business units, which can decide what they do and do not wish to learn from each other.

Networks and Difficult Links

Networks are excellent for promoting voluntary co-operation between units. But difficult links between units in the network are more problematic. Difficult links will only succeed if the parent promotes them by establishing co-ordination mechanisms or by active intervention, and may ultimately require a reorganization that incorporates them in a single unit under a strong general manager. Even the most friendly and open person-to-person contacts between units in the network will not normally be sufficient to make difficult links work successfully.

The difficult links test highlights the importance of recognizing that, even in networks, the parent has an important role to play in facilitating co-ordination. In a new book about multinationals,[17] Yves Doz, Jorge Santos and Peter Williamson argue that the transnational idea demands too much from local units, and that the parent should set up central units or processes to facilitate knowledge transfer. These "magnets" are needed to bring together the relevant units, to overcome barriers that might otherwise prevent them from collaborating, and to oil the wheels of networking. We agree with this proposition, and indeed go further. In our view, most networks depend on active involvement by the corporate parent in guiding and facilitating at least some co-ordination issues. Even then, with truly difficult links, there is a limit to what active parenting across separate units can achieve; it may be necessary to reconsider the disaggregated unit structure if it calls for unworkably difficult links between units. Overoptimism about what networking can achieve is dangerous, since it can end up discrediting the whole idea of a network structure.

Networks and Hierarchy

The drive to eliminate hierarchy is part of the concept of the network organization. While this is often desirable, we have to recognize that in large companies, some hierarchy, concerned with minimum necessary parenting activities, is unavoidable, and well-designed hierarchy can be a beneficial source of added-value parenting. In organizations with complex interdependencies between units, the role of the parent is especially important, both to sponsor difficult links between units and for other reasons, listed in Chapter 6.

The notion that network structures do away with the need for upper levels of parent management is false. Those who advocate a sort of "withering away" of the corporate parent are no more realistic than Engels, whose socialist ideals led him to look forward to the withering away of the state. By all means use the redundant hierarchy test to get rid of levels of management that have no useful role to play, but it is important to balance it with the parenting advantage test and to recognize that the parent is often a vital part of a structured network.

Networks and Accountability

The interdependent lateral relationships that are built into network structures can reduce the pressures on units to self-correct. They can also circumscribe the autonomy of units, making managers feel less strongly accountable for their unit's performance. The high-performance culture is not easy to create in networks with pervasive interdependencies.

To pass the accountability test, networks need to be designed to reduce tied relationships and shared decisions: as far as possible, network relationships should be based on voluntary, not mandatory, collaboration. Equally important, the control process should incorporate clear and "appropriate" performance measures for each unit, as described in Chapter 3, otherwise there is a risk that the network will be a congenial forum for managers who like to work together on common tasks, but will lack the cutting edge of accountability that is needed for delivery.

Networks and Confusion

The biggest danger for networks is confusion about how decisions should be reached, especially where different units have opposing views. Full and spontaneous harmony between upstream and downstream units, between product and customer units, between resource provider and resource user units, cannot be expected. Even in the most co-operative of networks, conflicts are bound to arise. If networks cannot resolve these conflicts and reach timely decisions, they descend into chaos. The network will then, for all its promise, become as unpopular and ineffective as the scorned matrix structure.

On the other hand, organization designers must avoid emasculating the initiative that networks are supposed to foster by imposing excessively detailed responsibility allocations and conflict resolution processes. The organization design must be clear enough to avoid confusion, but not so fixed and precise that it undermines initiative. How can this design conundrum be resolved?

The answer is to get the basic design clear, by specifying unit roles and relationships in accordance with our taxonomy, and to fill in only those details and processes that are needed to pass our good design tests. Once the essential structure is in place, decentralized unit managers can put the rest of the flesh on to the bones of the organization in their own way.

Structured Networks

In summary, structured networks call for

- co-operative managers, who are willing to participate fully in the network;

- rich information, which provides the basis for sound decisions within the network;

- respect for unit autonomy and unit boundaries, especially where specialist cultures need to be able to stand back from the network;

- realism about what sorts of co-ordination can and cannot be achieved by networking;

- a recognition that upper levels of management need to play some vital parenting roles, which are essential for the success of the network;

- relationships and performance measures that are designed to avoid the accountability problems that networks often encounter; and

- clear unit roles and relationships and sufficient designed-in processes, so that self-managed networking can take place in accordance with the intentions of the organization designer, without descending into the frictions, ambiguities, and paralysis of traditional matrix structures.

These are the features that networks need to fulfill their potential as true twenty-first century organizations. Many companies, such as BP, Citigroup, and IBM, have already incorporated most of these features into their organizations. We believe that the tests, the taxonomy, and the design process put forward in this book can guide other companies who aspire to create effective organizations that work as structured networks.

Endnotes

Chapter 1

[1] See Michael Goold, Andrew Campbell, and Marcus Alexander, *Corporate-level Strategy*, John Wiley & Sons, 1994, and Michael Goold, David Pettifer, and David Young, "Redefining the corporate centre", *European Management Journal*, February 2001.

Chapter 2

[1] Lex Donaldson's book, *American Anti-management Theories of Organization*, Cambridge University Press, 1995, provides an excellent summary of the main organization theories. See also Henry Mintzberg, *The Structuring of Organizations*, Prentice Hall, 1979.

[2] Chapter 2, Lex Donaldson, as above.

[3] Chapter 4, Lex Donaldson, as above.

[4] Chapter 5, Lex Donaldson, as above.

[5] Chapter 6, Lex Donaldson, as above.

[6] Lex Donaldson, as above.

[7] Alfred Chandler, *Strategy and Structure*, MIT Press, 1962.

[8] Robert Bergelman, "A model of the interaction of strategic behavior, corporate context and the concept of strategy", *Academy of Management Review*, **8**(1), 1983.

[9] Michael Goold, Andrew Campbell and Marcus Alexander, *Corporate-level Strategy*, John Wiley & Sons, 1994; C.K. Pralahad and Yves Doz, *"The Rationale for Multi-SBU Companies"*; Chapter 18 in *Oxford Handbook of Strategy*, (eds David Faulkner and Andrew Campbell), Oxford University Press, 2002; Tom Copeland, Tim Koller and Jack Marrin, *Valuation*, John Wiley & Sons, 1990; Gerry Johnson and Kevin Scholes, *Exploring Corporate Strategy*, Prentice Hall, 1999, 285–294; David Collis and Cynthia Montgomery, "Creating corporate advantage", *Harvard Business Review*, May–June 1998; Tarun Khanna and Krishna Palepu, "Why focused strategies may be wrong for emerging markets", *Harvard Business Review*, July–August, 1997.

10   Michael Goold, Andrew Campbell and Marcus Alexander, *Corporate-level Strategy*, John Wiley & Sons, 1994.
11   We were alerted to the importance of this dimension of fit by our project team collaborators at McKinsey. They emphasized that design work frequently has to take account of issues such as legal structures and the capabilities of the company's IT systems. As we worked together, we were able to identify several factors that can constrain the design choice, at least in the short term.
12   Christopher Bartlett and Sumatra Ghoshal, *Managing Across Borders*, HBS Press, 1989.
13   Jerry Johnson and Kevin Scholes, *Exploring Corporate Strategy*, Prentice Hall, 1999.

Chapter 3

1   One of the earliest attempts to pull together a set of organizational design principles comes from L.F. Urwick in 1952 (*"Notes on the Theory of Organisation"*, American Management Association). Urwick identified eight principles – the principle of the objective (structure follows strategy), the principle of correspondence (between authority and responsibility), the principle of responsibility (higher levels must control), the scalar principle (clear reporting lines), the principle of the span of control (not more than six subordinates), the principle of specification (focus), the principle of co-ordination, and the principle of definition (clarity).
2   The authors who have done the best job of sorting the advice into a form that is helpful to managers are Jay Galbraith in *Designing Organisations: An Executive Briefing on Strategy, Structure and Process*, Jossey-Bass, 1995, or *Designing the Global Corporation*, Jossey-Bass, 2000; and David Nadler and Michael Tushman in *Competing by Design*, Oxford University Press, 1997.
3   See Chapter 4, in which we identify the management challenges faced by simple and complex organizations and show how they relate to our tests.
4   Adam Smith, *The Wealth of Nations*, 1776. (Reprinted by Methuen, 1922.)
5   Fredrick Winslow Taylor, *The Principles of Scientific Management*, Harper & Row, 1911.
6   In Carl Stern and George Stalk, *Perspectives on Strategy*, John Wiley & Sons, 1998.
7   James Thompson, *Organizations in Action*, McGraw-Hill, 1967.
8   Paul Lawrence and Jay Lorsch, *Organization and Environment*, Harvard University Press, 1967.
9   Clayton Christensen, *The Innovators' Dilemma*, Harvard Business School Press, 2000.
10   Andrew Campbell and Michael Goold, *Synergy*, Capstone Publishing, 1998.
11   Michael Jensen and William Meckling, "Theory of the firm", *Journal of Financial Economics*, **3**, 1976.
12   See, for example, Jay Barney, "Firm resources and sustained competitive advantage", *Journal of Management*, **17**(1), 1991.
13   Jay Barney, "Looking inside for competitive advantage", in *Core Competency-based Strategy*, eds Campbell and Luchs, Thomson Business Press, 1997.
14   Jeffrey Pfeffer, *The Human Equation*, Harvard Business School Press, 1998.
15   Michael Jensen and William Meckling, "Theory of the firm: managerial behavior, agency costs, and ownership structure", *Journal of Financial Economics*, **3**, 1976.

[16]   See Michael Goold and Andrew Campbell, *Strategies and Styles*, Blackwell, 1987 for more discussion of the control process and its impact on management commitment. See also Robert Simons, *Levers of Control*, Harvard Business School Press, 1995.

[17]   Robert Simons, *Levers of Control*, Harvard Business School Press, 1995.

[18]   Robert Kaplan and David Norton, "The balanced scorecard measures that drive performance", *Harvard Business Review*, **70**(1).

[19]   See Chapters 4, 5, and 6 for further discussion.

[20]   See Michael Goold and James Brian Quinn, *Strategic Control*, Addison Wesley, 1990, for further discussion of performance measures.

[21]   See Henry Mintzberg, "Crafting strategy", *Harvard Business Review*, June 1988; Robert Burgleman, "A model of the interaction of strategic behavior, corporate context and the concept of strategy", *Academy of Management Review*, **8**(1), 1983.

[22]   Ron Askenas, Dave Ulrich, Todd Jick and Steve Kerr, *The Boundaryless Organization*, Jossey-Bass, 1995.

[23]   See Oliver Williamson, *Markets and Hierarchies*, Free Press, 1975; *The Economic Institutions of Capitalism*, Free Press, 1985; "Strategy research: governance and competence perspectives", *Strategic Management Journal*, December 1999, 1087–1109.

Chapter 4

[1]   See Chapter 3 for a discussion of the "autonomy needs" of units, including the dangers of contamination from cross-unit influence.

[2]   BA has now sold Go to a management buy-out.

[3]   Creative accounting can make profitability a less objective measure, but with agreed accounting principles and conventions the scope for subjectivity can be relatively low.

[4]   Different measures of profitability can be used to try to address these issues. Return on net assets is preferable to return on sales, since it includes a concern for investment as well as profit margins. Economic profit or value-based management measures are even more sophisticated, but no form of profit measure is able to insure that all relevant aspects of performance are covered. There is always some danger of profitability being an oversimplified performance measure.

[5]   See Adrian J. Slywotzky, *Value Migration*, Harvard Business School Press, 1995.

[6]   See Michael Goold and Andrew Campbell, "Taking stock of synergy", *Long Range Planning*, **33**, 2000, 85–88.

[7]   See Morten T. Hansen and Bolko von Oetinger, "Introducing T-shaped managers: knowledge management's next generation", *Harvard Business Review*, March 2001, 107–116, for a fuller description of BP's peer group process.

[8]   During 2001, BP introduced some modifications to its structure. These included some consolidation of business units to gain economies of scale, thereby reducing the number of business units. The regional dimension of the organization was also strengthened, with an emphasis on enabling organic growth in local markets. Finally, there was a consolidation of functional competencies in areas such as marketing and technology. These changes represent a move towards a more complex, multi-dimensional structure, although BP aims to maintain the benefits of strong decentralized accountability.

9   See Michael Goold, Andrew Campbell, and Marcus Alexander, *Corporate-level Strategy*, John Wiley & Sons, 1994, for a fuller description of how Emerson adds value, and Andrew Campbell, "Tailored, not benchmarked: A fresh look at corporate planning", *Harvard Business Review*, March–April 1999, for more information about Granada and Emerson.

10   In our book, *Strategies and Styles*, Blackwell, 1987, we showed that Financial Control-style companies, such as Hanson, which believe strongly in SBU-based structures, discourage synergies between their businesses.

11   Shona Brown and Kathleen Eisenhardt, *Competing on the Edge*, Harvard Business School Press, 1998.

12   The *feasibility test* is so contingent on specific company circumstances that it is not possible to give a general rating to SBU structures as such

13   We use the term "interdependent" rather than "matrix" or "network" structures for any organization with more than one dimension of focus. This is because the matrix label can also be used more strongly to refer to organizations in which the balance of power between the different dimensions is roughly equal, and in which there is divided reporting (see Chapter 6) along different dimensions. Not all interdependent structures are balanced matrices. We also prefer to reserve the term "network" for interdependent structures in which much of the collaboration between units takes place on a self-managed basis, rather than through imposed top-down formal processes. Again, not all interdependent structures are networks in this sense.

14   See, for example, Jay R. Galbraith, *Competing with Flexible Lateral Organizations*, Addison Wesley, 1994.

15   See William Ouchi, "Markets, bureaucracies, and clans", *Administrative Science Quarterly*, **25**, March 1980, 129–141.

16   As in our review of SBU structures, we can give no general assessment of interdependent structures in terms of the feasibility test, since this test depends on specific company circumstances.

17   See W.R. Ashby, *Design for a Brain*, John Wiley & Sons, 1952 and *An Introduction to Cybernetics*, Chapman & Hall, 1956.

18   See Chapters 7, 8, and 9 for further discussion.

Chapter 5

1   See, for example, Sumantra Ghoshal and Christopher Bartlett, *The Individualised Corporation*, Heinemann, 1998.

2   In previous research, we described a variety of different management styles adopted by corporate parent managers, ranging from highly decentralized (Financial Control style) to more influential (Strategic Planning style). See Michael Goold and Andrew Campbell, *Strategies and Styles*, Blackwell, 1987.

3   This section focuses on the functional structure within business units. However, there is usually some sort of functional structure within all the unit types we describe. The observations that we make concerning business functions are relevant, *mutatis mutandis*, for functions within other sorts of units.

4   In fact, there is also an area level of management between the division and the branches.

5   Gunn Partners Inc., for example, have carried out survey research with 30 companies that supports these conclusions. See *Introduction to Shared Services*, Gunn Partners Inc.

6   See Michael Goold, Andrew Campbell and Marcus Alexander, *Corporate-level Strategy*, John Wiley & Sons, 1994, Chapter 7.

7   See Russell Eisenstat, Nathaniel Foote, Jay Galbraith, and Danny Miller "Beyond the business unit", *McKinsey Quarterly*, 2001.

8   See Jay Galbraith, *Designing the Global Corporation*, Jossey-Bass, 2000.

Chapter 6

1   Michael Goold, Andrew Campbell, and Marcus Alexander, *Corporate-level Strategy: Creating Value in the Multibusiness Company*, John Wiley & Sons, 1994.

2   In previous research, documented in our book *Strategies and Styles* (Blackwell, 1987), we recognized that some corporate parents like to decentralize as much as possible, while others prefer a more influential role. We used the term the "Strategic Planning" style to refer to the approach adopted by more influential corporate parents. We can now see that the so-called Strategic Planning style is specially well suited for complex, interdependent structures.

3   See David Young and Michael Goold, *Effective Headquarters Staff*, Ashridge Strategic Management Centre, 1999 and David Young, Michael Goold, Georges Blanc, Rolf Buhner, David Collis, Jan Eppink, Tadao Kagono and Gonzalo Jimenez Seminario, *Corporate Headquarters: An International Analysis of their Roles and Staffing*, Financial Times Prentice Hall, 2000.

4   "New formula coke", *The Economist*, February 3, 2001, p. 84.

5   See David Young and Kay Dirk Ullman, *Benchmarking Corporate Headquarters Staff*, Ashridge Strategic Management Centre, 1999.

6   See Young *et al.*, 2000 (the second reference in (3) above).

7   See (1) for a discussion of how to identify "parenting opportunities" that can lead to real value being added.

8   See Michael Goold, David Pettifer, and David Young, "Redesigning the corporate centre", *European Management Journal*, February 2001, 83–91.

9   See David Young and Michael Goold, 1999, p. 21 (First reference in (3) above).

10   See David Young *et al.*, 2000 (as in (3) above), p. 126. Reporting spans of 4–10 were the most common.

11   See David Young *et al.*, 2000 (as in (3) above), and Young and Ullman, 1999 (as in (5)).

Chapter 7

1   The process we suggest in this chapter has been greatly influenced by our joint project with McKinsey & Co. While our process is not identical to the process described in McKinsey's latest internal guide to organization design, we owe a big debt to the McKinsey project.

2   An alternative design process that we are familiar with, and admire, is called "organizational profiling", developed by Michael Beer and Russ Eisenstat together

with the Center for Organization Fitness. This process is particularly effective at insuring that managers learn about and confront the strengths and weaknesses of their current situation.

Chapter 8

[1]   We worked closely with McKinsey in defining these tests and deciding which analyses are practical and useful. This does not mean that what we offer here is identical to McKinsey's internal manual, but the ideas are interwined. We owe a particular debt to Risto Pentinnen, Anne-Francoise Weynns, and Jim Wendler for their contributions.

[2]   See Andrew Campbell and Michael Goold, *The Collaborative Enterprise*, Perseus Books, 1999 for a fuller discussion of issues related to collaboration and linkages between units, including the two checklists put forward in this section.

[3]   See Y. Doz, J. Santos, and P. Williamson, *From Global to Metanational: How Companies Win in the Knowledge Economy*, Harvard Business School Press, 2001.

[4]   In our collaboration with McKinsey, the McKinsey team decided to introduce a complexity test, and have articulated a corresponding simplicity principle.

Chapter 10

[1]   Christopher Bartlett and Sumantra Ghoshal, *Managing Across Borders*, Harvard Business School Press, 1989.

[2]   See, for example, Jay Galbraith, *Designing the Global Corporation*, Jossey-Bass, 2000.

[3]   See, for example, Stanley Davis and Paul Lawrence, *Matrix*, Addison-Wesley, 1977; Jay Galbraith, *Designing Complex Organizations*, Addison-Wesley, 1973.

[4]   See, for example, Robert Grant, "Towards a knowledge-based theory of the firm", *Strategic Management Journal*, **17** (Winter Special Issue), 1996, 109–122; Gary Hamel and C.K. Prahalad, *Competing for the Future*, Harvard Business School Press, 1994; I. Nonaka and H. Takeuchi, *The Knowledge-Creating Company*, Oxford University Press, 1995.

[5]   See Peter M. Senge, *The Fifth Discipline*, Doubleday, 1990, and David A. Garvin, "Building a learning organization", *Harvard Business Review*, July–August 1993, 78–91.

[6]   Raymond Miles, Charles Snow, and Grant Miles, "The Future.org", *Long Range Planning*, **33**, 2000, 300–321.

[7]   See Philip Evans and Thomas S. Wurster, *Blown to Bits*, Harvard Business School Press, 2000.

[8]   See John Hagel and Marc Singer, "Unbundling the corporation", *Harvard Business Review*, March–April, 1999.

[9]   Charles Handy, "Balancing corporate power: A new federalist paper", *Harvard Business Review*, November–December, 1992.

[10]   Our own work has emphasized the dangers of value destruction by corporate parents. See Michael Goold, Andrew Campbell, and Marcus Alexander, *Corporate-level Strategy*, John Wiley & Sons, 1994.

[11] Sumantra Ghoshal and Christopher Bartlett, *The Individualized Corporation*, Heinemann, 1998.

[12] Bruce A. Pasternak and Albert J. Viscio, *The Centerless Corporation*, Simon & Schuster, 1998.

[13] Jay Galbraith, "The reconfigurable organization", in *The Organization of the Future* (eds Frances Hesselbein, Marshall Goldsmith and Richard Beckhard), Jossey-Bass, 1997.

[14] For an extension of this idea, see Russell Eisenstat, Nathaniel Foote, Jay Galbraith, and Danny Miller, "Beyond the business unit", *McKinsey Quarterly*, 1, 2001.

[15] Shona Browne and Kathleen Eisenhardt, *Competing on the Edge*, Harvard Business School Press, 1998.

[16] The network concept has been popular in academic circles for some time: see, for example, *Networks and Organizations*, (eds Nitin Nohria and Robert G. Eccles), Harvard Business School Press, 1992; *Markets, Hierarchies and Networks*, (eds Grahame Thompson, Jennifer Frances, Rosalind Levacic, and Jeremy Mitchell), Sage Publications, 1991; Gunnar Hedlund, "A model of knowledge management and the N-form corporation", *Strategic Management Journal*, **15**, 73–90, 1994. More recently, network structures have found increasing interest in management circles. See Winifried Ruigrok, Andrew Pettigrew, Simon Peck and Richard Whittington, "Corporate restructuring and new forms of organising", *Management International Review*, 1999/2, Special Issue, **39**.

[17] Y. Doz, J. Santos, and P. Williamson, *From Global to Metanational: How Companies Win in the Knowledge Economy*, Harvard Business School Press, 2001.

Index